Credit and Debt in an Unequal Society

The Human Economy
Series editor:
Keith Hart, University of Pretoria

Those social sciences and humanities concerned with the economy have lost the confidence to challenge the sophistication and public dominance of the field of economics. We need to give a new emphasis and direction to the economic arrangements that people already share, while recognizing that humanity urgently needs new ways of organizing life on the planet. This series examines how human interests are expressed in our unequal world through concrete economic activities and aspirations.

Volume 7
Credit and Debt in an Unequal Society: Establishing a Consumer Credit Market in South Africa
Jürgen Schraten

Volume 6
Money at the Margins: Global Perspectives on Technology, Financial Inclusion, and Design
Edited by Bill Maurer, Smoki Musaraj and Ivan Small

Volume 5
Money in a Human Economy
Edited by Keith Hart

Volume 4
From Clans to Coops: Confiscated Mafia Land in Sicily
Theodoros Rakopoulos

Volume 3
Gypsy Economy: Romani Livelihoods and Notions of Worth in the 21st Century
Edited by Micol Brazzabeni, Manuela Ivone Cunha and Martin Fotta

Volume 2
Economy for and against Democracy
Edited by Keith Hart and John Sharp

Volume 1
People, Money, and Power in the Economic Crisis: Perspectives from the Global South
Edited by Keith Hart and John Sharp

Credit and Debt in an Unequal Society

Establishing a Consumer Credit Market in South Africa

Jürgen Schraten

berghahn
NEW YORK • OXFORD
www.berghahnbooks.com

First published in 2020 by
Berghahn Books
www.berghahnbooks.com

Library of Congress Cataloging-in-Publication Data

Names: Schraten, Jürgen, author.
Title: Credit and debt in a unequal society : establishing a consumer credit market in South Africa / Jürgen Schraten.
Other titles: Human economy ; v.7.
Description: New York : Berghahn Books, 2020. | Series: The human economy ; volume 7 | Includes bibliographical references and index.
Identifiers: LCCN 2019044682 (print) | LCCN 2019044683 (ebook) | ISBN 9781789206388 (hardback) | ISBN 9781789206395 (ebook)
Subjects: LCSH: Consumer credit--South Africa. | Consumer credit--Social aspects--South Africa. | Debt--Social aspects--South Africa.
Classification: LCC HG3756.S6 .S37 2020 (print) | LCC HG3756.S6 (ebook) | DDC 332.70968--dc23
LC record available at https://lccn.loc.gov/2019044682
LC ebook record available at https://lccn.loc.gov/2019044683

British Library Cataloguing in Publication Data

A catalogue record for this book is available from the British Library

ISBN 978-1-78920-638-8 hardback
ISBN 978-1-78920-639-5 ebook

Contents

Illustrations

Figures

Tables

Acknowledgements

The primary inspiration of this study is the Human Economy approach developed and promoted by Keith Hart. His work brings the everyday experiences of people back into the focus of economic research, and this motivated me to analyse the institutional setting of a consumer credit market from a sociological perspective. The fieldwork that built the foundation of this study was conducted thanks to a fellowship of the Human Economy programme at the University of Pretoria, generously funded by the Andrew W. Mellon Foundation. This study shares the strong commitment to democracy and humanitarianism that characterizes the work of Keith Hart.

Andreas Langenohl shaped much of my theoretical understanding of sociology and social theory. He supervised the final conduct of this study, which served as a postdoctoral habilitation treatise at the University of Giessen but has been significantly revised. His advice and encouragement were indispensable, and our discussions helped shaping the main insights of this study. He is a great teacher, and it is a pleasure to be his colleague.

The late Helmut Dubiel, as our common mentor, formed my foundational understanding of society with its special focus on the role of social conflicts in a democracy. I miss him.

I thank Reimer Gronemeyer, who read the manuscript and served as a supervisor of my habilitation. His dedication in giving the marginalized of society a voice, especially in Southern Africa, motivates me.

John Sharp was responsible for providing a progressive and fruitful research environment at the University of Pretoria, and his contributions to the Human Economy approach influenced the direction of my research a great deal.

Many colleagues at the University of Gießen contributed to the discussions of the book. I want to thank Herbert Willems, Sebastian Giacovelli, Carola Westermeier, Jens Maeße, Il-Tschung Lim, Eva Gros, Jörn Ahrens and Thomas Linpinsel. Special thanks go to Carmen Ludwig for her extensive personal and scientific support.

At the University of Pretoria the Human Economy programme built a unique environment of research of the everyday economy, and

I want to thank Albert Farré, Theodore Powers, Tijo Salverda, Camille Sutton-Brown, Maud Orne-Gliemann, Doreen Gordon, Mallika Shakya, Busani Mpofu, Detlev Krige, Juliana Braz Dias, Booker Magure, Vito Laterza, Fraser McNeill and Sean Maliehe.

Two anonymous reviewers provided me with helpful comments and suggestions.

I am very grateful to the fantastic contribution of Anthony Waine, whose assistance went beyond copyediting my manuscript. I learned a lot.

Special thanks go to the patient, friendly and supportive staff of Berghahn Books. Many organizational tasks would never have been successfully finished without the help of Antje Schäfer in Gießen and Corena Garnas in Pretoria.

Notes on the Text

The South African currency, the rand, is usually abbreviated as ZAR, but in the sources sometimes only as R.

ZAR 100 converts into around 7 US dollars and 1 US dollar converts into around ZAR 15.

However, the exchange rate shows high volatility due to the economic problems of South Africa, therefore I have not given conversions into US dollars because this would impede the comparability of figures over time.

Abbreviations

ABSA	Amalgamated Bank of South Africa (a commercial bank)
ANC	African National Congress
COSATU	Congress of South African Trade Unions
DTI	Department of Trade and Industry of South Africa
FNB	First National Bank
ITSA	Insolvency and Trustee Service Australia
Ltd	Limited (legal form)
MFRC	Micro-Finance Regulatory Council
NCA	National Credit Act 34 of 2005
Nedlac	National Economic Development and Labour Council
NP	Nasionale Party (Afrikaans: National Party)
NPS	National Payment System
PIN	Personal Identification Number
s	Section (of a law or regulation)
SACP	South African Communist Party
SAMOS	South African Multiple Option Settlement
Treasury	Ministry of Finance of South Africa
US	United States of America
ZAR	South African Rand (currency)

Introduction

The main concern of this book is to investigate a particular feature of many contemporary societies that is clearly visible, yet rarely explained, and to analyse and illustrate it through a study of the unlikely case of South Africa. The feature under investigation is essentially this: whenever a borrower is unable to serve his debts, the issue is turned from being an economic matter into a legal one. At that point we no longer talk about the satisfaction of wants or exchanges, but about the enforcement of contracts and offences. Delinquent borrowers are deprived of their legal capacity, a special kind of autonomy that many authoritarian regimes actually grant their citizens, and which usually marks the threshold between infancy and adulthood.

Over-indebtedness is of salient public topicality since the expansion of finance has increased the easy access to consumer loans in many countries and growing amounts of consumption have become debt-financed (Bauman 2007). Consumer credit markets have become an important part of contemporary capitalism because they augment the options for involving otherwise illiquid citizens in the market economy (Hart, Laville and Cattani 2011: 3; Langley 2010). Consumer loans changed from being an emergency tool into a common component of commodity supply and, finally, into a commodity themselves (Langley 2014). For citizens living in financialized economies, it has become the norm to tap into their future income. At the same time, consumer credit markets increase the number of over-indebted citizens and prevent them from improving their standard of living, or they exclude them from social life altogether.

In this regard, South Africa is indeed an unlikely case due to its social structure. Sampie Terreblanche (2002) has explained why the country possesses one of the highest levels of social inequality, a fact that has been confirmed repeatedly by data from the World Bank (2019). Hein Marais (2011) provided a detailed analysis of the many restrictions and hardships a broad majority of the South African population is exposed to in their daily lives, among them unemployment, underemployment and poverty. Under these circumstances, the development of a consumer credit market, whose rationale one should expect to lie in the probability of loan repayments based on reliable income streams, is a surprising fact in the first place.

Indeed, South Africa is one of the first of the 'poorer nations' (Prashad 2014) to have an institutionalized and financialized consumer credit market. The combination of these three terms – marketization, institutionalization and financialization – constitutes the principal feature of this study and justifies its unconventional approach.

The first keyword is marketization. Since its foundation in 1993, the South African consumer credit business has been deliberately turned into a market, i.e. it was intended to be accessible for everyone, transparent, competitive and supposedly self-regulated. As will be evident in the following chapters, this was not a natural development, but a politically governed one (Callon 1998a; Polanyi 2001). A market represents a sphere in which participants are expected to interact autonomously in instrumentally and strategically oriented ways in pursuit of their individual benefits (Callon 2007: 142–43; Hirschman 2013). Therefore, this study will differ significantly from scholarly works on mixed or non-market forms of monetary exchanges and indebtedness as well as from legal studies on the topic.

Important research on the role of credit in the daily lives of South Africans has been published before, in particular by Deborah James (2012, 2013, 2015) and Detlev Krige (2011, 2014). Both scholars focussed on the connection between local communities and the ways in which money and debts were handled. Further important studies relating to the National Credit Act have been undertaken by legal scholars, and in this regard work carried out by Jannie Otto (2010) and Michelle Kelly-Louw (2007, 2008, 2009) must be mentioned. The analysis of marketization in this study, on the other hand, differs from these works because it concentrates on the economic effects a legal framework has on the equality of market participants.

The second focus is on institutionalization. Beginning with reforms in 1999, and finalized with the enactment of the NCA (National Credit Act 34 of 2005), the South African government took its consumer credit market to a different level of stabilized organization, especially in comparison to traditional forms of money lending. The legal framework introduced rules and procedures, and it established additional governmental and privately acting bodies. A growing number of market actors like credit bureau clerks, debt counsellors and payment distribution agents were assigned defined tasks and had to meet specific quality criteria. The process of credit granting was furnished with benchmark data, formulas and forms. The market as such was placed under permanent observation and literally made public. Money lending could no longer be reduced to a private exchange between two parties. To sum up, the business was turned from a space of private social interaction into being a permanently available infrastructure, i.e. a stabilized environment of social interaction (Luhmann 1989: 51–62).

The third focus is on financialization, viewed as the practice of calculating future risks in order to solve present tasks (Martin 2002; Schraten 2015). The politically shaped market became dominated by commercial banks, because they could fulfil the new conditions most easily. From 1990 onwards, South African banks re-entered the global markets after years of apartheid-related boycotts and legal restrictions (The Banks Act 94 of 1990). Grietje Verhoef (2009) has analysed the remarkable dominance of the very few key players in the South African economy. They brought financialization into the everyday lives of the people. National and international commercial banks were able to share their risks on the financial markets, or even to get rid of them by way of securitization. As will be seen in this study, this has shaped the form of the loans they offered to the South African customers. By issuing the NCA, the government intended to involve its citizens in these procedures of financialization because it granted the political right to apply for a loan to every citizen (s 60 NCA). Hence, it encouraged them to take the risks involved in financialized loans instead of demanding thriftiness and encouraging saving in order to satisfy wants.

This did not happen by accident, as Dale McKinley (2017: 7) revealed in his study on the 'corporatisation of liberation', as it was performed by the governing political parties. With this term he is referring to the political strategy of the ANC of promoting the emancipation and social uplifting of the hitherto discriminated and impoverished parts of the population by means of including them in the capitalist economy. Instead of redistributing resources or building a social welfare state that would protect the population from the devastating effects of market competition, citizens were called on to enter the economic struggles as entrepreneurs themselves. Free business was meant to generate economic growth, which was supposed to enable the government to distribute wealth without interfering in the existing social structure. The establishment of a financialized consumer credit market was deliberately intended to be a part of this strategy, as this study will show.

However, the financialization of everyday life is not limited to the economic expansion into world markets, a process Gillian Hart (2014: 121–42) aptly characterizes as 'de-nationalization', because it also entails the local regulations – including the legal framework – that represent a 're-nationalization'. This twofold tendency is not a contradiction of the findings of McKinley, who emphasizes the importance of the ideology of a National Democratic Revolution in the strategy of the ANC. From the beginning, the political and economic transformation of South Africa had a nationalistic character, seen most evidently in the expulsion of foreigners and in xenophobic riots (Crush 1999; Manzo 1996). The following chapters confirm that the legal regulation of the globalized economy was locally embedded, limited in its effects to the citizens and permanent residents of the nation state, and heavily dependent on a functioning state apparatus.

Summarizing this approach in methodological terms, the aim of this study is to explain the empirical character of the 'extra-locality' (D. Smith 2001: 159) of the institutions, rules and norms of the South African consumer credit market that cannot be grasped by participant observation, traditional ethnography or sociological interviews. Instead, it distils the 'ruling relations' (D. Smith 1999: 73–95) from the social setting created by laws, institutions, procedures, calculations and forms. The infrastructural relations between the laws and legal regulations, institutions, actors and processes are of the utmost importance. The empirical resources of this study are legal texts, policy documents, aggregated data and statistics, formulas and forms (Cooren 2004; Latour 2010; MacKenzie 2006; Riles 2011; D. Smith 2001). Of special importance are economic textbook principles that have been implemented into the infrastructure of the South African consumer credit market, as well as loan offers and contracts and their regulations which build the database for an analysis of this market (Callon 1998b; Muniesa, Millo and Callon 2007). The main argument of the study in methodological regard is the following: the purpose of this complex arrangement was the reconciliation of a backward-looking colonial property right with the requirements of a future-oriented financialized economy. The result was an intensification and consolidation of the social inequality that the consumer credit market was allegedly supposed to have mitigated.

The Conflict of Interests

A lot has changed in the treatment of debtors over the last centuries (Schraten 2016). In pre-modern societies, debtors were culprits that could be imprisoned, enslaved, tortured or executed. However, capitalism turned them into an economically valuable resource. For creditors, it became literally counterproductive to insist on the imprisonment of debtors because this immobilized the debtors' labour power. Instead, indebtedness presents an irresistible justification for demanding unselfish drudgery from the so-called plebs.

In addition to economic reasoning, the Enlightenment endowed human beings with the arguments necessary to claim acknowledgement of their dignity, something they had fought for since the revolutions in the United States (1776), France (1789) and Haiti (1791).

These elements resulted in a continual conflict between political efforts to defend exploitative rights and the intention to deter payment default on the one hand, and the struggles for debtors' alleviation together with humane and solidary conflict resolutions on the other hand. Expressed in the terms of Polanyi (2001: 136–40), we observe in these conflicts the expansion of free markets and its 'countermovement'. With the emergence of a financialized economy, the political conflicts between creditors' and debtors' interests intensified, and as a result most legislations are being constantly reformed (Kilborn 2007; Niemi, Ramsay and Whitford 2009; Niemi-Kiesiläinen, Ramsay and Whitford 2003).

The establishment of a consumer credit market in South Africa is an extraordinary example of this phenomenon, not only due to the social division of the population caused by slavery, colonialism and apartheid in the past, but as a consequence of the detailed and sophisticated market framework that was implemented in 2006. By focussing on its conflicting dynamics, this study aims to complement the study by David Graeber (2011), which dealt with the stable features of debt in the first place.

A political debt relief solution is urgently needed in South Africa. However, this book will argue that debt relief only represents the treatment of superficial symptoms. In the stage of over-indebtedness, the mechanism of consumer credit has already failed. The utilization of the emancipatory potential of consumer credit would require a fundamentally different understanding of the options this economic tool offers. Where consumer credit is concerned, we are confronted with a closely woven interdependence of the economy and law, which means that the realization of future opportunities is dependent on and shaped by a legitimacy that derives from the past. In the case of the South African consumer credit market, the new opportunities of credit customers are embedded in a ruthless property law from colonial times – with harmful consequences for consumers. The democratic constitution of South Africa from 1996 confronts this legacy with a Bill of Rights, which demands 'that state and society are working towards the effective realisation of these rights', as Heinz Klug (2010: 4) argued. This study will disentangle the interwoven threads of the economy and law in order to make alternative policies of such an emancipatory kind visible.

The Scope and the Effects of the Market

The Republic of South Africa has developed a thriving consumer credit market. The quarterly report of the supervisory governmental body, the National Credit Regulator, confirmed a year-on-year growth of 6.6 per cent of the value of credit granted in December 2018. The average year-on-year growth rate during the previous twelve months had been 7.2 per cent (my own calculations from NCR 2018a: 3; NCR 2018b: 3; NCR 2018c: 3; NCR 2018d: 3).[1]

The latest reports from 2018 contained figures indicating economic progress year-on-year in nearly all sections of the business. Banks and retailers had posted increased amounts of sold loans. The number of loan applications had grown, and the total amount of most of the different credit types like mortgages, secured credit, credit facilities, unsecured loans and short-term credit had also risen. The total amount of outstanding consumer credit had risen by 5.6 per cent, and the number of credit-active persons had gone up by nearly 800,000 within a year. The rejection rate of loan applications had increased slightly to 56 per cent. Only a few statistics indicated a decline, such as that of the fairly insignificant area of developmental credit (NCR 2018b: 1–7; NCR 2018e: 2).

This was a remarkable achievement for an African country with high rates of poverty and unemployment, indicating that many citizens were able to bridge their gaps in liquidity by applying to regulated and supervised credit suppliers. It was even more exceptional when one remembers that a banking collapse had taken place in 2002, which had been caused by bad debts resulting from irresponsible lending and borrowing practices and which had seriously damaged financial business (Porteous 2004: 82–85).

However, one fact undermines the impression of success and progress: the number of credit customers with 'impaired records', i.e. those in arrears for more than three months, blacklisted or with judgements and administration orders against them, remained at the level of nearly 10 million individuals. This number had crossed the threshold of 9 million persons in March 2012 for the first time, reaching its peak of more than 10.5 million in June 2015, but never dropping below 9 million subsequently. There has been no permanent decline in the numbers since the peak was reached. In December 2018 the figure of 10.16 million was 460,000 higher than in December 2017 (NCR 2018e: 2).

The total number of credit customers in 'good standing' had also gone up, a fact that coincided with high levels of over-indebted customers due to the growth of the market. Its share had declined by 1 per cent within a year, though. It meant that one in six South Africans – including children and pensioners – was in serious financial trouble because they had not been able to make a loan repayment for more than a quarter of a year, or had already been excluded from the market by creditors, courts or administrative bodies. This is an alarming finding for a country with one of the highest poverty rates in the world, and one that is a young political democracy constantly living with the pressure of social unrest (Alexander 2010; Makgetla 2018).

It meant that a sizeable part of the South African population was held in a liberal form of debt bondage in so far as their citizens' rights were not infringed but all efforts to improve their economic position were in vain because their earnings would ultimately belong to their creditors.

Consequently, it comes as no surprise that South African politicians started to discuss a debt relief bill, which was based on a draft Amendment to the NCA (Government Gazette No. 41274) and suggested extinguishing debts as a measure of last resort. Quite predictably, this suggestion was immediately opposed by the credit industry, which warned against the moral hazard of credit customers who would start to borrow carelessly as soon as a debt relief was expected (Tshwane 2018).

On the Political Formation of Markets

However, it requires a more complex debate to make the positive potential of consumer credit work, and to prevent exploitation, poverty and extreme social inequality at the same time. Debtors and creditors are not only divided by a conflict over the repayment of debts, but they actually share certain mutual interests, often without being aware of it. For instance, an increase in the borrower's income is in the interest of both – it would improve the living conditions of debtors, secure the repayment of loans and raise the demand for further credit. On the other hand, debtors should not be indifferent towards the creditors' intention to avoid repayment default because this affects the price of loans, and their general availability.

Yet the most important aspect of this discussion cannot be grasped from the individual perspectives of debtors or creditors. One needs to view it from a third perspective, i.e. that of society as a whole. Only this perspective allows one to take the mutual dependency of a multitude of creditors and debtors into account, and to give due consideration to a long-term time frame of socio-economic change and to the tensions between the economic, legal and political fields of society. This viewpoint is a purely reflexive one, though. Society does not exist as 'a single thing' (Rosanvallon 2006: 190), and adopting this viewpoint is an imaginary process that requires normative decisions (Castoriadis 1997).

Consumer credit can only result in beneficial improvements for the whole of society if it is organized in liberal markets, which means that every citizen is able to access credit under the same conditions, and actors are able to observe and calculate the practice of their behaviour. However, markets can be organized in different forms. Only some promote equal exchange, whereas others facilitate competition, and still others benefit oligopolistic actors. The establishment of a liberal market beneficial to a democracy requires political intervention in order to guarantee transparency and to prevent the abuse of power by the successful actors at the expense of weaker competitors, newcomers, customers and society as a whole. Karl Polanyi (2001) explained the necessity for managing markets by state intervention, and Mark Granovetter (1973, 1985) showed how the densely woven fabric of economic rationalities, legal regulations, political interests and social norms influences the decisions of actors. Both used the term 'embeddedness' to describe this multiplicity of societal interdependencies. The democratic government of the Republic of South Africa seemed to have been basically aware of these intricacies because it 'embedded' its consumer credit market in a complex legal and institutional framework.

The economic mechanism behind the opposition of market growth and high levels of over-indebtedness is easy to understand: loans are taken out due to a lack of liquidity, and insufficient income often constitutes the reason for a debt career of this kind beginning (Ritchie 2018). If earnings are not increased quickly to cover the expense of debt repayments, the economic situation will deteriorate further because of constantly increasing financial obligations. In other words, taking out an unsecured loan is beneficial only if the lack of liquidity is temporary or the loan is used to generate additional income. At the same time, repayment defaults lead to penalty fees, the compounding of interest and prolonged debt services, hence to higher profits on the part of creditors. This means that consumer credit will increase the social inequality in society if most loans are used for consumption.

Less easy to understand is the political mechanism. Why does a political democracy construct a market framework that perpetuates the imbalance between a small number of beneficiaries and such a huge number of permanently hard-pressed debtors? Even more astonishingly, why is a government claiming it is advancing 'the social and economic welfare of South Africans', as it says in section 3 of the NCA, by implementing this kind of consumer credit market? These two questions, in particular, represent the main concern of this book, and thus the debate about possible debt relief mechanisms is framed by this socio-economic analysis.

The core of the analysis is formed by the crisis of the consumer credit market between 2012 and 2014, which ended with the collapse of the African Bank Investment Ltd and then by the continuation of a financialized consumer credit market in South Africa afterwards. A reconstruction of the history of South African money and credit supply following the foundation of the National Central Bank explains the long-term effect of policies and the structural starting point of a freely accessible consumer credit market in 1993. Consequently, a discussion of the failure of the free market experiment between 1993 and 2002 will illustrate the reasons and the conditions for the construction of the NCA.

The debate on credit relief measures in South Africa only gained momentum after considerable delay, and the Amendment of the NCA was still under consideration at the time of writing. Nevertheless, irrespective of the final outcome of this, the fourth chapter will set out the suggested 'debt intervention' in the context of an international comparison of consumer bankruptcy laws, especially those which informed the South African legislators. The chapter will show that the debt relief bill does not affect the fundamental mechanisms of the South African consumer credit market.

The core idea behind this study has three main sources of inspiration, two classical and one contemporary. The classical inspirations are Georg Simmel and Max Weber, because both developed social theories which allow us to analyse the opposed dynamics of economic progress and normative inertia. The purpose of the reference to Simmel and Weber is not to start another discussion on social theory, but to demonstrate the establishment of shared economic textbook principles in the period of the implementation of a capitalist society. The contemporary inspiration is the human economy approach of Keith Hart (2000, 2015; Hart, Laville and Cattani 2011; Hart and Sharp 2014). This approach claims to bring the everyday economy of citizens back into focus, which is far too often sidelined in debates about economics, as these mainly deal with profit and growth rates of companies and nation states. The scientific analysis of the people's economy cannot be limited to mathematical models of a predefined number of variables. It has to research the full range of social practices which human beings perform in order to take care of their economic needs and wants. These practices, which partly deviate from the economists' models, contain the resources for political alternatives.

The Role of the Consumer Credit Market in South African Democracy

A lack of liquidity was and still is an everyday source of distress for millions of South Africans. Therefore, the consumer credit market has been an important concomitant of the political transformation from apartheid to political democracy, and huge efforts have been made to utilize the progressive options of consumer credit in the 'corporatised liberation' (McKinley 2017).

The basic mechanism of consumer credit can help to build a tool for overcoming poverty and for levelling inherited social inequalities, because it allows access to resources without having to own the equivalent amount of money. Stretching the payment of durables over time can be economically advantageous. There is a beneficial effect from the perspective of society, too. In consumer credit markets, unused savings are mobilized to serve as loans to benefit those lacking liquidity and to achieve a better allocation of capital.[2]

The opportunities included in financialized consumer credit even exceed these lauded effects of consumer credit markets. As will be argued by interpreting *The Philosophy of Money* by Georg Simmel (1990) in this study, the deliberate extension of the money supply by the usage of loans basically allows the inclusion of additional participants in the economy without endangering the soundness of money. This option was of crucial importance to the leadership of South Africa after the overthrow of apartheid, in order to be able to extend economic inclusion to the majority of their country's population, which had been disregarded, humiliated and impoverished on political grounds.

However, the apartheid regime had not only constantly tried to discriminate against and externalize non-white South Africans, it had also demonized credit money on religious grounds. Tellingly, regulations concerning the lending business had been fixed in a law called the Usury Act. As a consequence, the post-apartheid governments had to establish a consumer credit market almost from scratch. Although this gold exporting country was equipped with sound and mighty banks, and the close ties to the centres of the world economy could be quickly re-established after 1990, it lacked the infrastructure which allowed a lending business to operate. Bank branches and ATMs in the living areas of the non-white population were scarce, and many citizens did not have bank accounts, let alone prepaid or credit cards.

Under these conditions, it was compelling for legislators to follow the instructions of neoclassical economics, and to believe in the possibility of a self-regulating market that would be established automatically by privately interacting individuals. Following this ideology would save political leaders from interventions in the economy and from the resistance that usually accompanies political advances in the property sphere. The initiation of a lending business in South Africa was accompanied by hopes for new investment opportunities, and for the smooth inclusion of formerly disadvantaged citizens as an effect of private economic activities. However, the first attempt to create a literally free consumer credit market resulted in over-indebtedness, economic hardships and violence, and had to be reframed due to its obvious malfunctioning after 1999. Despite this failed attempt, the ideological idea of the possibility of a self-regulating market has haunted the development of the consumer credit market through to the present day, as this study will show. The ongoing debate about debt relief measures is no exception to this.

The Misconception of the South African Consumer Credit Market

The high level of long-term indebted customers, as revealed by the National Credit Regulator since March 2012, fundamentally calls into question the rationality of a consumer credit market that aims at advancing the 'social and economic welfare of South Africans' according to section 3 of the NCA. Obviously, a considerable part of the population is doomed to constant debt servicing.

This problem has not gone unnoticed. The National Credit Regulator has warned the public against the consequences of constantly growing numbers of seriously indebted citizens since March 2012. The justification for this alarm was confirmed by the collapse of the sixth biggest lender of the country, African Bank Investments Ltd, in August 2014. As a consequence, the bank was quickly split into a decontaminated good bank, with the aim of enabling the business to continue, and a bad bank, thus isolating the bad debts that had caused the collapse – a political move that has become very familiar to the global public since the financial crisis in 2007. In a concerted action, the government and banking business representatives tightened the affordability criteria for loans. From the governmental perspective, these operations were successful because any potential contagious effects of the African Bank collapse on the other banks could be contained, and the good bank indeed seemed to recover. Even more importantly, the review of the National Credit Act, which had been initiated after the first warnings of the National Credit Regulator, could be completed without changing the basic architecture of the market.

The effects of these careful and reluctant market interventions were reviewed in the Consumer Credit Market Report of December 2018. It indicated a reduction in the share of unsecured loans of the total amount of credit to a level of 21.5 per cent (NCR 2018b: 4). At the height of the crisis in 2012 and 2013, this proportion had constantly risen until it had reached values above 24 per cent, signalling the preference of credit providers to maximize the sale of this most expensive and most risky type of consumer loan (NCR 2012b: 4). From a short-term business point of view, the preference for selling unsecured loans was a rational move, but in the long run it endangered the resilience not only of the single credit supplier but of the business as such, as the collapse of African Bank confirmed.

This simple fact – a contradiction between the short-term and the long-term rationality of economic action – revealed a crucial mistake in the idea of a self-regulating consumer credit market which forms the core of the National Credit Act 34 of 2005 (Langenohl 2008). The legislators and business representatives had continued to conceptualize the market as an institution that represented a self-evident and infallible guiding principle, albeit with a more complex framework than before 2002. According to its creators, the South African consumer credit market would benefit all participants as long as they followed this principle. It was based on the conviction that undisturbed price negotiations by private actors, supported and monitored by governmental bodies that guaranteed the transparency of information, would result in an economic equilibrium to the benefit of all. The main purpose was the fulfilment of contracts under all circumstances.

The review of the market undertaken in this study will reveal, in at least three respects, misunderstandings of the economics of a financialized consumer credit market. To begin with, there was no single rationality of market actors even under the conditions of transparent information, because the outcome of economic interaction is uncertain by definition. Without adopting a deliberate position with regard to the unforeseeable future, economic actors would not be able to realize economic advantages (Appadurai 2012). The uncertainty of economic action runs counter to the conceptualization of a single guiding principle of markets because free actors cannot be determined by a uniform interpretation of their individual futures. On the contrary, economic success depends on the ability to utilize an opportunity that has been rejected by others (Knight 1921).

Secondly, as already mentioned, a financialized consumer credit market is not constituted by two private parties negotiating a price. Instead, it consists of a complex arrangement of institutions, which assemble legal rulings, a variety of social norms and monetary mechanisms into a single 'market device'. This term will therefore be used in this study to describe the unified environment that actors in a consumer credit market are predisposed to accept (Muniesa, Millo and Callon 2007). The market device appears as a uniform setting, which, however, may be handled by the actors very differently. In fact, the purpose of the market device in the South African consumer credit market was, as far as possible, to generate *homines oeconomici*. Human beings are not limited by nature to pursuing their individual economic interest, but they can be conditioned to do so under very specific circumstances (Callon 2007: 142–43).

The third misunderstanding of the economics of a financialized consumer credit market emanates from the debate about debt relief as a last resort of over-indebted citizens. The study shows that this policy only deals with the problem after the economic and social position of debtors has already deteriorated. The basic uncertainty of a loan means that information about the success or failure of the risk-taking action will only become evident subsequent to the conclusion of the contract (Esposito 2011: 18–36). This means that a responsible consumer credit market would require some kind of credit counselling to be instigated before the contract is made, and during its term. As soon as prospects of success vanish, an intervention in the contract commitment is necessary in order to prevent over-indebtedness. This would limit the earnings of creditors, of course. The protection of the profit interest of creditors caused the core problem of the South African NCA, namely, that existing over-indebtedness was conceptualized as a precondition of political intervention.

The Procedure of the Argumentation in this Book

The main argument put forward in this study is that the specific understanding of market economies as a realm of freely interacting individuals (and companies, which are also constructed as individuals in the fiction of a legal person under private law) suffers from a repression of its core foundation by an understanding of private property as the exclusive right of an individual to refuse every competing access to a resource. In other words, market economies are embedded in a property right that predestines instrumental rationality over solidarity, emotions and communal traditions.

Consumer credit would basically allow this principle to be surmounted by treating the loan as a common resource that could be utilized to the benefit of creditor and debtor and of society too.

An important conclusion of this argument is that the compartmentalization of our market societies into different realms, called 'the economy' and 'the law', is a precondition for being able to hide the basic reason for an allegedly instrumental economic rationality that seems to be without alternative – and the alternatives that would become obvious once a consciousness of this connection between the legal epistemology of economic interaction had been developed.

These arguments are developed by first describing the South African consumer credit market. The first chapter begins by illustrating the meaning of financialization through an analysis of a typical, ostensibly very simple, very cheap and very unproblematic loan offer, which nevertheless turns out to be expensive and dangerous. The most serious repercussions though could only be extracted from the small print of the contract, which revealed the consequences of a temporary repayment default. The second section of the first chapter then presents a market overview, demonstrating that the single loan offer was actually quite typical. The third section turns our attention to the – now unsurprising – warnings of the National Credit Regulator against the growth of over-indebtedness, and to the consumer credit market crisis, which developed subsequently. After an outline of governmental reactions, the culmination of the crisis with the collapse of African Bank is reconstructed. The chapter ends with a summarizing market overview at the end of the crisis.

The second chapter is devoted to the historical development of money and credit in South Africa from the foundation of the central bank in 1921 to the collapse of the first attempts of establishing a consumer credit market in 2002. It shows a clear hostility towards private lending and a generous money supply. Traces of the twentieth-century history of South Africa are still present in the geographic and social structures of the country today. This reconstructed development was responsible for the specific normative order, in which the later forms of the consumer credit market was implemented. The path dependency was based on certain long-term convictions about right and wrong economic decisions. Their condensed forms reappeared in the legal framework of the NCA, as the subsequent chapter will show.

The third chapter analyses the legal framework of the National Credit Act. The first sections deal with the different institutional actors, which were implemented to achieve an economic rationality for all economic participants. It reveals an almost complete protection of private property as an incentive to comply with the rulings. Even more importantly, the details of the analysis show why these hopes were inevitably doomed to failure. The following sections of the chapter reconstruct the governmental reforms in reaction to the crisis from 2012 to 2014, showing a shift in concern from over-indebted citizens towards the preservation of the market principles. The chapter concludes by turning its attention to the international consumer credit market frameworks that informed South African legislators, and the unique characteristics of the National Credit Act. Basically, these other legislations show alternatives in the construction of property rights in consumer credit markets. In this context, the still unrealized South African debt relief solution is discussed, revealing how it would represent a political programme for impoverishment.

This governmental obstinacy with regard to obviously failing market principles demands an intensive analysis of the origins, the social foundation and ideological construction of the idea of a self-regulating market. The fourth chapter begins by explaining the argumentative trick of Adam Smith's famous 'invisible hand'. It then focuses on the possible social implementation of a market equilibrium with reference to the work of Georg Simmel. The rationality of markets, its hidden core and the limits of this rationality are reviewed with reference to Max Weber.

The conclusions to be drawn from this complex analysis are summarized in the final chapter. It explains what the South African consumer credit market devices ultimately consist of, how they work, and why they fail. It ends by highlighting some fundamentally different alternatives in the construction of a credit market.

NOTES

1. The year-on-year figure compensates for seasonal fluctuations, especially during the festive season, which usually results in a short-term peak of consumer credit demand.
2. Of course, bank money builds the core of capital that is utilized in loans nowadays, but this does not deny the truth of this argument.

CHAPTER 1

Borrowing in the South African Consumer Credit Market

In 2006, the South African government implemented a reformed consumer credit market after the unregulated market, which had developed since the winding-up of political apartheid in 1990, had finally collapsed under the burden of increased over-indebtedness of customers' bad debts in the accounts of their creditors in 2002.

The new legal framework, the NCA, claimed to promote 'the social and economic welfare of South Africans' (s 3 NCA 34 of 2005).

Section 60 of the NCA provided every citizen of South Africa with the right to apply for a loan. This illustrated the importance of the reformed consumer credit market in the political concept of the government. In a country with very high levels of poverty and unemployment, the law encouraged citizens to make use of credit instead of cautioning against indebtedness. In the introduction of the NCA, a declaration of its purpose explained that it aimed at 'promoting the development of a credit market that is accessible to all South Africans, and in particular to those who have historically been unable to access credit under sustainable market conditions' (s 3(a) NCA).

This chapter aims to portray the resulting consumer credit market. In the first part it takes the perspective of the demand side by considering a single loan offer. It shows that consumer credit – and therefore money itself – has turned into a consumerist commodity that can be bought in different forms and at different prices, is advertised in glossy promotion materials, is easy to access, and is intended to be used up quickly (Langley 2014: 421).[1] In the second section, the perspective is changed to the supply side. A survey undertaken at the height of a public debate on consumer credit in December 2013 shows the product line of the dominating credit providers of South Africa. Here we see a growth-oriented market with different products and high prices. However, some sales limitations signal that this is not an ordinary market.

The very fact that consumer credit was openly – and in parts aggressively – advertised reveals two of the core characteristics of a financialized consumer credit market. First, loans are no longer seen as an emergency solution, restricted to overcoming threatening situations with no financial alternative, but are presented as integral parts of many commodities in the consumer society, secured by the future earning prospects of the borrower alone. And secondly, it constitutes a paradoxical construction, because the inevitably time consuming process of lending and repayment is organized as a market, which means that the agents can 'enter and leave the exchange as strangers' (Callon 1998b: 3). This impersonality is indispensable for the instrumental rationality of a market society, because personal bonds and normative obligations would hamper the pursuit of individual interests (Hart 2000: 8). However, a credit contract by definition institutes a longer lasting relationship and a long-term commitment between the contracting parties.

To make the difference between traditional personal lending and a financialized consumer credit market clear from the beginning: in the case of the still existing traditional mode of personal lending, money is exchanged occasionally under undefined conditions which have to be specified by the social actors themselves, often characterized by the procurement of reputation by the lender, by the establishment of trustworthiness between the contracting parties, and governed by the financial power of the owners of money. Personal lending requires a social relationship between lenders and borrowers, preceded by trust and followed up by the possibility of social control of the repayment (Burton 2008: 49; Fontaine 2001; James 2015).

In contrast to this, the financialized South African consumer credit market provided a complex framework of institutions and rules (D. Smith 2001). Actors would not need to know each other in advance, and the whole procedure could remain impersonal – basically, it was possible to agree on a loan contract without any inter-subjective contact. The market was meant to be transparent and stable, providing customers and clients with all the relevant information and with predictable conditions of the performance of contracts. It created generally comparable situations for all customers, independently of the individuality of actors and the concrete place and time of access. Competition was to be limited to the price of a loan. Finally, social control was replaced by institutional control, which means it was no longer the responsibility of a credit provider to secure a repayment, but a generalized societal expectation that loan contracts have to be fulfilled (Burton 2008: 50). In case of a default of repayment, the legal system would be activated.

However, establishing a consumer credit market, in which actors are encouraged to maximize their individual advantage, is dangerous because the commodity at stake – credit money – is a 'fictitious commodity' (Polanyi 2001: 70–79), which means that it cannot be freely produced to meet an existing demand. The limited availability of money creates lasting indebtedness, with the potential risk of a loss of autonomy and freedom on the side of the borrowers. The dangerous quality of loans had long been a reason to condemn the lending business on moral or social grounds, and financialization could not eliminate its core danger, i.e. over-indebtedness.

Over-indebtedness is defined as the situation in which the repayment obligation of borrowers continually surmounts their freely available income, resulting in the loss of most of their earnings to creditors, and their inability to improve their financial situation. Bad debts, i.e. loans without prospect of repayment, are the repercussions of over-indebtedness on the supply side of the market and threaten banks. Collapsing banks damage all their customers, not only those in arrears. This means that consumer credit markets are dangerous for borrowers, creditors, and for all citizens in need of banking services.

It therefore comes as no surprise that the third section of this chapter deals with the consumer credit crisis which occurred between 2012 and 2014. It begins with the warning against rising levels of over-indebtedness by the supervising authority of the South African consumer credit market, the National Credit Regulator. From 2012 on, this governmental body took a new political role by warning against over-indebtedness. It mandated a research report on the problem, which is discussed in more detail because it shows that the worrying developments, illustrated in the first two sections of this chapter, had been known to the governmental supervisors of the South African consumer credit market since August 2012 at the latest. However, as a reaction to this we encounter here for the first time a strategy that will be familiar to the reader. Malfunctions of the consumer credit market are attributed to the uninformed and irrational behaviour of individual borrowers and not to the asymmetry of power inherent in credit relations. As a consequence, the report suggests educational programmes instead of a market reform.

The chapter then continues by focussing on the peak of the credit market crisis, which is represented by the collapse of African Bank Investment Ltd. The collapse was initially caused by the expectation of defaulting loan repayment, but it was the punishment of underperforming actors in financial markets that brought the bank to its knees.

The chapter ends with a summary of this market overview.

A Single Case Study: Analysis of a Zero Per Cent Loan

The following advertisements represent typical examples of the financialized South African consumer credit market in the years between 2011 and 2014, addressing all potential customers. The examples were legal according to the NCA and not unusual, as will be shown by the survey in the second section of this chapter.

In January and February 2011 African Bank launched an advertising campaign, offering an 'Interest Buster' loan on its websites, emphasizing a '0%' interest rate as its most striking characteristic.

According to the webpage, the allegedly simple offer unfolded into a complex, comparative economic calculation, which presented two incentives for customers to take out a loan. To begin with, it announced a repayment of ZAR 534 per month instead of ZAR 608, calculated for a loan of ZAR 5,000 with a repayment period of twelve months. The difference in the instalments referred to the financial advantage of the offer in comparison to the regular price of the loan, resulting in monthly savings of ZAR 74.

A second calculation presented a detailed comparison with the loan of a fictional 'Other Bank' in a table: (see table 1.1. below).

The line below the table said: 'Pay [ZA]R 763 less!'

The message of the comparison was clear: both banks offered the same principal amount for the same contractual term, and they applied the same monthly fee. Yet, African Bank's product would come at a zero per cent interest rate, and would result in a much cheaper product. The monthly repayments would be ZAR 64 lower, and the overall savings would be ZAR 763.

Table 1.1. Extraction from an advertisement flyer.

	Other Bank	**African Bank**
Capital	ZAR 5,000	ZAR 5,000
Term	12 months	12 months
Monthly Fee	ZAR 57	ZAR 57
Interest Rate	27%	0%
Monthly Payment	ZAR 598	ZAR 534
Total Payment	ZAR 7,170	ZAR 6,407

The commercial included the following: 'Apply for an interest free loan today. Limited period only!', and: 'One loan per client'. The advertisement did not provide information about the duration of the offer. That way, customers were urged to take the opportunity immediately, because it created the impression that neither African Bank nor competitors would offer such a cheap loan on a regular basis. The loan was marked as being scarce.

However, this calculation not only made clear that African Bank was cheaper, but also that a 'zero per cent loan' was anything other than priceless. It was clear for anybody to see that a principal of ZAR 5,000 would have to be repaid as a total of ZAR 6,407, i.e. added to by an additional share of 28.14 per cent within a single year. This was less than the total cost of 43.4 per cent in the offer of comparison, and even this did not exploit the margins, because it would have been legal to charge an interest rate of 32.1 per cent.[2] Nevertheless, the discrepancy between a '0%' as advertised and a 28 per cent mark-up was noteworthy.

Yet, there was more to think about because the calculation of the comparison posed a conundrum on second viewing. On the one hand, the presentation contained some superfluous information like the rows of figures referring to capital, term of repayment and monthly fee, which showed identical figures. They were functionally unnecessary and served only as an illustration. On the other hand, the presentation did not reveal every factor of the proposed contract, because calculating the monthly costs from the principal and the outlined monthly fee of ZAR 57 did not add up to the outlined instalment of ZAR 534, but only to ZAR 473.67.[3] That is to say, the calculation revealed additional costs that were not mentioned explicitly. The line of 'monthly fees' indirectly revealed that there were further costs not covered by the ZAR 57. This was legal because credit providers could charge seven different forms of fees. So, the difference could be explained, but the table gave the impression of an elaborate calculation that outlined the details of the costs. On second reading, it was revealed as a simplified advertisement that held back essential information. Despite complying with the legal requirements, it was a deceptive advertisement that gave the impression of a richness of detail at first glance only. Customers could hardly be expected to make an unambiguous, rational calculation based on this.

At the beginning of 2012, just after the festive season, the campaign for the 'Interest Buster' loan was relaunched, and you could listen to the following advertising jingle on the South African radio stations:

> Some people don't quite know what we mean by zero per cent loan. We mean: Niks![4] Nada![5] Iqanda![6] Nothing! Take your kids back to school with African Bank's interest buster loan. It costs you no interest for loans between 3 to 12 months. Get credit between 11 Jan[uary] and 29 Feb[ruary], and you could win your share of 500,000 Rand in bursaries. To apply, SMS *zero* to 49494, or visit an African Bank branch. African Bank is a registered credit provider. Service, initiation and insurance fees apply. T[erm]'s and C[ondition]'s on website. SMS costs 1 Rand 50.

The advertisement lasted thirty seconds. The poster, related to this temporary offer, said: 'it's easier to take your kids back to school with a 0% buster loan. NO interest, niks, nada, iqanda, nothing. African Bank. Credit that works for you'.

This campaign was launched immediately after the end of the feast days, usually within the South African summer holidays, and lasted until the end of February, when everybody would be back to living a normal daily life. It explicitly addressed parents of school children – who might have spent extraordinary amounts of money on Christmas presents and holidays – but that is only an assumption. As an incentive to take out a loan, the proposition appealed to parental responsibility by referring to educational expenses for the children, i.e. an unselfish investment oriented to the future of one's own offspring.

The temporal limitation of the offer pressurized customers into making a quick decision. The implicit message was that lending would become more expensive from March onwards. The repayment period was limited to three to twelve months, which seemed to be a manageable time horizon – next Christmas the whole story could already have been finalized.

Then, there was a lottery attached, and it was promoted with a total jackpot of ZAR 500,000, which was fifty times the maximum amount of this loan offer. This could be translated into the possibility of winning much more than a loan would cost. However, the advertisement only held out the prospect of a 'share' of the sum, in the ring-fenced form of a bursary. A bursary, again, would be unselfish and would benefit the children.

Accepting the offer could be done by sending a short text message via mobile phone, i.e. without direct social interaction, or by visiting a branch, and therefore without making personal contact with bank clerks. At the end of the advertisement African Bank was explicitly presented as a 'registered credit provider', demonstrating that they were officially acknowledged as lenders complying with the rules and minimizing any possible suspicion on the part of customers.

However, the mentioning of service, initiation and insurance fees then gave a first indication that a 'zero per cent loan' would not result in a zero-priced loan.[7] Unsurprisingly, there were more details to be acknowledged than an advertising jingle could contain, so the advertisement referred to the terms and conditions. Finally, the short message would cost ZAR 1.50, which was a significantly higher price than usual, but not an appreciable amount of money either.

To summarize, this advertisement presented the loan as a solution to financially stressed customers after the Christmas season. It appealed to the rationality of responsible parents not saving at the wrong end, instead of calling for financial cautiousness after an economically demanding period. The offer did not present itself in a realistic way because the term 'zero per cent loan' made it appear cheaper than it actually was. This was additionally stressed by the attached lottery which gave the idea that the acceptance of the offer could better the financial situation of the customer, instead of worsening it.

Accepting the offer by applying for a loan would require customers to acknowledge the terms and conditions of the campaign. Therefore, the legal terms valid in 2012 are reviewed here. They could be found on the webpage of the credit provider and were available on flyers at every branch of the bank, which means that finding out about them required further activity on the part of the customer.

These 'terms and conditions' outlined the limitation of the offer to loans up to ZAR 10,000, and gave further details about the fees: 'The offer is for a limited period only and includes a 0% interest rate and no service fees. Only insurance and initiation fees apply'. The initiation fee was limited to ZAR 150 plus 10 per cent of the amount of the agreement in excess of ZAR 1,000 (s 42(2) Regulations of the NCA). In the example taken from the website, this would result in a maximum initiation fee of ZAR 550 for a loan of ZAR 5,000. This means that the law allowed an institution to advertise a loan at a 'zero per cent interest' rate, and at the same time to accrue more than 10 per cent of the principal as an initiation fee.

The rest of the terms included precautionary clauses of a general character with regard to the loan and the lottery, but did not give further details of repayment. The last sentence directed the attention to another list of clauses: 'Participation of this offer implies full knowledge and acceptance of the terms and conditions'. This referred to the 'standard terms and conditions' for credit facilities and loans of African Bank, not to be confused with the loan offer 'terms and conditions' analysed in the previous paragraphs.

In its initial sentences, this second set of terms required the customer to talk to a bank clerk directly in case of difficulties in understanding any part of the text. Relinquishing this option would result in a juristic assumption of understanding and consent. This means that the bank required the customer to opt in, instead of explaining the terms to him unless he opted out. This is of great importance. Despite the rather complicated regulations concerning credit contracts, and despite the acknowledgement of the legislators that many credit customers had little financial experience and knowledge due to the discrimination they faced in the past, this opt-in clause shifted the responsibility to the borrowing party, if they did not ask for assistance proactively.

The second list of terms contained an explicit notification about the option of compounding interest. The pre-agreement statement could contain a 'penalty interest' which would be applicable even to an otherwise 'interest free' loan. Compounding could also affect capitalized fees (s 40(1) of the Regulations of the NCA). This means that the loan was free of interest only as long as no default of payment occurred.

Of crucial importance was a passage which dealt with the case of non-fulfilment of contractual obligations, because it made clear that even an interest free loan could become very expensive in case of unforeseen difficulties with the repayment. A consenting customer had to declare the following:

> If I default on my obligations under this agreement I will have to pay default administration charges to African Bank. In addition African Bank will be entitled to terminate this agreement after giving me notice. Any amount that is in default or arrears will bear interest referred to in the [pre-agreement statement]. Such arrears interest will be calculated daily and capitalised monthly. If I die, or commit any act of insolvency, or default with my obligations in terms of this agreement, the full amount in terms of this agreement will immediately become due, owing and payable. If I am in default of any of my obligations in terms of this Agreement, African Bank may institute legal action against me, which could result in a court judgement against me, attaching and selling my property and attaching my salary to recover the loan. This would mean that I have a bad credit record.

A few sentences later some further obligations were added in the section on legal costs:

> If I default on my loan, I agree that I will be liable for, and pay all African Bank's legal fees on an attorney and client scale, as well as any necessary disbursements and other charges (including collection costs such as tracing costs and collection commission) that the Bank may incur in collecting the debt from me. I further agree that I will be liable to pay interest at the

contractual rate on the said disbursements and charges that the Bank may levy in the process of collecting the debt from me.

By demanding that their customers agree to these terms, the bank made clear that they would claim more money in reaction to a default of repayment – instead of alleviating the burden of a struggling borrower – and that they would mobilize a whole range of legal instruments against their customer – instead of searching for a consensual re-arrangement. Moreover, a customer would have to pay for all the costs resulting from investigations, debt collection arrangements and legal proceedings. Nor should one forget, it affected a customer who applied for a loan due to a lack of liquidity.

What the credit provider revealed here was a clear but not inevitable economic rationality that was in full accordance with the intentions of the NCA, which encouraged economic actors to pursue their own interests. In the case of a default of repayment, the credit provider did not have to care about the reasons on the side of the borrower, and did not even have to negotiate further proceedings with him or to worry about additional costs, but could unleash his ambition for profit and mobilize the institutional arrangements of society to enforce the contract. The default of a repayment by a borrower could be taken as another means to the end of increasing profits, in contradistinction to a value-rational behaviour that would aim at a consensual recognition of the other's options to fulfil the contract (Weber 1978: 24–25).

These possible consequences of an allegedly cheap loan offer will now be reviewed in the context of the general goal of political and business administrations, which had created the rules of this market.

The establishment of the South African consumer credit market was part of an attempt by the South African government to overcome the problems of poverty and unemployment. In other words, it was built as an additional market to fight deficiencies that derived from other parts of an already existing market economy. Karl Polanyi (2001: 74) explains the basic dynamic of such market building processes: 'A market economy can exist only in a market society'. The reason for this is that market actors are urged to satisfy their specific needs in a market-conformist, i.e. an instrumentally rational way. As a consequence, a specific market contains the tendency to transform its environment in markets, too. In the case at hand, the lack of money to repay the loan by a borrower was treated like the lack of any other commodity, and the only way to solve the problem consisted in the bringing in of the contractually agreed upon supplies. However, in Polanyi's view money was not a commodity that could be produced or bought at one's discretion but a 'fictitious commodity' that required the borrower to enter the labour market, i.e. to provide himself as a 'fictitious commodity' in another market (Polanyi 2001: 71–80).

In a traditional lending procedure between individuals, with personal interaction, the conditions of repayment may be re-negotiated. In other words, the monetary interaction of lending and borrowing could be contained by switching to non-monetary interaction in case of a credit default, e.g. by offering an alternative service. However, consumer credit in a competitive market resulted in the non-availability of socially flexible options of settlement. 'In practice this meant that the non-contractual organizations of kinship, neighborhood, profession and creed were to be liquidated since they claimed the allegiance of the individual and thus restrained his freedom' (Polanyi 2001: 171). The default of repayment in a financialized consumer credit market was not treated socially but institutionally. It entailed the suspension of the initial equality of contracting parties. From the moment of default of repayment, the creditor was a prosecutor backed by the legal system of South Africa, and the debtor was turned into a culprit that somehow had to generate income.

In such cases, the proceedings were outlined in the small print of a loan contract. After the listing of some further bureaucratic regulations, the 'standard terms and conditions' of African Bank contained another clause that gave evidence of the character of South African consumer credit money and referred to the order in which repayments had to be made. In this clause a credit customer agreed to declare: 'Any payment that I make will be used firstly to settle interest, secondly to satisfy fees, costs or charges, and thirdly to reduce the amount of the principal debt'. Again, this was unsurprising in a market economy but certainly not inevitable. In a market such a clause served the maximization of returns of the credit provider because the interest-bearing principal was the last part of the loan that would be reduced. However, in a social community it would have been more appropriate to reduce additional costs and principal to the same extent. A reduction of the principal would mean reducing the interest and fees levied on it, but this would have been in contradiction to the mandatory pursuit of profit in a market economy.

In our example loan offer from 2012, a clause of imminent importance followed in a section titled 'Assignment'. In a very unpretentious way, it revealed what it meant to act in a financialized consumer credit market: 'African Bank will be entitled to cede, sell, assign, all or any of its rights under this agreement, without your consent or prior notice to you. You may not cede, delegate, sell, assign, or transfer any of your rights or obligations in terms of this agreement'.

The first sentence entitled African Bank to use the loan contract as a financial tool in its own right. This happened in the way of securitization, a financial technique explained in an official banking report as follows: 'In the broadest sense, securitization is financial intermediation that involves at some stage the buying or selling of financial claims' (Cumming 1987: 11). African Bank – like all other big credit providers in South Africa – sold 'loan participations', i.e. originally illiquid claims towards customers that were packaged into bonds and sold on financial markets. This way, the seller obtained liquidity again, whereas the buyer of the bond became entitled to receive the instalments paid by debtors. If the price of the bond covered the costs of the included loans, but was lower than the total amount of all expected repayments of the future, such a deal would benefit seller and buyer at the same time, even without increasing the costs for the debtors whose loans had been passed on (Cumming 1987; Leyshon and Thrift 2007). It would allow banks to accelerate the return of money lent, and to increase the sales figures of loans, whereas the investors of the bond participated in risk-sharing with the chance of deriving profits from it. However, the reselling of loans meant also passing on the risks of repayment, and it should be noted that bonds containing higher risks yielded higher returns as well. Securitizing loans was a way of removing uncertainty from the transformation of assets into claims, a miraculous shift of meaning which Joseph Schumpeter once illustrated very clearly: 'you cannot ride the claim to a horse, but you can pay with a claim to money' (Schumpeter 1996: 305).

This financialized option of the consumer credit market generated repercussions for the relationship between credit provider and borrower. In the balance sheet of a bank, securitization reconfigured a stream of expectable repayments into a fixed asset (Bryan and Rafferty 2017: 341). The legal permission to securitize loans removed incentives to perform a pervasive, time consuming and expensive risk assessment from the bank, simply because they could get rid of the risk if it turned out to be unfavourable (Gorton and Penacchi 2015: 505).

The second sentence of the term that forbade borrowers to pass on their loan obligations disguised the alleged legal equality of the contracting parties as an asymmetry between an organized lender and an individual borrower. The latter was not allowed to let someone step in for his financial obligations. The NCA even ruled that other household members would be held liable under certain circumstances, as Chapter 3 on the legal framework will show.

The analysis of the loan offer reveals that African Bank used the provisions of the NCA to offer loans allegedly free of charge. However, the detailed 'terms and conditions' of the loan contract placed African Bank in a superior position towards its customers. A borrower would be a contracting party on a par only as long as he was able to pay his instalments in time. In case of a repayment default, African Bank could put the legal system's automatism into motion, which had to be paid by the debtor and which would worsen his troubles. However, the general demand of the market to calculate at the margins encourages the bank to serve risky clients. Accordingly, there existed a high probability that the loan offer would induce additional cases of over-indebtedness.

Overview of the Consumer Credit Market

The example of the loan offer of African Bank was remarkable due to its advertising of an 'interest free loan', on which repayment was charged at more than 28 per cent of additional costs. The commercial was on the margin of legality, because the Regulations of the NCA had ruled that 'the following statement or phrases, or any wording that has substantially the same meaning, may not form part of any advertisement or direct solicitation for credit (a) "no credit checks required"; (b) "blacklisted consumers welcome"; (c) "free credit"' (s 21(6) Regulations of the NCA). It could have been argued that the wording 'zero interest loan' was close to 'free credit'. However, African Bank could have replied that the mention of fees in the radio jingle revealed that additional costs were to be expected, a step that was enforced by section 21(2) of the Regulations.

Be that as it may, the offer of African Bank was peculiar but not unusual as will be shown by a survey of consumer credit offers, carried out on 13 December 2013. It comprises seven credit providers: the big four that dominated the market (ABSA, FNB, Nedbank and Standard Bank), the two shooting stars of the unsecured lending business (African Bank and Capitec), and, for the purpose of comparison, the self-claimed 'micro-lending' branch of Old Mutual, a well-established insurance company.

The survey showed that some requirements were common to all credit providers: customers had to be in possession of a South African ID card, which was accessible only to citizens and permanent residents. Only ABSA offered bank overdrafts to temporary residents as well. In addition, prospective borrowers needed proof of residence and a bank account; the latter was compulsory because a debit order was the usual way of debt collection. Additionally, with the exception of African Bank, all providers asked for some recent payslips and bank statements, the number differing for employed and self-employed customers.[8] The latter had to bring in more payslips and bank statements to prove the mid-term viability of their business. African Bank was the only credit provider willing to serve customers without formal employment. All lenders set a minimum age of eighteen, but only FNB had a maximum age of sixty-five, thereby limiting their customers to the active workforce.

In summary, it could be said that South Africans and permanent residents above the age of eighteen with formal employment or regular self-generated income and a bank account generally qualified for a loan. ABSA, by including foreign residents, and African Bank, by not requiring payslips, extended these limitations to some degree, whereas FNB restricted it by excluding pensioners. This means that ABSA and African Bank increased their risk portfolio, whereas FNB reduced it, because for pensioners it would be difficult to increase their income if demanded. The criteria listed here represented minimum requirements, of course, which qualified the prospective customer for a further test of his eligibility.

The range of the loans on offer reached up to ZAR 230,000.[9] The repayment period ranged between one and eighty-four months. The next table shows that Capitec and African Bank offered the smallest as well the biggest loan sizes, and the longest repayment periods. The qualification of Old Mutual as a 'micro-lender' was disputable because its products did not differ from ordinary unsecured loans.

Almost all providers had some kind of product on offer that is worth special mention here.

In the case of ABSA, this product was the so called 'instant loan' that could be obtained by qualified bank customers at an ATM; it was not very

Table 1.2. Range of loan offers.

Bank	Range of loans in ZAR	Range of repayment periods in months
ABSA	1,500-150,000	1-85
FNB	250-150,000	1-60
Standard Bank	3,000-80,000[10]	12-60
Nedbank	1,000-120,000	12-60
Capitec	up to 230,000	up to 84
African Bank	up to 180,000	up to 84
Old Mutual	up to 120,000	up to 60

Source: Websites of the banks. Retrieved 13 December 2013.

different from a bank overdraft. There was no interest but a 10 per cent fee, and a repayment period of thirty-five days. It was available twenty-four hours a day, seven days a week. The loan was withdrawn from an ATM like other cash, i.e. without further proceedings, so it remains unclear if customers became aware of the fact that the fee actually amounted to an interest rate of more than 104 per cent per year. This figure was probably the main reason why ABSA called the additional costs a ‘fee’, because as ‘interest’ it would have been illegal.

ABSA and Standard Bank both offered a ‘revolving loan plan’. A minimum salary of ZAR 8,000 was required for this product, and the repayment was made by way of fixed instalments. In the case of the ABSA, this instalment was termed at 1/40 of the loan amount. The loan could reach up to three times the amount of the documented salary. With Standard Bank, the borrower could receive between ZAR 6,000 and ZAR 300,000. The crucial characteristic of the ‘revolving credit plan’ was that the loan amount was refilled once the borrower had paid back 15 per cent of his first loan. This meant that the framework of the loan remained constant, like a permanent bank overdraft or like a credit card that was constantly debited with the loan amount. In the example of ABSA, a ‘revolving loan plan’ could result in constantly transferring 7.5 per cent of the monthly salary as a repayment. This was a way for the bank to provide their higher earning customers with an extended liquidity, and the borrowers thus became accustomed to a state of permanent indebtedness.

Another peculiarity of ABSA’s product line was that there was no ‘early settlement fee’ attached to their personal loans, which was the norm with other banks: repaying a loan before it fell due resulted in an additional fee for the borrower. This was a common practice among credit providers. It can be seen as a penalty for lost interest payments. Yet it meant that borrowers, who were able to commute their loan earlier and wanted to improve their economic situation by getting rid of repayment obligations, were deterred from doing so by a penalty fee.

FNB had the most straightforward product line of all. They required a minimum net income of ZAR 700 after expenses, and they offered loans between ZAR 250 and ZAR 150,000 with repayment periods between one and sixty months. The noticeable element in their portfolio was a ‘payment holiday’ in January, as a kind of relief after the festive season. During a payment holiday, however, compound interest was applied to the outstanding amount of the loan, so that it resulted in increased financial obligations for the borrower. The term ‘holiday’ was surely misleading.

Nedbank was the only bank to publish the costs of credit life insurance on its website. Credit life insurance was mandatory by most credit providers, and on average it increased the cost of credit by 10.1 per cent, whilst it contributed 11.2 per cent to the overall earnings of credit providers (NCR 2012g: 63, 65). Nedbank calculated payments of ZAR 2.62 per loan of ZAR 1,000 plus a basic fee of ZAR 30.

Capitec, besides offering the biggest loans and the longest repayment periods, did not charge credit life insurance. This was an exception. Of course, the insurance costs could be hidden in the other six fees. Their website, like Nedbank's, provided an online credit calculator. This calculator offered no option for the person to define their own risk profile, hence it provided no information about the eligibility of the customer, but it allowed one to estimate the total cost of credit, including the costs of the single loan components. Since Capitec was prominent as the role model of the unsecured lending market, their online credit cost calculator was used to demonstrate the resulting costs of the loan, as an example here shows. Products from ZAR 1,000 up to the maximum amount of ZAR 230,000 were calculated for different repayment periods, presenting minimum and maximum figures as below. Each loan amount was tested for the shortest repayment period first, and the longest repayment period second.

Table 1.3. Costs of loan offers.

Amount	**Repayment period in months**	**Maximum interest rate**	**Monthly instalment**	**Total repayment**
1,000	1	60	1,230	1,230
1,000	84	25,5	112	9,396
10,000	1	31	11,485	11,485
10,000	84	25,5	343	28,774
100,000	1	31	103,810	103,810
100,000	84	25,5	2,649	222,553
230,000	1	31	237,168	237,168
230,000	84	25,5	5,982	502,457

Source: Online Credit Calculator, http://www.capitecbank.co.za. Retrieved 13 December 2013.

The main insights to be drawn from the example above are that small loans and short repayment periods were far more expensive than bigger loans and longer repayment periods. A loan of ZAR 1,000 that was stretched over the maximum period of repayment cost nearly ten times the principal – although this was a theoretical scenario, it was nevertheless a telling one. A loan of ZAR 230,000 stretched over seven years – a more realistic scenario – still resulted in a repayment of more than double the amount of the principal.

Taken together, the single loan offer and the overview of the credit supply in South Africa showed easily accessible, but expensive consumer loans. Customers were attracted by clever advertisement strategies, which depicted borrowing as a responsible act under certain circumstances. Borrowing became especially dangerous after a repayment default had occurred. The details of the then forthcoming consequences were hidden in the proverbial small print, which was actually distributed over a number of different documents.

This overall structure of the market resulted in a development, which caused the supervisory body of the market to issue a warning in March 2012.

Trouble in the Consumer Credit Market 2012–2014

The NCA implemented a credit market that allowed even low-income customers without assets to borrow money. Basically, this was not a problem as long as the instalments were affordable, although the economic rationality depended on the purpose of the loan, of course.

The NCA promoted a self-regulated market that would best serve the public good if all actors pursued their own interest. This meant that credit providers would strive to increase their earnings by selling more loans at the best price they could get, and that their customers would borrow as much as they could afford. However, as we could see in the previous sections, the concrete features of loan offers and the product line were not well suited for eliciting economically rational behaviour on all sides because credit providers could maximize their profits by selling high-risk loans to possibly defaulting debtors, and credit customers were attracted by presentations of unproblematic repayment scenarios. Unsurprisingly, the result was a growing consumer credit market with rising numbers of customers having impaired records.

The new legislation allowed for a rise in sales figures of more risky and more expensive products. In early 2012, the National Credit Regulator pointed out this development. It named over-indebtedness as an unwanted consequence of the expanding market. In reaction to this, the Minister of Finance met with representatives of the banking industry. They were more concerned with the financial stability of the economy than with over-indebtedness. Nevertheless, they agreed on measures to reduce the granting of unsecured loans and consented to reforming procedures inside the existing legal framework.

Yet, these measures could not avoid the final collapse of a major lending bank in August 2014, which will be discussed in the following section.

The National Credit Regulator Raises Concerns

In March 2012 the National Credit Regulator warned of the increase in consumer credit taken out until the end of 2011. Hereby the Regulator raised public concern for the first time since its implementation in 2006.

Until 2012, it had reported on the growing numbers of loan applications and the extension of credit granted, or it had advised consumers to curb consumption during the festive season, but it had never referred to a political problem in the consumer credit market.

But then two media releases were issued in short order, the first entitled 'Strong Growth in Unsecured Personal Loans' (NCR 2012h), and the second 'Credit Market Activity Suggests the Need for Caution' (NCR 2012d).

The first media release addressed the strong growth of unsecured lending and referred to the figures of the last 'Consumer Credit Market Report' of 2011, which revealed a shift in the preferred form of loans that were being granted. Mortgages had decreased in number, whereas unsecured credit had grown by nearly 25 per cent within a quarter of a year and by nearly 60 per cent compared to the year before. Now it made up a quarter of all newly granted loans (National Credit Regulator 2011a: 4). 'Unsecured lending' referred to 'all transactions in respect of which the lender does not have any security (other than credit facility or short-term credit)' (NCR 2011a: 14).

The main advantage of unsecured loans was their accessibility to people without assets; their main danger lay in the high risk of a default of repayment because there were no securities with which to settle a loan that could not be repaid due to unforeseen events.

The term 'credit facilities' referred to payment tools like credit cards, store cards and bank overdrafts. They represented orders towards a bank to pay a bill which usually had to be settled from the person's own account within a month, and therefore were a special form of short-term credit.

The report further revealed that commercial banks dominated the market with a share of nearly 90 per cent, whereas micro-lenders, pension-backed lenders, developmental lenders and other non-mainstream credit providers added up to a market share below 6 per cent. At the end of the first media release, the National Credit Regulator announced that it had 'embarked on an extensive research regarding the rapid growth in the unsecured personal loans market' (NCR 2012h: 2).

The second media release referred to the quarterly 'Credit Bureau Monitor', which showed 9 million out of 19 million customers of registered loan providers having 'impaired credit records' at the end of 2011 (NCR 2011d: 1). With a total population of 50.6 million in 2011, this meant that nearly every fifth South African citizen failed to serve instalments to a registered credit provider in a timely manner (Statistics South Africa 2011: 3). Noticeable in regard to this categorization was the fact that 'impaired records' referred to customers who were in arrears for three months or more, who were registered by credit bureaux as 'slow paying', 'absconded', 'default', 'handed over' or 'written off' (summarized as 'adverse listing'), or who had court judgements or administration orders caused by unpaid debts against them. Their share was contrasted with customers 'in good standing'. Yet, even customers in arrears for one or two months were classified as being 'in good standing' (NCR 2007: 3, 5). This means that the share of credit active consumers that served their instalments in time was even smaller than outlined in the category 'in good standing'. Despite these high figures, the National Credit Regulator only suggested a 'need for caution' in the headline of the media release: 'This [development] will be closely monitored to assess whether the increase evident in impaired performance categories is likely to prove consistent' (NCR 2012d: 1).

Four months later, after publishing its next reports on the credit market, the Regulator made itself much clearer by announcing 'that the latest statistics for the quarter ended in March 2012 indicate deterioration in credit performance of consumer accounts in the first quarter of 2012' (NCR 2012e: 1). The reports had again revealed the growth of unsecured lending figures in a year-on-year comparison and of impaired credit records (NCR 2012a: 1, 4).

Only two months later the Regulator presented the next reports and altered its tone once again. It commented that the reports 'indicate a continued deterioration in the financial health of consumers' which 'plummets' (NCR 2012f: 1). The focus continued to be on the growth of unsecured lending and impaired credit accounts.

These press releases indicate a new role that the National Credit Regulator took on from 2012 onwards. It had started to publish its quarterly reports on the demand side and the supply side of the consumer credit market in September 2007 and in June 2008 respectively (NCR 2008a; NCR 2007; Porteous 2004: 83). Credit bureaux, which were gathering data about the credit and payment history and the more general economic situation of customers, and registered credit providers, were obliged to submit reports about their data to the National Credit Regulator. From these data the Regulator was able to produce figures for the credit market about actors, whose businesses consisted of private contracts and, therefore, remained opaque organizations. The figures of the Regulator presented the official picture of the state of the credit market. Political actors, other participants in the market and the general public oriented their expectations and opinions according to these data.

The development of indebtedness from the beginning of the official monitoring by the Regulator to the beginning of the public debate is set out in table 1.4.

The first data row shows the growing population. Then two categories offer the National Credit Regulator's overview of the observations on the demand side in Table 1.4 and the supply side in Table 1.5.

Table 1.4. Demand side of the consumer credit market.

Month	**June 2007**	**June 2009**	**June 2011**	**June 2013**
Population	47.9 million	49.3 million	50.6 million	53.0 million
Demand side				
Credit active customers	16.8 million	17.8 million	18.8 million	20.2 million
Customers in arrears in %	52.5%	58.3%	60.9%	62.2%
Number of customers with impaired records	6.1 million	7.9 million	8.8 million	9.7 million
Percentage of total population with impaired records	12.6%	15.9%	17.4%	18.3%

Source: NCR 2008a, 2009a, 2011b, 2013b, 2009b, 2011e, 2013e, 2007; Statistics South Africa 2007, 2009, 2011, 2013; own calculations.

The demand side lists the numbers of credit active customers and, in the third row, the numbers of customers with an impaired credit record as outlined by the National Credit Regulator. In distinction to the figures of the official body, the second row shows my own calculations of the percentage of all credit customers in arrears, and the fourth row outlines the percentage of borrowers in serious financial trouble out of the total population of South Africa.

There are three important conclusions to be drawn from this. Firstly, at any one time more than half of all credit active consumers were unable to serve their instalments in the time frame agreed upon. Secondly, the share of borrowers unable to serve their instalments grew faster than the share of credit active citizens, that is to say that a constantly growing number of customers received loans they could not afford. Thirdly, in spite of a growing population the percentage of citizens with longer term financial obligations increased disproportionately.

The second table lists the development of the supply side of the market.

On the supply side three categories show the growing amount of credit granted, the even faster growing share of unsecured loans in the debtor's book, and finally the amount of unsecured loans among the newly granted loans of the three months covered by each report, revealing a peak of unsecured lending at the time the National Credit Regulator first raised concern, but still remaining on a very high level after the public debate had begun.

Table 1.5. Supply side of the consumer credit market.

Month	**December 2007***	**June 2009**	**June 2011**	**June 2013**
Supply side				
Amount of outstanding debt in ZAR	1.05 trillion	1.14 trillion	1.23 trillion	1.47 trillion
Percentage of unsecured lending	3.90%	4.38%	7.11%	11.46%
Percentage of unsecured loans of new contracts in last term	8.4 %	16.10%	22.28%	20.13%

* These are the earliest figures available.

Source: NCR 2007, 2008a, 2009a, 2009b, 2011b, 2011e, 2013b, 2013e; Statistics South Africa 2007, 2009, 2011, 2013; own calculations.

An interesting detail about the published credit bureaux data was that only the first three reports contained a section that subdivided the share of customers into good, impaired or bad standing according to income categories, so these figures could be compared only for the period between December 2007 and June 2008. These data were based on the report of only one credit bureau, which was the technical reason given for abandoning the practice. Nevertheless, the trend shown by these figures is documented here in table 1.6.

The results were not surprising, but important. The first row shows customers in arrears, and the second row those in arrears for a quarter of a year or longer, with adverse listings or with official enforcement acts against them.

First of all, it confirmed that the increasing levels of indebtedness mainly affected the low and low-to-middle income group.[11] Secondly, it showed that the middle-income category represented the fastest growing group of long-term indebted people, which suggests that the affordability calculations of credit providers, in regard to this market segment, were distorted.

Table 1.6. Low-income customers of the credit market.

Month	**December 2007**	**March 2008**	**June 2008**
Individuals earning up to ZAR 3,500			
In arrears in %	59.0%	63.0%	63.3%
Impaired credit records in %	39.7%	41.6%	43.7%
Individuals earning from ZAR 3,500 to ZAR 7,500			
In arrears in %	61.3%	64.2%	64.4%
Impaired credit records in %	42.7%	44.3%	45.0%
Individuals earning more than ZAR 7,500			
In arrears in %	48.5%	51.1%	52.8%
Impaired credit records in %	28.5%	30.0%	31.9%

Source: NCR 2007: 3; 2008b: 3.

On 6 August 2012, the National Credit Regulator published the research report on unsecured lending it had announced in its first critical media release. The report was based on statistical information and questionnaires with ten major credit providers, interviews with industry experts, and workshops with consumers and lenders. In its research, unsecured lending was identified as an expensive product 'that may result in unsustainable credit growth' and was of concern with regard to financial stability and consumer protection (NCR 2012g: 9).

The research report found that the rapid increase of unsecured lending had been caused by the very success of the NCA, because these loans were easily and quickly obtainable by customers and allowed high earnings on the side of credit providers. Two banks, in particular, African Bank and Capitec, had targeted the middle- and low-income market, in which the demand for secured credit and mortgages was relatively low due to missing collateral. Most interestingly, the report explicitly outlined the rationale of credit providers that resulted from the business model of the NCA, and its consequences:

> Consumers that represent higher risks will be charged higher interest rates and it will be anticipated that there will be a relatively high level of overdue accounts and defaults in respect of such clients. It is, accordingly, not surprising that these consumers are reported to have a significant level of impaired accounts with credit bureaus. ... It has been estimated that some 3.6 million of these consumers are deeply impaired (NCR 2012g: 12).

The report also exposed the effects of rearranged payment procedures, as they were negotiated by debt counsellors: 'Extending the term of a loan will have the effect of reducing the amount of the periodic installments [*sic*] ... but interest will be paid over a longer term, thereby increasing the cost of finance over the term of the loan in nominal terms' (NCR 2012g: 20).

Further on, the authors stated that the trend towards unsecured lending was caused by competition in the market, which had encouraged big banks to imitate the business model of smaller credit providers. They all had in common the competitive pressure to calculate the cost of credit in the upper margins (NCR 2012g: 13). Nevertheless, the report advised against further regulation of the business and acknowledged the results of research as a somewhat inevitable outcome of the market because it

> is geared towards encouraging access to credit and there is an inherent likelihood that large numbers of consumers will have challenges in meeting their debt commitments. Access to credit is facilitated through the relatively high interest rate caps in respect of unsecured personal loans

> as well as the other revenue streams that are available to credit providers, including credit life premiums. If these are changed, access to credit will be impacted (NCR 2012g: 12).

That is to say the report deliberately accepted over-indebtedness as a result of the NCA, and prioritized access to credit over the financial health of consumers.

On the other side of the market, i.e. the demand side, the report found that customers showed the tendency to suppress the future consequences of current borrowing in favour of obtaining immediate economic options. One manifestation of this was to ignore the tightening effect of repayment obligations, another was to trade off the affordability of instalments against the total cost of credit. Both responses resulted in instant consumption at the cost of future expenses without calculating the long-term advantageousness.

With regard to these findings, the report resorted to a solution that had already been included in the NCA: 'A broad based consumer education programme will provide consumers with valuable support' (NCR 2012g: 13). The report drew conclusions that derived from the understanding of loan contracts as a matter of equals: 'Consumers that take up more credit than they can repay are, to some extent, complicit in the over-indebtedness that arises' (NCR 2012g: 18). The authors of the study stood by these assumptions despite their data showing that according to credit providers, 27 per cent of unsecured loans were used for debt consolidation. This means that new debts were used to pay old debts and, therefore, led to a state of over-indebtedness over time. If this was true for more than a quarter of all unsecured loans, the resulting over-indebtedness could barely be described as the result of accumulated wrong decisions by autonomous consumers. Instead, these figures showed that a quarter of all customers took out unsecured loans because there were already financially stressed, which means that they did not act with their usual aplomb.

In general, the report contented itself with more technical recommendations like standardized risk assessment procedures or a more emphasized disclosure of credit prices to the customer. With regard to cost-extending credit life insurances and in relation to over-indebted customers, the report restricted itself to recommendations of measures of industrial self-commitment. All considerations were subordinated to the availability of credit as the primary purpose of the NCA, which became most clear when the initially lamented cost of unsecured loans was considered:

> Pricing has a direct impact on access to credit. For instance, where the interest rates that are charged to clients are reduced, there will be a reduction in access to finance to certain higher risk clients that could have been serviced by credit providers at those higher rates (provided that they could afford the repayments relating to the credit in question). … This includes all aspects of price, including interest rates, fees, charges and credit life insurance (NCR 2012g: 18).

This notion was complemented by the assumption of an unpreventable desire for credit on the side of customers. In the case of market restrictions 'credit needs of consumers will be met through alternative sources, which could include loans from family members or the likes of *loan sharks*' (NCR 2012g: 18; emphasis in original). Hence, the intention to take out a loan was represented as the uncontrollable desire of customers. According to this assumption, the access had to be extended under all circumstances because the alternative would consist of an extension of illegal lending practices.

To sum up, the report identified several main purposes of the NCA – profitability, competitiveness and easy access to loans – as central reasons for the worries of the National Credit Regulator, but it characterized further regulation of the supply side as undesirable and had no specific idea of how to change the behaviour of the demand side. The authors were inconsistent because at the beginning of the report they referred to an 'unsustainable credit growth' and worries about consumer protection, but refused to recommend any change of principles, despite the fact that they were identified as causes of the concern.

However, the worries raised by the National Credit Regulator had received public resonance, so government and business representatives felt obliged to react.

Reaction by Government, Banks and Business Representatives

The development outlined by the National Credit Regulator was observed with calm by the central bank, which was responsible for financial stability. It was not concerned with the fate of customers but had to observe the banking business as a crucial part of the economy. From this point of view, there was little difference between consumer credit and unsecured lending to small and medium enterprises.

In its 'Financial Stability Report March 2012' the South African Reserve Bank acknowledged healthy business conditions, increased earnings and no problems with lending. It recognized the rapid growth of unsecured lending but identified no reasons for apprehension (South African Reserve Bank 2012a: 23).

In its second report of the year, it explicitly referred to the reports of the National Credit Regulator, but remained relaxed nevertheless. Acknowledging the increasing figures for unsecured lending as well as rising credit losses, it concluded that the business 'remained adequately capitalized in terms of the current minimum regulatory requirements' (South African Reserve Bank 2012b: 23).

Yet, the alarm sounded by the National Credit Regulator was successful insofar as the National Treasury reacted. In August 2012, in a meeting with the chief executives and chairpersons of the Banking Association of South Africa and of commercial banks, the minister addressed the problem of over-indebtedness, and the issue of financial stability was subordinated to this:

> The representatives of banks and the Minister noted the rapid increase in unsecured lending. The meeting agreed that the poorer households were at risk of getting caught in a debt spiral. Although some of this lending was by non-bank financial institutions, including retailers, banks could do more to ensure that they lend responsibly and do not contribute to household over-indebtedness. While there are currently no systemic risks, the meeting noted and supported the close attention that unsecured lending is receiving from the SA Reserve Bank's Bank Supervision Department. There will be further engagement with financial and non-financial institutions on this issue so that South Africans are not over-indebted. (Treasury 2012b: 2).

This meeting was followed up by negotiations between government, central bank, banking association and representatives of the six biggest banks on 19 October 2012. The agreement was published on 1 November 2012, and it contained a shift in emphasis. Over-indebtedness remained the central matter of concern, but it was framed by an affirmation of the basic business principles of consumer credit. Besides illegal practices, the agreement identified some unwanted procedures which were, however, in accordance with the existing limitations of the law: 'Excessive lending to households even when such loans are not affordable. ... Selling inappropriate credit products to maximise margins (example: using expensive unsecured lending for house renovations instead of cheaper mortgage loans). Extending unaffordable loans to pensioners and other social grant recipients. Abuse of consumer credit and asset insurance, including excessive fees and charges' (Treasury 2012a: 1).

Still, before drawing conclusions from these risky practices, the gathering assured people that it would follow the path of development that had been struck since the implementation of the NCA. The agreement stated that the Banking Association of South Africa and the Ministry of Finance noted 'the importance of credit to the economy, particularly to grow small businesses, enable the purchase of houses and other assets, help students to study at higher education institutions and so on' and that they agreed 'with the Reserve Bank's latest Financial Stability report that there are no financial stability risks at present, but accept the need to take steps to ensure that current lending trends do not increase future prudential risks'. Only as an addition to this confirmation of the principles of the existing consumer credit market did they admit that 'some credit practices are undesirable and reckless, and agree on the need to deal with poor market conduct practices that contributes [*sic*] to over-indebtedness of borrowers' (Treasury 2012a: 2).

The banking business agreed to 'review their approach to the assessment of affordability, and ensure the selling of appropriate credit products to their customers', and that they would be willing to 'formulate a standard to measure affordability, which could then be incorporated into regulations as minimum standards'. They promised to 'develop approaches to provide appropriate relief to qualifying distressed borrowers by reducing their instalment burden, without additional cost to the borrower' and to consider 'appropriateness and the full impact of all charges on affordability'. Finally, the banking association members announced their intention to 'improve client education on secured and unsecured credit, and create and manage a consumer education fund focused on the household lending environment' (Treasury 2012a: 2–3).

This means that solutions were primarily formulated as voluntary self-commitments by the banking industry. The most concrete suggestion was to 'formulate a standard to measure affordability, which could then be incorporated into regulations as minimum standards', which would provide a clear precondition for loans to be legally accepted. However, a change in the law was not considered by any of the participants.

Abstaining from fundamental interventions in the market or its legal framework, the basic development of increasing rates of bad debts could not be stopped, and it resulted in another bank collapse in August 2014.

Crisis Peak: The Collapse of African Bank Ltd in August 2014

Unsurprisingly, the competition between lenders for growth rates, especially in the segment of unsecured loans, resulted in financial problems. Finally, it was African Bank that had to pay the price for calculating at the margins.

On Sunday, 10 August 2014, the South African central bank announced that the African Bank, characterized by the National Credit

Regulator as a 'predominantly unsecured lending bank' (NCR 2012g: 23), was to be split into a good bank, which received a ZAR 10 billion financial injection by competitors and was put under curatorship, and into a bad bank, to single out loans with a low probability of repayment with a book value of ZAR 17 billion, which was backed by the central bank with another ZAR 7 billion (Bonochis and van Vuuren 2014). Stakeholders of the company had to take a 10 per cent share of the losses (Ndzamela 2014a).

This event makes it worthwhile to call to mind the history of African Bank Investment Ltd because the Bank was closely connected to the emergence of consumer credit in South Africa. It had developed from a traditional bank that had been shut down. In 1998, the name was used for the merger between a stock listed formal investing company, Baobab Solid Growth Ltd, and Theta Securities, which was built from failed smaller micro-lending projects. The company's chief executive, Leo Kirkinis, turned from a fundraiser for developmental projects in the 1980s to the owner of an unsecured lending bank, which deliberately aimed at 'making unsecured loans to shack dwellers for housing' (Porteous 2004: 96). Its business model was purely profit oriented. Kirkinis summarized its philosophy in 2004 as 'the higher the risk, the shorter the repayment period, the smaller the loan and the higher the interest rate' (Porteous 2004: 97).

In the South African financial crisis of 2002, it was African Bank which took over the micro-loan book of the collapsed Saambou Bank. The unique characteristic of African Bank among the big players in the South African consumer credit market was that it was completely focussed on the lending business, and that it did not offer deposit accounts or other financial services.[12] In 2004, African Bank was celebrated by market observers for 'good business principles' (Porteous 2004: 96), and Porteous assumed not without reason that it claimed truthfully to hold 30 per cent of capital against its loans, which would have been three times the amount required by the central bank.

However, after the introduction of the NCA the competition in the consumer credit market become stiffer again. Henceforth, legislation offered banks a legal framework in which they could practice unsecured lending without being blamed for 'reckless lending'. The increase in unsecured lending gave proof of the profitability of the business and the success of the NCA.

At first, African Bank, together with Capitec Bank, was the main beneficiary of the market growth because they prospered in competition with the traditional four major banks of South Africa.[13] However, in 2013 the first signs of trouble became evident. African Bank had to announce a reduction of earnings from the beginning of the public debate on unsecured lending in 2012, because it had reacted with 'lower offer rates, smaller loans sizes and increased pricing. These measures substantially curbed credit offers' (Lefifi 2013; West 2013a; 'Abil Share Price Plummets 17% on Trading', *Business Day Live*, 3 May 2013). According to the bank's representatives, this change of business policy, which was in full accordance with the political agreements with the Treasury (Treasury 2012a), had successfully reduced the risk of bad loans, but it forced them to announce a reduction of the cash dividend on their shares from ZAR 0.85 to ZAR 0.25. The stock market investors reacted mercilessly, and African Bank's share price dropped dramatically in May 2013 (West 2013b). Later on, the media reported on a downgrading of the bank's credit quality by rating agencies and on considerations about charges against the bank for 'reckless lending' offences (Benjamin 2013).

Capitec Bank, although offering a more versatile product line and constantly reporting rising growth rates, was affected by a decreasing share price, too (Lefifi 2013). A public debate on unsecured lending in general emerged again. Concerns about 'South Africans living for years beyond their means' (Shevel 2013) were raised.

The important part of this episode lies in the fact that African Bank's voluntary reduction of earnings at the margins of the consumer credit market was answered with a fundamental attack from the financial markets. Shareholders, rating agencies and business mass media punished African Bank for taking political responsibility by withdrawing capital and support from the company. It is important to recognize that the pressure of economic competition had materialized here and contributed actively to the collapse of a bank that refused to apply a purely instrumental economic rationality.

These events of May 2013 had a double negative effect on the sustainability of African Bank's business. On the one hand the drop in share prices reduced the liquidity of the company, and on the other hand the overall reduction of credit availability diminished the options of troubled borrowers to serve their debts once again. 'People who until now were borrowing from one lender to repay another older loan are now being turned away' (Shevel 2013). Of course, the payment of debts with loans did not represent a successful strategy for the debtors, but it resulted in a problem for the creditors nevertheless.

Although the central bank saw signs of more reluctance towards unsecured lending by banks in early 2014 (Holmes 2014), African Bank could not stop its decline. Finally, in August 2014 the central bank and some competitors stepped in with their capital injections in order to assure the public that someone would pay back the loans, and in order to prevent a run on the deposits of other banks. At that moment it turned out that the creation of a sphere of deliberation between competing banks had been the most decisive success of the governmental reactions to the warnings of the National Credit Regulator. In a moment of crisis, commercial banks could effectively be urged to act together to back the market.

Indeed, the outcome of the bankruptcy in August 2014 was significantly different from the collapse of the South African financial business in 2002. Despite concerns about the encroaching effects of African Bank's bankruptcy, which were underpinned by the downgrade of other commercial banks by international rating agencies (Brand and Khanyile 2014), the measures taken by the central bank were successful in containing the crisis. Other banks were able to avoid being affected by the bankruptcy, and the curator of African Bank held out the prospect of the re-entry of the good bank into the market only a month after its collapse (Holmes 2014; Ndzamela 2014b; Ndzamela and Mittner 2014).

The lenient outcome of the collapse encouraged the continuation of the basic track of the NCA once more.

Summary of the Market Overview

This chapter on the market development up to 2014 has shown, first of all, that the growing competition between credit providers resulted in similar product lines. Most credit providers offered special products which encouraged customers to go deeper, and for longer, into indebtedness. None of the product advertisements presented warnings about the potential financial risks of the loans, and none of them asked for rational criteria, such as permanent income planning or careful budgeting, to be observed. On the contrary, terms like 'zero per cent loan' or 'payment holiday' had a misleading effect, and customers were pressed into decisions by temporary campaigns and lotteries.

Taking together the analysis of a single loan offer in the first part of this chapter, and the overview of loan products on offer in the second part, allows us to estimate the general character of the financialized South African consumer credit market. In a nutshell, it showed that the South African market did not address the two lowest strata of the South African social hierarchy, i.e. the informally employed and the unemployed (von Holdt and Webster 2005), because proof of some kind of regular salary was a common precondition. However, it defined a minimum income only in a few cases, and then at a very low level. It was the orderliness of formal employment that made customers an attractive target to credit providers, especially with regard to the option of a debit order as a cheap, convenient and non-embarrassing collection method. The income level or stability connected to it was of secondary importance, because a higher risk level contained the prospect of penalty fees and compounding.

This can be confirmed by the data of the National Credit Regulator. Its quarterly Consumer Credit Market Report outlined the granting of different credit types and of unsecured loans to income strata, categorized into three groups, consisting of those with monthly earnings below ZAR 10,000, between ZAR 10,000 and ZAR 15,000, and those with more than ZAR 15,000. Some results are shown in diagrams here.

The first diagram (Figure 1.1) shows the share of unsecured lending of all credit types. It reveals the boom in unsecured lending, especially after the global subprime mortgage crisis of 2008, which hit the South African credit market very hard between the third quarter of 2008 and the second quarter of 2009. The financial crisis resulted in the deterioration of house prices, and the supply of mortgages collapsed as a consequence, and on a global level. The amount of borrowed money in the form of mortgages granted in South Africa decreased by 36 per cent from the third quarter of 2007 to the third quarter of 2008, and by another 48 per cent by the second quarter of 2009. In total, the number

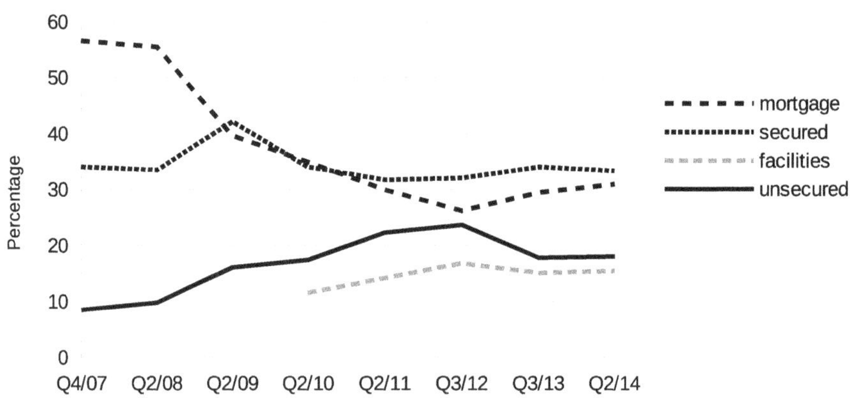

Figure 1.1. Distribution of credit types. Fourth quarter 2007 – second quarter 2014. Source: NCR 2008a: 3; 2009a: 4; 2010a: 4; 2011b: 4; 2012c: 4; 2013c: 4; 2014b: 4. Created by the author.

of mortgages plummeted by more than 76 per cent during a period of only eighteen months, or by a total of ZAR 35.5 billion (NCR 2008a: 3; NCR 2009a: 4).

Unsecured loans were by no means a functional substitute for mortgages, because the amount borrowed was lower, the repayment period shorter, and the risk profile higher. Accordingly, they were more expensive. However, to a certain degree, the demand for unsecured lending was certainly boosted by the subprime mortgage crisis. The increase in mortgage sales after a governmental intervention of 2012, however, reveals that the decision to grant unsecured loans rather than mortgages was also based on business decisions by credit providers. If the shortage of mortgages had been caused by the financial crisis alone, the rise of their share from 2012 onwards would likely not have happened.

The second diagram (Figure 1.2) shows the development of the share of unsecured loans among the total number of new contracts between the third quarter of 2009 and the end of 2014, i.e. after the market had reacted to the collapse of African Bank.

Remarkably, the collapse of African Bank had no significant effect on these sales figures, and during the festive season of 2014 they peaked as usual. This was a sign of the resilience of the market, and a significant change in comparison to the banking crisis of 2002.

In general, the sales figures developed in parallel. They decreased after the governmental intervention at the end of 2012. Now the gap between the lines widened, indicating a significant reduction in the

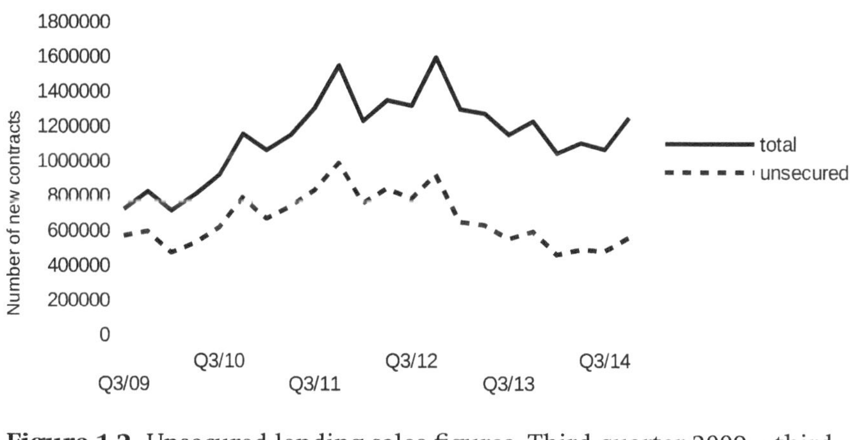

Figure 1.2. Unsecured lending sales figures. Third quarter 2009 – third quarter 2014. Source: NCR 2010b: 15; 2011c: 15; 2012c: 15; 2013f: 15; 2014c: 15. Created by the author.

share of unsecured lending. This shows that governmental intervention, performed together with business leaders, had an effect on their business. The general attractiveness of unsecured lending remained intact, though, as the parallel development still generally shows.

The third diagram shows that the tendency to grant unsecured loans even to income groups who could barely afford it was accompanied by rising levels of long-term indebted citizens. The share of customers of registered credit providers in arrears for three months or more had constantly grown, and the figures rose sharply after the tendency of unsecured lending had been curbed due to political intervention. This effect can be explained by the sudden decline in newly short-term indebted customers due to the decrease of sales figures.

Besides the changes in this development, it should be noticed that a fifth of all credit customers was permanently long-term indebted. This means that a significant share of credit customers were unable to service financial obligations on a regular basis. This caused no instability in the financial system, but it can barely serve as an indicator of a rational and self-regulating market.

The review of the economic form of loan contracts in South Africa revealed that the expectation of unambiguously rational action by borrowers was a daring one, because the advertising of loans did not address economic rationality in the first place. Additionally, the detailed analysis of contractual 'terms and conditions' showed an asymmetry implemented in the access to institutions.

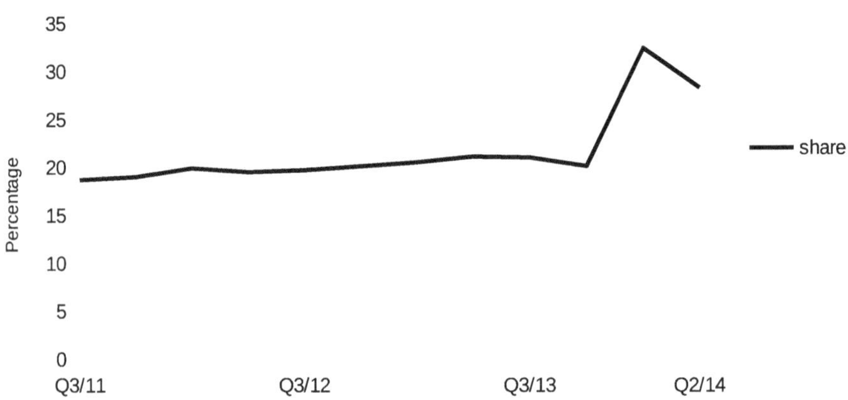

Figure 1.3. Share of long-term indebted customers. Third quarter 2011 – second quarter 2014. Source: NCR 2011c; 2012c; 2013c; 2014b. Created by the author.

To finish the overview of the period between the first warning of the National Credit Regulator in 2012 and the time of adopting reforms to the NCA in 2014, the development of the figures from tables above will be further outlined.

The main characteristic was that the growth of the consumer credit market continued but the share as well as the amount of unsecured lending had significantly declined. The intervention of the National Credit Regulator and the government had obviously changed the credit granting policy of credit providers. As many unsecured loans from the boom period until 2012 had a repayment period of a few years, it naturally required some time for the share of unsecured loans of all outstanding debt to decrease. This became evident from an age analysis of the unsecured debtors' book, a calculation of the National Credit Regulator that showed the age of existing debts. It displayed a relative increase of longer-lasting debts. In the category of debts overdue for more than three months, the figures only started to decline in the second quarter of 2014, i.e. one and a half years after the change of business policies (NCR 2013f: 29). However, the unsecured lending business was still far from having dried up; the monthly granted amount had levelled out at around ZAR 18 billion to ZAR 19 billion per quarter (NCR 2014a: 5).

On the other hand, the number of impaired credit accounts was still increasing despite a fall in the share of customers in arrears. This revealed a pitfall of relational figures because in a growing market the share of mismanaging customers could decrease despite continually increasing numbers of repayment defaults, of course. That is to say, a growing number of customers still ran into financial trouble.

This chapter has shown that the regulated market had established relations between government, representative bodies of the banking business and credit providers which allowed interventions with concerted action into a pressing crisis of the market, suspending competition in favour of collective support measures. All this happened against the background of a continually growing and profitable market.

Less successful were the demands for support for over-indebted citizens. All that could be achieved in 2014 referred to the situation, in which borrower had to make a choice before concluding a contract, for instance a more clearly accentuated disclosure of credit costs. The recurrent demands for extended consumer education remained somewhat ineffectual because they rested on an instrumental stimulus-response-model. All suggestions for debt relief foundered on the principle of full satisfaction of all financial obligations by the borrower.

The market overview has outlined the tendency to sell high-priced loans to risky clients as a main strategy of creditors to extend their market share in a competitive business field.

The development of the South African consumer credit market, and the firm directness of politicians and industry representatives, even in the face of the worsening financial health of borrowers, requires us to reconstruct the long-term developments of the market economy in South Africa, because they will show the foundation of the principles which

Table 1.7. Overview of lending and indebtedness, 2013–2014.

Month	**June 2013**	**December 2013**	**June 2014**	**December 2014**
Population	53.0 million	*(no population figures)*	54.0 million	*(no population figures)*
Demand side				
Credit active customers	20.2 million	20.6 million	22.1 million	22.8 million
Customers in arrears in %	62.2%	61.9%	57.8%	57.4%
Number of customers with impaired records	9.7 million	9.9 million	10 million	10.3 million
Percentage of total population with impaired records	18.3%	*(no population figures)*	18.4%	*(no population figures)*
Supply side				
Amount of outstanding debt in ZAR	1.47 trillion	1.52 trillion	1.57 trillion	1.59 trillion
Percentage of unsecured lending	11.46%	11.23%	10.98%	10.64%
Percentage of unsecured loans of new contracts in last term	20.13%	18.22%	18.02%	15.90%

Source: NCR 2013; 2013b; 2013d; 2013e; 2014a; 2014b; 2014d; 2014e.

govern the financialized consumer credit market. This is the task of the next chapter.

NOTES

1. This designation as consumerist commodity refers to the definition of consumerism as provided by Zygmunt Bauman (2005, 2007). Bauman distinguishes consumerism from consumption by its purpose of expenditure and wastage instead of the satisfaction of wants. The term consumerist commodity has to be distinguished from the commodity theory of money, which understands the function of money as a kind of ideal commodity that is capable of replacing all other commodities (Hart 1986: 638).
2. At the time of the offer, the repurchase rate of the South African Reserve Bank was 5.5 per cent. According to section 42(1) of the Regulations of the NCA, an unsecured small loan could be charged with 5.5 multiplied by 2.2, with an additional 20 per cent charged per annum.
3. ZAR 5,000 divided by twelve months plus a ZAR 57 fee gives ZAR 473.67 per month.
4. Niks (Afrikaans): nothing.
5. Nada (Spanish): nothing.
6. Iqanda (Zulu): zero.
7. This practice was enforced by the Regulations of the NCA, which demanded in section 21(2) that in case 'an advertisement discloses only the interest rate … and no reference is made to other costs of credit, no further information has to be disclosed, but the advertisement must indicate that an initiation fee and service fee will be charged, if applicable'.
8. This was standardized by the Amendment of the Regulations of the NCA from March 2015. From then on, chapter 3(4) generally demanded three payslips and bank statements giving proof of three salary or income payments.
9. Up to ZAR 15,000 they were defined as 'small credit agreements', and up to ZAR 250,000 as 'intermediary credit agreements (section 7(1)b red with section 9(2),(3) NCA; Government Gazette 28893). The difference lay in the information that had to be disclosed.
10. Only the access loan of Standard Bank was listed here, because its 'revolving loan' represented a specific kind of loan, which will be explained in the next paragraph.
11. To give an estimation of the purchasing power, an urban single bedroom flat in the city centres of the South African main towns cost around ZAR 3,000–4,000 in 2011 (Numbeo 2019). At the same time, the top 10 per cent of the population had an average monthly income of ZAR 12,000, but this figure does not tell us much about the living conditions in a country with one of the highest income inequalities of the world. The differences run along the lines of skin colour, which had been transformed into social groups discriminated against under the apartheid regime. Unfortunately, this results in a continued practice of distinction referring to skin colour due to the long-term effects of discrimination. The top 10 per cent of black and coloured

South Africans earned between ZAR 9,000 and ZAR 10,000, whereas the upper decile of white citizens made around ZAR 25,000 a month. Social inequality becomes even more obvious when the lower-income sections of the population are compared. The bottom 25 per cent had an average income of ZAR 1,500, with black and coloured Africans receiving between ZAR 1,200 and ZAR 1,500, but the bottom 25 per cent of whites earned ZAR 5,000 on average. The overall statistics showed that the income of a black person equated to 82 per cent of the income of a coloured person but only 22 per cent of what a white person earned (Statistics South Africa 2010: 8–9).

12. In 2008, it took over Ellerine Holdings Ltd, a furnishing company. The main interest of African Bank in this company was located in the financial services branch of the company that sold furniture on instalment plans, and the problems African Bank incurred through this acquisition derived from defaulting repayments (Johannesburg Stock Exchange 2008; Johannesburg Stock Exchange 2010; Donnelly 2014).
13. These four banks represented 84 per cent of all banking assets in 2012: Standard Bank (with a market share of 26 per cent), Absa (22 per cent), FirstRand (19 per cent) and Nedbank (17 per cent) (Banking Association of South Africa 2013).

CHAPTER 2

Raising the Storm of a Free Consumer Credit Market

This chapter will reconstruct the development of the monetary economy of South Africa from the foundation of a central bank in 1921 to the implementation of the NCA. Its purpose is to outline the traditional understanding of money as a means of facilitating consumption. The surprising fact is that a long period of strict credit control was abruptly replaced by a political consensus to extend the consumer credit market after 1993. The reason for this change is explained in the following chapters, which describe the efforts made to provide the economically inclusive effects of consumer credit without interfering with the existing social structure and property rights to compensate for the inferiority of debtors.

The chapter starts by focussing on the governmental treatment of monetary supply, showing a stable preference for scarcity of means of payment, even in economically difficult times. It continues by showing the initial appearance of consumer credit after 1993, and with it the first 'ruling relations' (D. Smith 2001: 162), which appeared in the form of contractual elements like deposits made from a bank account. The violent debt collection methods of the 1990s then led to an increase of ruling relations established by the legislators. The chapter rests on the understanding that current options are shaped and limited by the developments of the past. The contemporary space of social interaction can, according to Lefebvre (1991: 66), be understood 'by starting from that present, working our way back to the past and then retracing our steps'.

Therefore, we will commence with an outline of the rationale of the final arrangement, in order to make the starting point of the narration transparent. It will explain the space of legitimate social interaction that was developed by the NCA. The chapter proceeds with a historical overview of the development of a monetized economy in South Africa. It then continues with developments, which were mainly restricted to white descendants of settlers and a small middle-class minority of non-whites. The period in question was that of the gold mining industry era. The second period refers to the apartheid regime, which generated the structure of the population and of the country, and which still influences contemporary developments. Economically, the record of this period shows a moral refusal towards the idea of credit, accompanied by a continual confrontation with inflationary problems. The third period covers the financial development of the transition to political democracy, with the experiment of a free consumer credit market. It was followed by the inevitable attempts to re-regulate the market. The chapter closes with an overview of the situation of the consumer credit landscape on the eve of the National Credit Act.

The history of consumer credit in South Africa prior to 2006 can be divided into three stages. Until 1992, personal lending was an exceptional act. For privileged citizens of the apartheid regime it was a costly solution, and the subjugated part of the population could only approach non-institutional moneylenders who offered loans at barely affordable prices. That is to say that personal loans were a rarely used emergency tool, expensive and morally deprecated, because they signified undisciplined financial behaviour. Lending was a minor part of the banking business, and no consumer credit market, understood as a business area shaped by accessibility, competition and volatile price developments, existed.

The second stage lasted from 1993 to mid-1999, in which small loans could be sold without regulation, and the form of debt collection had to be organized by lenders. A loan represented a contract between two parties, and a violation of the agreement was treated like any other breach of contract.[1] This was a literally free market, resulting in high prices due to great demand, characterized by rough and sometimes violent debt collection methods, and it left behind many customers as over-indebted victims of exploitation. The unregulated consumer credit market had destructive effects on the social fabric.

The third stage from 1999 to 2005 was shaped by attempts to re-regulate the market, and by a banking crisis as a late effect of the free market. Legislators tried to re-establish control of the lending procedures by introducing new market actors, but with little success. The credit business had gained a momentum that was difficult to curb again. Yet, the thriving business of the 1990s had left behind a significant amount of debt without any prospect of repayment, burdening the balance sheets of banks, and resulting in a collapse of some banks in 2002, followed by a contagious effect on business as a whole. As a result, market actors became willing to accept a complete overhaul of the lending business via the implementation of a state regulated consumer credit market through the National Credit Act 34 of 2005.

The law came into effect on 1 June 2006 and was fully implemented by 1 June 2007 (Otto 2010: 9–11).[2] Its intention was to provide a unified legal framework for a 'fair, … sustainable, … and accessible credit market and industry', which means its threefold goal was to establish a market that would benefit society by offering fairness to all participants; it should offer a stable area for creditors to conduct worthwhile business; and it was designed to provide easy access to money for citizens in need of it (s 3 NCA). According to the purpose of the law, expressed in Section 3 of the NCA, its primary target group consisted of the broad majority of the South African population that had been disadvantaged during a long history of slavery, colonial subjugation and apartheid. It expressed the expectation that a market would develop in which money could be lent to mutual advantage by concluding private contracts, provided that the participants complied with the norms expressed in the Act. These 'provisions are not a hollow statement of nice-sounding ideals; section 3 has an effect on the interpretation of all the provisions in the Act', as J.M. Otto (2010: 6), Advocate of the High Court of South Africa, pointed out.

Threats to such a realm of peaceful exchange of liquidity were identified on both sides of the market, the most crucial being reckless lending and concealed costs of a loan contract on the side of creditors, and over-indebtedness and false information about the ability to repay a loan on the side of debtors. Therefore, the disclosure of information by all parties of the contract was seen as being of utmost importance, i.e. the business of personal lending had to be transparent and observable, and a supervisory body was established by the Act to ensure this.

Before the launch of the NCA, a review of existing market practices had revealed dissatisfaction with truthful information about the actual cost of loans as a main concern of credit customers (DTI 2003: 3). Again in 2013, the notion that consumers were 'not always properly in formed' represented a main motivation for reform (Government Gazette No. 36504: 26). If creditors presented all obligations resulting from a contract, and could assess all the foreseeable consequences of it on the side of the prospective borrowers, and if in turn customers had a clear notion of the implications of a loan so that they could pick out viable offers, then nobody would have to intervene in a self-regulating market of supply and demand of credit money. That is to say, the expectation expressed in the NCA was that the consumer credit market would benefit society as long as it was clear, straightforward and accessible, and without opaque mechanisms.

However, the Act implicitly acknowledged that there was a problem with regard to this vision of a peaceful market by referring to 'imbalances in negotiation power' (s 3(d) NCA), which it hoped to equalize by 'providing consumers with education', 'providing consumers with adequate disclosure of standardized information' and 'providing consumers with protection from deception' (s 3(e)(i)-(iii) NCA) through the means of binding lenders and credit bureaux to publish truthful information about loan contracts and the credit market.

Obviously, the imbalances were seen as disadvantaging borrowers, because they were the contract parties that had to be endowed with additional resources. The policy framework, which explained the intentions of the government, noted that 'the consumer credit market is one in which consumers are particularly vulnerable' (DTI 2004b: 9).

Moreover, the argument of the policy framework meant that legislators defined the imbalance of economic power as a problem regarding the distribution of knowledge. More precisely, the economic power in the market was equated with the awareness of the consequences of a loan contract until the final settlement of repayments. As soon as both parties could extrapolate the prospective effects of a contract, they would have the chance to decide on it autonomously – at least according to the fundamental assumption of the Act.

Consequently, in a transparent market, over-indebtedness was seen as the result of wrong decisions taken by customers despite the availability of information about a loan, and effected in 'the principle of satisfaction by the consumer of all responsible financial obligations' (s 3(g) NCA). Only if an over-indebted consumer could substantiate the fact that he was not given sufficient and truthful information about the conditions of a loan contract could he claim the agreement to be reckless. Otherwise, it was assumed that he had made a wrong decision and would therefore have to cope with the consequences himself.

The amount of money that had been lent as a principal by a credit provider under the conditions of the NCA was protected property. Enforced modifications of a loan contract could affect interest, fees or the repayment period, and fines for violating the law applied to the company as an economic unity, but the principal would usually remain untouched even in the case of a breach of rules.

This was the straightforward rationale of the legal text. The following sections reconstruct the history of the monetary economy in South Africa in order to explain the conditions under which such a rationale could have developed.

A Tradition of Tight Money Supply

This section sets out to explain the long-lasting tradition of tight monetary supply in South Africa, which still influences political and economic notions of money. It is important for the discussion of a consumer credit market because it represents the historical foundation of the unwillingness to generously provide money to the consumers. The overview shows the stability of this conviction despite fundamentally changing circumstances.

Gold and the gold industry influenced the development of the monetary history and of the social structure of South Africa until the Second World War. After the war, the policies of the apartheid regime, and the reaction to it, became decisive. Both these periods resulted in unique economic conditions, in which lending played a marginal role only. However, this part of the history shaped a general social understanding of credit and of debtors, which is still reflected in contemporary political discussions.

Until the beginning of the 1990s, the provision of consumer credit in South Africa had been hampered by the long-lasting tradition of a policy of tight money supply and credit restrictions, which had become established after the move away from bullion money to paper money in South Africa after 1933.

From 1910 to 1961 the Union of South Africa was a semi-autonomous part of the British Empire. As such, it was shaped by a policy of free trade-oriented world market participation, and the landscape of banking was characterized by the country's role as a gold exporter, because it produced half the world's supply of newly mined gold (Breckenridge 1995: 272; Feinstein 2005: 93). As another indicator of this special role, the central bank, which opened in 1921, not only had to fulfil the typical functions of issuing the currency, being the government's banker and lender of last resort, and processing the foreign exchange business, but also that of marketing South Africa's gold output (Houghton 1973: 192; Nattrass 1981: 248).

After 1924, South Africa remained the only part of the British Empire that minted gold coins as specie, a policy that was encouraged by mining companies and their migrant workers alike. This policy not only kept the demand for the product of the mines high but also allowed owners to pay their workers from the mined gold directly. It was also in the interest of migrant workers, especially those from Portuguese colonies, who had no use for South African paper or token money in their home villages

(Breckenridge 1995: 273–77). This development was important because it placed the mining companies – instead of the banking industry – at the centre of monetary supply in South Africa.[3] 'The mines were ... able substantially to recast both the form and the velocity of money supply after 1925 by simply paying their workforce in gold' (Breckenridge 1995: 288). Due to the payment of migrant workers, much of the money was out of reach of commercial banks and the central bank.[4]

The impact of gold mining on the South African economic conditions was so important, that its historical development has to be very briefly outlined here. Since coming into existence in South Africa after 1886, the gold industry had been closely linked with those economic powers interested in establishing an international free trade market. There was proof of close connections between the mining industry, the government, and the Royal Mint in London (Breckenridge 1995: 283–84).

The gold standard, which intermediated value differences between currencies, meant that a balanced circulation of gold was in the interest of all participating countries and could be used to level international trading relations. The system kept the price of gold at a fixed rate. In 1873, the US, France, the German Empire, Italy and Belgium had pegged their currency to a fixed amount of gold, and other countries soon followed. Then the gold standard collapsed with the outbreak of World War I. It re-emerged as a topic of political debate soon afterwards, especially in reaction to inflationary tendencies in many countries, including South Africa. The gold producing companies were proponents of the re-establishment.

In a currency system based on this standard, 'monetary integrity' was mostly understood as stabilizing the value of currencies in international exchanges, and this was achieved by sound nation-state budgets and the repayment of international loans. Only if these preconditions were fulfilled would nation-states gain profits from their exports at an international level. The effect of this policy resulted in a tightened money supply in domestic markets, always accompanied by the danger of deflation (Polanyi 2001: 141–57).

This was no different in the case of South Africa. Keith Breckenridge (1995: 284) portrayed the perspective of an influential mining manager: 'In a democracy – even a racially exclusive one – only gold could ensure financial discipline'. For the rest of the population this resulted in deflationary effects: 'For all southern Africans the years between 1910 and 1933, with exception of the post-war inflationary crisis, were characterized by stable or declining price levels' (Breckenridge 1995: 276). Between 1921 and 1931 the average price level, although measured with data of relatively poor quality, declined by 3.2 per cent per annum, deliberately brought about in a political attempt to restore pre-World War I conditions (Rossouw 2008: 154). Declining prices meant, of course, reduced earnings and limited economic growth.

After the Great Depression of 1929, South Africa hesitated longest of all countries to abandon the gold standard (Feinstein 2005: 94–95). The depression was accompanied by a severe drought with devastating effects on the economy, and in rural areas monetary practices seemed to vanish altogether. Nevertheless, the mining industry pressed politicians to stick to a gold-based currency for a further period: 'To these people the snapping of the legal thread that bound currencies to gold threatened not merely the stores of capital but the future of gold and the Witwatersrand mines' (Breckenridge 1995: 297). As a consequence, deflationary tendencies increased. Due to a lack of profits, the lending rate rose to 11.8 per cent in a contracting economic environment (Rossouw 2008: 156). This, of course, made lending unaffordable to most economic actors. It also increased the price of existing loans dramatically.

A turn of the economic strategy set in after the effects of the depression had become evident at a global level. Now, the mining industry understood that a devaluation of commodity prices as well as of wages offered the opportunity to reduce mining and labour costs generally and, subsequently, to increase the export of gold. The political conflict also involved the domestic farming lobby, which suffered from high interest rates on their debts and low prices for their produce (Leslie 1933: 88–89).[5] The final incentive for the end of the gold standard in South Africa was provided by a classic bank run after many middle-class citizens had started to transfer their savings to gold in the course of the year 1932 (Breckenridge 1995: 298–99; Eichengreen 2008: 7; Rossouw 2008: 155).

From 1933 on, the South African Reserve Bank slowly moved into the centre of the monetary game. Since its foundation, it had been confronted with the double problem of a barely controlled issuance of specie and too few financial instruments at the same time. Until 1933, every banknote literally represented gold, and gold was coined by those in possession of it, so nobody cared about the issuing authority of banknotes very much. Simultaneously, other intermediaries of payment such as trade bills were rare. This situation made it difficult for the central bank to govern the monetary supply by buying and selling on the open market (Rossouw 2008: 150–51). During its first years, the Reserve Bank had constituted a paper money institution in a bullion money economy. A long-term effect of this was that the central bank had fundamental difficulties in exercising influence on credit granting practices by commercial banks, even after the gold standard had been abandoned.

Consequently, the first steps of monetary policy after 1933 were taken by Parliament and not by the central bank. With the switch from gold standard to paper money, the focus of monetary policy shifted a little from international trade relations to the domestic development of prices, although governmental spending remained the focus of attention. South Africa opted for a known policy path by coupling the value of its currency to the British pound sterling: 'South African banknotes continued to carry a promise of convertibility' (Rossouw 2008: 155). Apart from the importance of the central bank gradually increasing, little changed in the monetary supply until World War II.

During the war, authorities applied a wide range of controls in monetary affairs, including decisions on wages and prices. These price controls, disabling adjustments in relation to a depreciating soundness of the currency, mark the starting point of a long history of South African inflation after the war. Additionally, the exchange control of the sterling area implemented by Great Britain had long-term effects on South Africa. The country started to liberalize exchange controls only after the turning to democracy in 1994 (Rossouw 2008: 159).

The controls were of importance for credit policies because they meant that domestic economic actors could not freely access foreign sources of credit, and foreign investors had to act in accordance with domestic conditions.

At the end of World War II, the central bank was officially put in charge of monetary matters by the SA Reserve Bank Act 29 of 1944. The currency was now a part of the Bretton Woods system of fixed but adjustable exchange rates. Gold was reduced to having a merely distant symbolic meaning as the root of the value of the US dollar which was the anchor currency of the world economy.

A decisive influence on the political and cultural approach to credit was exerted by the election victory of the NP (Nasionale Party) in 1948. This political movement was committed to the accumulation of capital in the hands of white-skinned, Afrikaans-speaking, Christian South Africans, and its approach to a capitalistic economic policy was mantled by a conservative Calvinist ideology (Marx 2008: 22–44; O'Meara 1983; Terreblanche 2002: 302–306; Welsh 2009: 1–51; Westhuizen 2007: 11–61). Under the NP the path of tightened monetary supply was continued, although based on a different ideological justification.

In 1949, South Africa followed Great Britain in a devaluation of its currency in relation to the US dollar, a step which was overdue after the fixation of its rate during the World War II. Economically, this step cheapened South African commodities on the world market, and triggered a new boom of mineral exports, namely of gold, and of uranium as the gold of the atomic age. New goldfields turned the mining business from a labour-intensive into a capital-intensive one (Feinstein 2005: 166). Additionally, the manufacturing industry of South Africa contributed to an economic boom that lasted until the 1970s, based on a policy of import substitution that was supported by the second remnant of war times, i.e. the strict control of transnational capital flows. However, much of the growth was caused by extensive expansion due to new markets, modernization and mechanization. That is to say, it was not rooted in rising productivity in the first place, and therefore was bound to come to a predictable end as soon as the leeway in economic development had been made up.

The economic boom was based on a catch-up modernization of the now politically privileged white Afrikaners, which was generated by cheap labour of discriminated non-whites. Although this model worked inside the boundaries of a nation-state for a while, it had a clear economic limit, especially as South Africa's productivity fell behind in comparison to other countries. Low-paid and unskilled labour thwarted economic rationalization, and a growing majority of the population were excluded from participation – and the generation of demand – in the economy. The political ideology of apartheid could not be made to fit into a growth-oriented market economy, in which the allocation of capital and labour required freedom of movement of both (Feinstein 2005: 180–88; Polanyi 2001: 59–70).

The economic boom had decisive consequences on the financial sector and monetary supply. First of all, it resulted in rising inflationary pressure. As a consequence, the Reserve Bank urged commercial banks to restrict credit, among other things, by increasing the interest rate (Rossouw 2008: 162). The effects of the restriction of credit money for the industry were to be compensated by the foundation of a National Finance Corporation. By using this institution, the central bank exerted a direct influence on the credit policy of commercial banks during the 1950s, led by the same anti-inflationary impetus known from the past (Rossouw 2008: 164–65).

In the early 1960s South Africa's reputation in the world suffered from the rising public awareness of the social reality of the racist apartheid regime. This began with the Sharpeville massacre on 21 April 1960 and was followed by the Rivonia trial against political leaders of the liberation movement from 1963 to 1964. On 31 May 1961, South Africa not only left the British Commonwealth but also the sterling area and introduced its own decimal currency, the Rand (ZAR). The new currency was part of the Bretton Woods system until 1971 (Houghton 1973: 196).

The economic boom had strengthened the financial system, and especially the capital stock of the Afrikaner organizations, which supported the apartheid government. New discount houses, insurance companies and pension funds equipped the financial sector with resources and organizations which allowed for a new kind of independence in the domestic economic development of South Africa (Feinstein 2005: 177–80). Accordingly, a wider range of institutions were creating 'money or near-money' (Governmental report cited in Rossouw 2008: 167). These money-generating instances were officially acknowledged in the Banks Act 23 of 1965. The government demonstrated its willingness to control the lending business with the introduction of more direct control mechanisms on credit. Credit rationing for private loans was effectively introduced by the Usury Act 73 of 1968 (Rossouw 2008: 169).

Only at the beginning of the 1970s did international economic trends gain a direct influence on the South African development again. The level of the inflation rate had a direct impact on lenders because their profit opportunities depended on it. The collapse of the Bretton Woods system resulted in a severe devaluation of the currency by 12.28 per cent on 21 December 1971. As a consequence, South Africa tried to peg the Rand to different currencies. Independently of these attempts, the country faced rapidly increasing inflationary pressure; the rate rose from 1.8 per cent in 1968 to 6.1 per cent in 1972, jumped to 9.4 per cent in 1973 and peaked at 12.5 per cent in 1975. It remained well above 10 per cent afterwards. In 1979, the government finally accepted a free floating of the currency, resulting in another peak of the inflation rate at 13.2 per cent, rising to 15.2 per cent in 1982 (Rossouw 2008: 343). As part of its efforts to fight inflation, the central bank tried 'to limit the supply of bank credit by commercial banks to the private sector' between 1976 and 1980 (Rossouw 2008: 170). Diverse actions of the government, ranging from deposit rate controls to strengthened exchange controls, meant a suppression of market mechanisms.

This changed decisively from 1980 onwards, in line with an international turn towards financially more risky policies aimed at promoting wealth accumulation (Harvey 2005: 19–25; Schraten 2015: 23–24). In South Africa, the policy turn was marked by an abolition of credit ceilings with regard to the industrial sector on 1 September 1980, and the replacement of direct controls by targeting a broadly defined money supply figure. This meant that the economy turned towards stimulating the self-governance of the banking system instead of directly intervening in the monetary processes.

However, the financial conditions of South Africa became even more chaotic. The international change of policies initiated a sharp rise in the price of gold, causing a decisive increase in South African liquidity due to higher returns of the mineral export. At the same time, South African inflation was fighting with high interest rates, and economic actors had to adjust to the now floating exchange rate of the currency. The situation was aggravated by the political opportunism of the central bank, which, for instance, lowered the interest rate before elections in 1984, and raised it again immediately afterwards.

After the refusal of fundamental political reforms by President Botha in 1985, foreign capital fled the country. As a consequence, South Africa had to close the foreign exchange market and stopped the repayment of foreign debts (Rossouw 2008: 172–75). Due to the lasting economic difficulties of the country, an expert commission was appointed, and the government accepted some of its recommendations. From 1986 on, the South African Reserve Bank acted independently from the government. With this step, political responsibility for the monetary supply was finally handed over to market forces.

The remaining years of the Botha government were characterized by an accentuated fight against inflation, but monetary policy no longer presented a political problem of primary importance to the collapsing apartheid regime (Rossouw 2008: 180–82).

Initiating a Lending Business

The direct influence of these broader economic developments on the policy of consumer credit was threefold.

To begin with, the banking business of South Africa was shaped by a long tradition of sound money, with high entry barriers to the market, strong regulations and the requirement to keep large reserves against credit and liabilities, and this made lending expensive and short-term business almost impossible. For instance, international banks were required to hold a minimum reserve against their total liabilities within South Africa, and not in their total balance sheet. As a consequence, the banking landscape was stable. The market had been dominated by Standard Bank and Barclay's since the beginning of the twentieth century, later accompanied by the Netherlands Bank, and, as the only big South African player, Volkskas. Therefore, competition and the need to open up new business fields were limited (Feinstein 2005: 177–78; Houghton 1973: 192–97; Verhoef 2009: 158).

Secondly, the Calvinist ideology of the apartheid regime frowned upon the practice of money lending. The name of the law that regulated most of the personal lending business indicated a sin: Usury Act (first Usury Act 37 of 1926, then Usury Act 73 of 1968). Additionally, the nationalist ideology had pushed foreign capital out of the banking business from the 1970s onwards, a tendency that was fostered by international disinvestments in the 1980s (Verhoef 2009: 180). That way, conservative Calvinism in combination with nationalism resulted in an economic restriction of banking services in general.

Thirdly, the racist policy of apartheid resulted in a political restriction of banking services, too. Access to banks, especially in rural areas, was difficult for those people the regime discriminated against by a limitation of their rights and freedoms. The effects of the geographical division of the country along the lines of skin colour by the apartheid regime could still be recognized a decade after the transition to political democracy. In a 2003 survey, less than 17 per cent of the poor and only 21 per cent of blacks, when asked, agreed that there 'is a bank nearby', whereas more than 90 per cent of whites gave this answer (Porteous 2004: 11–17, 37).[6] 'The majority of South Africans only had access to the parallel informal system of credit consisting of *stokvels*, pawnbrokers and *bomashonisa* acting outside of the Usury Act' (Bamu and Collier 2005: 7). However, these social institutions represented limited alternatives in comparison to legal credit providers.

Stokvels, i.e. informal savings clubs, required some form of income as contribution to the group scheme, and the sequence of payouts was restricted (Bamu and Collier 2005: 21; Breckenridge 1995: 294; James 2015: 135–41; Krige 2011, 2014). Pawnbrokers necessitated some property as collateral, so they represented no source of credit to those without luxury goods. *Bomashonisa* (Zulu: 'the ones who impoverish others') were (and still are) illegally operating loan providers in the townships of South Africa, who usually only interacted with family members and individuals with whom they were acquainted. There was no open competition or a market for them. A case study conducted in April 2005 revealed that they were known for granting very small loans between ZAR 20 and ZAR 1,000, and charged high interest rates between 360 and 600 per cent per annum, and even more in the case of a default of repayment (Bamu and Collier 2005: 9, 17–21; Kelly-Louw 2009: 178). The repayments were enforced by using the social control mechanisms of local communities, which, however, did not necessarily mean that they were violent. On the contrary, as known members of the community *Bomashonisa* often allowed for a more flexible cancellation of debts than formal lenders, and depended on the goodwill of their customers to a huge degree (Hart 1990: 180–81; James 2015: 111; Krige 2011). Due to the nature of their business, there is only sporadic knowledge available; on account of the illegality of their business, *Bomashonisa*, in particular, avoided written documents as far as possible.[7]

Some NGOs had tried to build up micro-lending businesses from 1978 onwards, but their scope barely allowed one to speak of a market. 'These early lenders functioned outside the law, charging interest rates above the ceiling prescribed in the Usury Act of 1968, but were too small to attract any official attention or sanction' (Porteous 2004: 80). In particular, mortgages – a relatively low-risk, cheap and long-term form of credit – were not available to the victims of apartheid, due to the dispossession of land and homes in the past (Terreblanche 2002: 260–64, 384–86).

In fact, the Usury Act 73 of 1968 and the Credit Agreements Act of 1980 restricted the possibility of legal personal lending effectively. The Usury Act prohibited the charging of interest rates above a ceiling set by the Ministry of Trade and Industry, and actually had capped the interest rate for small loans at 21 per cent between 1974 and 1981, a period during which the prime interest rate of South Africa was well above 10 per cent for most of the time. During the 1980s, with interest rates rising above 25 per cent at times, the cap for small loans fluctuated between 24 and 33 per cent. This meant that there was little scope for recovering the cost of credit and profiting from lending.

The Credit Agreements Act regulated contracts for the sale and lease of durable, movable goods and did not deal with financial aspects (Bamu and Collier 2005: 11). It regulated the common practice of buying furniture on instalment and dealt with indebtedness resulting therefrom. However, hire purchase could be interpreted as an effect of the absence of a consumer credit market as well as being part of it, because it represented a non-monetary loan that was linked to the purchase of a specific good from a defined supplier. Freedom of choice as a characteristic of a market was present only in a narrow sense. Consumer credit enables the borrower to take advantage of an economic opportunity, but hire purchase is a way of selling goods very expensively precisely because the customer is unable to choose a cheaper competitor due to the lack of credit.

With the downfall of apartheid, dramatic change set in. The Banks Act 94 of 1990 opened the market for international banking again, which resulted in a rapid increase in the presence of foreign banks (Verhoef

2009: 185, 193). Hence, the pressure of competition arose between lending companies, and they had to search for new streams of revenue.

The consumer credit market itself came into being very suddenly with the Exemption Notice 73 on the Usury Act on 31 December 1992 (Government Gazette No. 14498). From then on, loans up to ZAR 6,000 with a repayment period of up to thirty-six months could be priced without restriction, and many lenders dodged the limit of ZAR 6,000 by simply selling a multitude of small loans to the same customer. There existed no barriers to market entry.[8] In other words, a free and non-regulated market for small loans had been abruptly created. 'This laissez faire approach has allowed retailers, large banks and insurance companies to undertake microlending as part of their activities. These organizations – which dominate[d] the industry – are profit-oriented, and concentrate on the borrower's ability to repay the loan rather than the purpose for borrowing' (Bamu and Collier 2005: 7). In other words, there was no political or economic strategy.

As a secondary effect, the term 'micro-lending' in South Africa simply referred to small loans exempted from the Usury Act, without any developmental component (Porteous 2004: 77).

Some credit providers, for instance Baobab Solid Growth Ltd, collected their capital by issuing shares on the Johannesburg Stock Exchange, and hence had to publish basic economic data about their business. The success that became visible in these figures motivated competitors to enter the market, and by the end of the 1990s all South African retail banks were engaged in the consumer credit market (Porteous 2004: 80–82).

However, in the beginning the granting of loans was still restricted by the limited access of citizens to formal banking solutions. Only bank accounts would make the reception of income calculable and would enable owners to make payments at a distance. More importantly, bank accounts were a precondition for collecting repayments by debit orders (Hawkins 2003: 10). Additionally, they allowed the withdrawal of cash via ATMs. Thus, the extended availability of bank accounts was a crucial precondition for the development of a consumer credit market, and after the turn to democracy in 1994 politically motivated developmental programmes were conducted by commercial banks, especially with the so-called 'Mzansi account', i.e. a cheap bank account with limited capabilities (James 2015: 107; Porteous 2004: 21–45).

Together with the spread of bank accounts and advances in telecommunications technology, so-called credit facilities emerged, i.e. financial tools backed by consumer credit, like bank overdrafts, credit cards and retail cards (Hawkins 2003: 8). A special form of credit was represented by 'mortgage bonds' or 'access bonds', which started as a traditional mortgage but were turned into a credit facility once some repayments had been made (Hawkins 2003: 19).

Beginning with the building of a consumer credit market, some creditors established rough debt collection methods. Louhen Financial Services granted personal loans in exchange for the bank card and PIN (personal identification number) of their customers, effectively depriving them of control of their own bank account. Other providers soon copied this procedure. In 1993, the salary system for public servants started to provide access codes to lenders to withdraw parts of an employee's salary even before it reached the employee's bank account. Private sector companies took over this practice of 'payroll-deduction', and King Finance was the first credit provider to make use of this nearly risk-free and cheap way of debt collection (Porteous 2004: 80–81).

Quite similar to payroll deduction was a third harsh debt collection method, called 'emolument attachment order'. In the public discourse and in the literature, this procedure is often wrongly called 'garnishee orders' because the employers these orders referred to were called 'garnishees'. However, a real 'garnishee order' aimed at the seizing of the possessions and assets of a debtor by a creditor to repossess him (s 72 Magistrate's Court Act). This was a non-existent solution with regard to unpropertied debtors, of course. Instead, the issuing of 'emolument attachment orders' aimed at engaging the employer of a debtor to withdraw a weekly or monthly percentage of the employee's wage or salary (s 65J Magistrate's Court Act). An emolument attachment order was more far-reaching than a garnishee order, because it deprived the debtor of future income, in contrast to a garnishee order that seized existing property only (GTZ 2008: 9–15).

To make things worse, there were different forms of abuse. The capital amount of emolument attachment orders in many cases was not checked by courts, and debt collectors added up to 25 per cent for their own benefit. For the same reason, some orders were issued despite credit accounts being up to date. Other creditors handed their claims to more than one debt collector, resulting in multiple emolument attachment orders referring to the same debt. In some cases, creditors obtained orders from incompetent courts, far removed from the debtor, depriving him of the option to appear as summoned, and to challenge the accusation (GTZ 2008: 35–44).

To summarize: in the free consumer credit market that came into existence from 1993 onwards, neither the products nor the procedures of debt collecting were regulated. The ruling relations between creditors and borrowers were shaped by the direct power relations according to their economic conditions. Creditors could lend at any rate that debtors were willing to accept – if they understood the consequences at all – and had to organize the debt collecting procedures on their own. There was no limitation on interest rates and fees for loans, with fees and insurance nearly doubling the cost of credit in many cases. Many debtors lost control of their finances altogether.

Wasted Efforts on Re-regulation

From these developments arose the sense of an urgent need to re-regulate the free consumer credit market. On 1 June 1999 and 16 July 1999 two Exemption Notices on the Usury Act 73 of 1968 were issued.[9]

The suspended practices gave an insight into what had been common routines of the years from 1993 to 1999. They should be read as a foil, making the reality of a free consumer credit market visible. As a result of the inflation rate of the 1990s, the regulations now referred to loans up to ZAR 10,000, and a repayment period of 36 months.

First of all, the regulation signalled political indecisiveness in regard to expensive loans. Upper price limits had handicapped the business until 1993, but free pricing had elicited high levels of indebtedness. So the Exemption Notices capped the maximum height of interest rate and fees to be charged at ten times the average prime overdraft lending rate. This was merely a theoretical level that signalled the intention to implement a flexible ceiling that would adjust to market prices, but it did not reduce the costs of loans effectively.

A second range of regulations indicated that many loan contracts had been concluded without informing the customer about the consequences at all. Now, lenders were obliged to explain the terms of the agreement before it was fixed, and they were to ensure that the borrower understood the meaning and the consequences of the loan contract. The lender had to allow the borrower to read the agreement, or to have it read to him, if he was illiterate. The borrower had the right to terminate the agreement within three days after completion. Disclosure of confidential information about the borrower was legal only with his consent.

Additionally, a basic verification of the borrowers' identity was necessary now. Registered lenders were obliged to demand and check the fulfilment of preconditions of loans. For instance, borrowers had to give proof of a 'regular source of income, contactability, affordability and payment history' (Hawkins 2003: 44).

A third part of the regulations referred not to the relation between credit provider and customer, but to the relation between society and credit provider. Society stepped into the market by establishing the MFRC, although only half-heartedly. The MFRC was not a governmental body but an 'association not for gain', according to Section 21 of the Companies Act 61 of 1973, i.e. the MFRC was a kind of non-profit company. Nevertheless, its existence transformed the private economic relationship of two parties into a multi-party, social constellation, and aimed at making the credit market publicly visible. The most important step was that the Exemption from the Usury Act was valid only for credit providers that registered with the MFRC, and the credit providers had to make their customers aware of this fact. Only registered lenders could make use of the legal protection. In return, they were obliged to make the rules of the MFCR available to the prospective borrowers. They had to record the agreements they entered into.

Interestingly, the new regulations required lenders to 'approve or decline loan applications in accordance with objective lending criteria in terms of lending policies' (Rule 5.2 of the MFRC). This means that the calculation of costs was no longer a matter of the direct power relation between contracting parties. Instead, lenders were politically forced to act in a market – the cost of credit had to be brought in line with competitors. Cheap credit in a competitive market was obviously not a natural consequence of an unregulated and 'free' business field.

Finally, lenders had to allow the MFRC to inspect their businesses. However, as a non-profit company the MFCR was restricted to conducting 'disciplinary hearings' in cooperation with the South African Police Service, and their reports could be used in criminal courts. This means they were not entitled to regulate on their own behalf (Bamu and Collier 2005: 11–14).

All these measures were intended to move opaque economic interactions into the public sphere in order to make them politically manageable, but there was only a limited enforceability attached to them because of the restriction to criminal violations of the law.

Between 2000 and 2005, the MFRC issued fines of ZAR 600,000, and cancelled twelve registrations with the MFRC for reasons of non-compliance. These figures have to be seen against the background of a total loan amount of ZAR 7 billion granted by registered small credit providers in 2001, and a figure for registered credit providers ranging between 1,239 in 2001 and 1,905 in 2004. Attempts to extend the scope of the rules by the MFRC was declared unconstitutional by the High Court in 2004 (Bamu and Collier 2005: 9, 15–16).

Furthermore, market practices existed which circumvented the regulations, for instance by increasing the cost of interest by charging an almost unlimited range of fees (Hawkins 2003: 9). Obviously, the regulations were unsuitable for directing illegal market practices because they offered incentives only for those interested in legal market competition.

Additionally, the MFRC was placed into a thriving unregulated market consisting of actors who were not interested in seeing their profitable business practices hampered, and therefore evasion of the law was a common practice.

The actual amount of credit granted after 1993 under the conditions of the Exemption Notices was difficult to gauge due to the unregulated character of the market. A study mandated by the Department of Trade and Industry provided some insight for the year 2002, after the first steps of re-regulation had been undertaken. It has to be kept in mind that knowledge about the amount of illegal loans was very limited, though. The MFRC estimated that nearly 80 per cent of credit providers had meanwhile registered with it, and that its data would comprise 96 per cent of all small loans.[10]

The volume of the market was relatively small. The total amount of outstanding loans was ZAR 15 billion, which could be compared to ZAR 325 billion which the banking institutions had lent in the form of mortgages, credit facilities, leases and instalment sales; banks also lent more than 50 per cent of unsecured small loans.

The total number of accounts registered with the MFRC indicated a bigger market, showing nearly 5 million credit active citizens, which means that more than 11 per cent of the total population of South Africa was affected. The average loan size was ZAR 1,112. A sample of the interest charged on small, unsecured loans revealed rates between 228 and 360 per cent for one-month cash loans, and between 83 and 208 per cent for loans between ZAR 1,000 and ZAR 5,000 with a repayment period between four and twelve months. In comparison, the average outstanding monthly amount for each credit card was ZAR 7,500, at an interest rate of around 24 per cent. This indicated, unsurprisingly, that low-income groups had to access small and expensive loans from the unsecured market, whereas upper-income groups on average withdrew seven times the amount from relatively cheap credit cards (Hawkins 2003: 41–47). In many cases, the provider was the same bank. This, again, made it clear that a competitive market with equal prices for all customers required political regulation because the natural development of the barely regulated business generated a fragmented market.

Legal Solutions to Over-Indebtedness before the NCA

As a consequence of the Exemption Notices, over-indebtedness became a publicly recognized problem. The South African law only provided three options for relief from indebtedness derived from commercial practice. However, none of the measures available seemed to be suitable for over-indebted consumers.

The first possibility consisted of debt administration. As long as debts did not exceed ZAR 50,000, Section 74 of the Magistrate's Courts Act allowed for the option of engaging a debt administrator. This option applied in the case of a debtor with insufficient assets to satisfy the claims against him, and it protected the debtor from legal action and execution proceedings (s 74 Magistrate's Court Act). It extended to past debts only and excluded so-called *in futuro* debts, which had to be paid by future instalments. A debt administrator appointed by a court was entitled to collect payments from a debtor, and to distribute them in equal shares among the creditors. Yet, during this time the debts still accrued interest, and the procedure ended only with the full payment of all debts and fees (Boraine and Roestoff 2002). Debt administrators could charge fees up to 12.5 per cent of the amount collected, and additionally they could seek the service of an attorney who was entitled to another 10 per cent. Some lawyers took both roles and charged 22.5 per cent.

Quite often, deceitful behaviour of administrators was reported. Some of them promised their debtors lower monthly payments if they recruited more indebted clients for the administrator, thereby building a pyramid scheme. Due to the upper limit of ZAR 50,000 for debt administration, most clients came from lower-income groups, and had little education. Obviously, this option presented a debt trap rather than a solution to individual borrowers (Bamu and Collier 2005: 11–12).

The second legal way of solving over-indebtedness was a sequestration. From the Insolvency Act 24 of 1936 the options of a voluntary surrender by the debtor, or a compulsory sequestration by demand of a creditor, were derived on the precondition that the debtor was actually insolvent (s 10(b) Insolvency Act). However, both were available only through a High Court decision, which usually required the services of attorneys and advocates. Moreover, section 6(c) of the Insolvency Act demanded that a sequestration had to be 'to the advantage of creditors', i.e. all creditors had to benefit from a sequestration, and proof of this had to be given. Although the Act contained no definition, judicial interpretation over the years made it clear that it had to be a pecuniary benefit.

Additionally, the Act provided an option to use future income of the insolvent for the benefit of creditors (Boraine and Roestoff 2002: 2–8). All in all, the Insolvency Act presented no solution to over-indebted citizens without assets and an insufficient prospect of income.

The third legal possibility consisted of the option of a voluntary agreement with one or all creditors, but they could 'not be forced into such proposals', so this remained an unlikely solution (Boraine and Roestoff 2002: 3).

The Near Collapse of the Banking Business in 2002

By the end of 2001 it had become clear that the Exemption Notices had been insufficient to re-regulate the market. In March 2002, the responsible Department of Trade and Industry mandated research for a fundamental reform of the credit industry.

> There is broad agreement that current laws are weak and outdated. The Department of Trade and Industry made certain changes to address specific problems such as increasing the protection on micro-loans, one change that was introduced in the revised exemption notice. The approach has, nevertheless, been piecemeal and a thorough and holistic assessment became essential. (DTI 2004a: 1)

This was supported by the finding that the free credit market of the 1990s had still excluded huge parts of the population from access to formalized lending products. 'The majority of consumers only have access to products such as micro-loans, hire-purchase and store cards – at much higher interest rates' (DTI 2003: 3).

Of course, market actors profiting from the current conditions were not interested in having their business curbed, but upcoming developments generated a sufficient willingness by the lending business to agree, and representatives of the business had a crucial influence on the debates.[11]

Further pressure to reform the market derived from the collapse of three banks in early 2002. The increasing competition in a limited market, consisting of customers who were vulnerable due to insecure working conditions and an emergent HIV-related health crisis, caused a deterioration in the quality of risk assessment procedures, and of other credit standards.

Most spectacular was the bankruptcy of Saambou Bank in February 2002. Saambou was the sixth biggest among the retail banks engaged in providing small loans to low-income borrowers. Growing concerns about losses due to unpaid debts triggered a run on the deposits of the bank, under which it collapsed. In concert with other failures and bankruptcies, trust in the lending and deposit business was seriously dented (Porteous 2004: 12, 82–85, 143–44). As a result, the Ministry pressed the need for legislative changes from fear of a 'systemic risk' and commissioned a Technical Committee to make suggestions for a reform, which officially published a draft paper under the title 'Driving Competitiveness, Consumer confidence and business excellence' on 9 September 2004 (Government Gazette No. 26774: 4).

One remarkable characteristic of this tense situation was that political groups from all directions showed an interest in the maintenance of the consumer credit market. The reform of the consumer credit market was propelled by representatives of the interests of borrowers as much as of lenders. The Financial Sector Charter was driven by the political desire to provide financial services to low-income customers.

In August 2002, Nedlac (National Economic Development and Labour Council) achieved a common declaration by representatives from government, trade unions, civil society organizations and the financial sector, which led to the Financial Sector Charter, signed in October 2003 (Porteous 2004: 7–10). It demanded 'appropriate and affordable priced products and services for effective take up' by persons living on less than US $2 per day (s 2.22.5 Financial Sector Charter; Porteous 2004: 15).

Remarkable in this context was the 'Red October Campaign' initiated by the SACP (South African Communist Party) that, among other initiatives, urged the banking industry to agree to the Financial Sector Charter (Porteous 2004: 14–20).[12] The Trade Union Federation COSATU submitted proposals for the National Credit Bill in which it demanded 'access for all, to financial services, including an amnesty for those listed by credit bureaux and the development of affordable financial services for poor households' (COSATU 2005: 6).

One reason for the activity of labour movement organizations was the still intolerable housing conditions of most of the victims of the apartheid regime. At the beginning of political democracy in 1994, the demand for credit and the defaulting on loans already represented a problem in these areas of poverty and discrimination. In 1995, government and banks built the joint venture Servcon Housing Solutions (Pty) Ltd, which was supervised by the National Department of Human Settlement. It dealt with 'non-performing loans and properties in possession of banks due to defaulting loans'. Servcon functioned as a kind of debt counselling organization. However, it gave clear priority to the interest of banks, because in case of conflict it 'assists identified defaulting beneficiaries with the rescheduling of their existing loans, or where affordability dictates to relocate to alternative affordable housing opportunities' (s 5.3.1 National Department of Human Settlements services). In other words, the protection of property was prioritized over the interests of residents. In case of doubt, residents were evicted from their homes.

By 2002, it had become clear that Servcon was not able to stabilize the relations between banks and debtors.[13] At the same time, the then Minister of the Department, Sankie Mthembi-Mahanyele, thought of enforcing more services by banks to low-income communities and borrowers by implementing a Community Reinvestment Bill. The bill was redrawn after protests from the financial sector (Gumede 2007: 294; Porteous 2004: 7; Rose 2002). The situation culminated in violent clashes between envoys of Servcon and local residents organized in the Anti-Eviction Campaign (Hooper-Box 2002), which were part of the rising so-called 'service delivery protests' (Alexander 2010; G. Hart 2014: 19–35). This conflict, with opposition from the financial sector to governmentally enforced investments on the one hand, and violent protests from over-indebted borrowers on the other hand, increased the pressure to establish a reformed consumer credit market.

Another key reason for the implementation of a credit market – instead of abandoning it – was the high level of unemployment with no prospect of turning a significant number of people into formal wage earners in the near future (von Holdt and Webster 2005; Marais 2011: 176–201). Hence, it was hoped that the lending business would initiate entrepreneurial activity in the informal sector. A director of the Department of Trade and Industry envisaged the possibility that a consumer credit market could 'provide the capital required to facilitate the integration of all people into the mainstream economy' (cited in Bamu and Collier 2005: 7).

In 2001, the then President Mbeki pleaded in favour of a resilient market, too: 'We need to develop the capacity to make success easier while retaining a well-managed financial sector' (cited in Bamu and Collier 2005: 7). In an official paper on behalf of the Ministry of Trade and Industry, Penelope Hawkins argued:

> The volume of credit advanced in the economy provides an indication of the degree to which those with expenditure plans in excess of current income, are able to give effect to such plans. However, where the cost or price of this credit is far in excess of that which would prevail in a competitive market, access to credit may unduly burden the future income streams and lead to further misery for those who use credit for short term consumption needs. (Hawkins 2003: 13)

Lack of liquidity was seen as an obstacle to economic development, and to a transparent market as a guarantor of best prices and rational decisions by the supply and the demand side.

In the debate about the upcoming National Credit Bill, the interrelation between economy and law became evident in two ways. Some actors blamed legal restrictions for expensive loans, whereas others claimed that insufficient enforcement of regulations had compelled credit providers to make loans expensive.

As an example of the former, one line of argument rejected the concept of consumer protection by interest rate caps, claiming that especially those citizens without assets that could serve as collateral would be excluded from the consumer credit market. The logic of the argument claimed that credit providers would only take on the risk with the prospect of sufficient earnings (Goodwin-Groen 2006: 19–30).[14]

As an example of the latter, another argument claimed that the absence of legal resources to enforce a loan contract would result in high interest rates and expensive loans. The rationale of this argument was that a legal guarantee of property was necessary to reduce the risk of losses (Boraine and Roestoff 2002: 1).

There was consensus in the endeavour towards cheap and easily accessible loans despite differing arguments. This view was expressed by commentators of the National Credit Bill who argued that support of the regulations would depend on 'whether the perceived benefits of compliance will outweigh the costs, thereby rendering compliance worthwhile' (Bamu and Collier 2005: 26).

Undisputed in this approach to consumer credit was a theoretical market-based principle, notwithstanding a social reality that gave account of the effects contradictory to the theory. 'In general, low-income consumers pay the highest rates for credit with the shortest maturity, unless they have access to security such as property, pensions or insurance policies' (Hawkins 2003: 9).

Despite this understanding, the report omitted to deal with the fact that the extension of the consumer credit market had to be the goal, and only the precise framing had to be debated. The solution was not seen to exist in a renunciation of consumer credit, but in a stimulation of the market, forecasting lower costs of credit for low-income customers as a result of the increasing competition of 'market players'. Contrary to restrictions on market mechanisms, the existence of maximum interest rates was seen as an obstacle for the access of lower-income groups to credit. 'Although the cap aims to protect the most vulnerable, there is evidence to suggest that these are the individuals who suffer most from its imposition' (Hawkins 2003: 11). FinMark Trust (Goodwin-Groen 2006: 19–30), as an important market player that was involved in the development of the coming National Credit Bill, expressly supported this point of view. Remarkably, these arguments only took the access to credit into account, not its repayment.

Alternative models of granting low-income groups access to finance, like a restriction of consumer credit to developmental purposes or savings-based lending schemes, were repudiated (Bamu and Collier 2005: 27–28).

From the perspective of the government, the result of the development of the consumer credit market was up to this point a divided market. 'It is a market that both reflects, but also reinforces, the two economies of South Africa – one economy that is modern, globally integrated and producing most of the country's wealth; the other characterized by underdevelopment and structurally disconnected from the first and the global economy' (DTI 2004b: 12). The lower stratum was seen to be characterized by people with a more urgent need of credit, but fewer options to attain it, at lower quality and higher prices, in comparison to the better-off stratum. Interestingly, the legislation to come made no differentiation between these two kinds of customers.

This means that the prospective consumer credit market was seen as a measure to unite these two economies. After a decade of free-market experiences, the fundamental crisis of the banking business had finally created the willingness to undertake a complete overhaul of the market. The quick provision of consumer credit was not queried by governmental forces, which suffered from a lack of financial resources to expand the welfare state significantly, or to start public investment projects on a large scale. This approach was supported by all economic actors that were interested in an extension of markets.

NOTES

1. Breach of contract was experienced as a criminal act of major severity by the suppressed part of the population since the Master and Servants Act of 1856 had imposed heavy punishment on it (Feinstein 2005: 58; Terreblanche 2002: 196–97, 200).
2. It replaced the Credit Agreements Act 75 of 1980, the Usury Act 73 of 1968 and its exemptions, and the Usury Laws Act 57 of 1996.
3. Before the restoration of the gold standard by the British government in 1925, South African gold mines had benefited from the sale of gold to New York, exploiting a classic economic mechanism that emerged from the difference between the face value of a currency and the commodity price of

the metal. This was one of the reasons for Britain to return to a (modified) gold standard (Breckenridge 1995: 276; Eichengreen 2008: 9).

4. The more so, as much of the money was taken by migrant workers to their domestic markets, especially in Portuguese East Africa.
5. As early as 1810 David Ricardo had recognized that farmers suffered the most from deflationary tendencies (Eichengreen 2008: 13–14).
6. In regard to David Porteous's book, it has to be taken into account that he was a member of the Technical Committee appointed by the Department of Trade and Industry, which was charged to review the situation in the credit market, i.e. he was an actor involved in the changes and not a scientific or journalistic observer (DTI 2003: 3).
7. The MFRC (Micro-Finance Regulatory Council) surveyed the extension of illegal practices in 2004 and found between 17 per cent unregistered lenders in Soweto and more than 40 per cent in Polokwane and Woodstock (Bamu and Collier 2005: 17–18).
8. How radical this reform was can only be understood by contrasting the deregulation with the various attempts of the previous Banking Acts and Bank Acts of South Africa to group banking institutions into different business groups like 'commercial banks' or 'building societies' or 'deposit-taking institutions', and to impose different requirements and limitations on them (Houghton 1973: 188–97; Verhoef 2009).
9. Notice 713 from 1 June 1999 was published in Government Gazette No. 20145 and Notice 910 from 16 July 1999 was published in Government Gazette No. 20307.
10. The study of the DTI, however, terms all of these loans 'microloans', defining everything falling under the Exemption Notice of the Usury Act as such. In this study, the term microloan is reserved for loans with developmental purpose, therefore the terms small loans and/or unsecured loans are used here. Regarding the original concept of microloans, see Bateman (2014) and Hulme (2008).
11. Many of the studies prior to legislation had been conducted by actors of the market.
12. The name of the campaign explicitly referred to the communist October revolution in Russia in 1917 (SACP 2013).
13. This is documented by a newspaper report: 'Servcon has a portfolio of about 23,000 properties in low-income areas with an outstanding balance of [ZA] R863-million. It has returned 14,893 properties to the banks by selling the properties back to the former owners, rescheduling the loan or getting vacant possession by occupants voluntarily vacating, right-sizing or evicting uncooperative occupants' (Hooper-Box 2002).
14. It should be mentioned that this study was mandated by FinMark Trust, a foundation exploring the options for micro-lending, funded by the British government.

CHAPTER 3

The Institutional Framework

Implementing a Consumer Credit Market

The purpose of this chapter is to outline the main characteristic of a financialized consumer credit market that was implemented by the National Credit 34 of 2005, and how is differs from traditional forms of money lending. A financialized market is constituted by a number of elements and actors, which are not part of the loan agreement itself but which are indispensable for the contracting parties to achieve a legal agreement that can be enforced by law if need be.

The chapter begins with a detailed analysis of the realm of legality as developed by the NCA. It then continues by including the economic effects of the legal framework, especially with regard to prices. This is then supplemented by an explanation of the National Payment System, an important but often neglected factor of the financialization of the consumer credit market. The next part focusses on the legislative changes introduced in the aftermath of the crisis, which were piecemeal and without a unified approach. The last section deals with the intended introduction of a debt discharge option, which was finally drafted in 2018 but was still being debated at the time of writing. The important argument is that it will not affect the basic mechanisms of the legal framework anyway.

The analysis requires a detailed review of the legal framework of the market due to a peculiarity of the NCA: although the act gives the clear image of a self-regulated market, in which credit providers lend surplus money to borrowers in need, and to the benefit of all, it acknowledges 'imbalances in negotiation power between consumers and credit providers' (s 3(e) NCA) that have to be addressed. As a consequence, the act serves two ideas at the same time. On the one hand, the market is seen as a realm of a private pursuit of individual interests, which has to be left untouched by governmental interventions in order to generate the maximum of benefits. On the other hand, it tries to solve the problem of 'imbalances', a term that seems to negate the equality of market actors. Yet, if market actors are not on a par, the idea of a self-regulating market is a chimera, of course.

Theoretically, this problem is addressed by Karl Polanyi's (2001: 79) notion of a 'double movement', which treats the problem that money is not a commodity like any other, but a 'fictitious' one, because in a profit-oriented economy it cannot be produced in ways that a market balance of supply and demand would require. A consumer credit market illustrates this problem in an apparent way: for one thing, the intention of a credit market is to better allocate money in the economy by motivating owners of surplus to lend it to borrowers. At the same time, the motivation to do so derives from the possibility of making profits, which requires the willingness of borrowers to pay for the service. This uneven relation between credit providers and lenders exists due to the scarcity of money, which is the consequence of the simultaneous competing seizure of limited resources by different actors (Stanley 1968).

Polanyi (2001: 79) outlines the political consequences of attempts to implement ideas of free market economies in the nineteenth century: 'the extension of the market organization in respect to genuine commodities was accompanied by its restriction in respect to fictitious ones'. This means that the markets of land, labour and money necessarily required political intervention and could not be conceptualized as self-regulating institutions. The same development is confirmed for the case of the South African consumer credit market.

To begin with, the idea of establishing a market derived from the unimpeded interaction of credit providers and borrowers resulted in the creation of the National Credit Regulator and the National Consumer Tribunal as two supervising institutions which revealed a hybrid character with regard to market intervention and legal judgement capacities. Then, credit scoring as a calculative technology to replace a relationship of trust between lender and borrower by a proactive control of consumers' behaviour took centre stage of the market operations. Furthermore, 'reckless lending' and 'over-indebtedness' as previously identified main obstacles of a functional credit market were turned into fine-grained legal terms that put the contracting parties into different power positions. Only after understanding the precise meaning of 'reckless lending' and 'over-indebtedness' did the crucial meaning of credit scoring and the powerlessness of debt counsellors become obvious. Even the power of courts was limited with regard to loan contracts that had been established in compliance with the National Credit Act. And, making the situation even worse, credit contracts of the most risky kinds – student loans and emergency loans – were excluded from the core regulations of the Act. Finally, the explanation of the payment systems complements the understanding of the institutional framework.

The initial statement of 'imbalances in negotiation power' is reviewed once again in the light of the constellation of rules and institutions, revealing the effect of the ideology of a self-regulating consumer credit market.

The Institutions of the National Credit Act

This section focusses on the National Credit Regulator, the National Consumer Tribunal, the role of credit bureaux and of payment systems in the constitution of the market. Together with debt counsellors, which are discussed in the next section, they have in common that they are not participants of a loan contract but an indispensable element of the new consumer credit market.

As the outcome of negotiations lasting more than three years, the National Credit Act was finally set up in June 2006, and it was regarded as a decisive shift concerning the existing private lending practices: 'The Act represents a clean break from the past and bears very little resemblance to its predecessors' (Otto 2010: 3).

So far, commentators have mainly focussed their review of the Act on one of three perspectives. The first category was formed by market actors, focussing on the effects of the NCA on business returns. Many of them had been actively involved in the debate on the Act (Goodwin-Groen 2006; Maris IT 2006). The second and biggest group was formed by legal scholars reflecting on the juridical effects of the law (Heerden and Otto 2007; Kelly-Louw 2007, 2008, 2009; Neethling 2006; Nyaruwata 2009; Otto 2009, 2010; Roestoff and Coetzee 2012; Roestoff and Renke 2005, 2006; Stoop 2009, 2010; Vessio 2008). I have reviewed the work of this group in more detail elsewhere (Schraten 2014). A final cluster could be formed from those turning their attention towards the effects of consumer credit on the borrowers (Campbell 2007; Collins 2008; Collins et al. 2009; James 2012, 2013, 2015). The first group takes on the economy of the supply side, whereas the second deals with the legal aspects of the supply side, and the latter group addresses the demand side.

In this chapter I will provide the perspective that is missing from these works: an analysis of the market as a whole, i.e. as a circuit of supply and demand that consists of legal relations and the exchange of money (Peebles 2010). The policy framework, which accompanied the implementation of the National Credit 34 of 2005, stated that 'credit cannot be seen as a basic universal service to which access should be extended in the same way as access to water, healthcare and electricity. There is a greater need to balance access to credit with protection for consumers, especially the vulnerable' (DTI 2004c: 7).

This reflected the insight of Karl Polanyi (2001: 71–80) that money was not an ordinary commodity; however, it was expressed in a paradoxical way. A term like 'the vulnerable' signalled that the political project was deliberately dealing with persons characterized by their economic weakness, but it turned them into customers with a high demand for consumer credit nevertheless. It acknowledged that it could do so only by implementing functional regulations.

Therefore, the next step of analysis consists of observations on how the political system of South Africa implemented a law into the legal system, and a consideration of this from a sociological perspective. The legal significance of the National Credit Act is of interest insofar as it affected the economic behaviour of participants in the consumer credit market. This interest in the legal character is accompanied by an extension of the interest in its economic, political and social effects, i.e. the interaction with the environment into which the legal system was embedded. Instead of defining a causality, or a domination of one by another, the different networks of interaction are observed as communicating vessels (Luhmann 1992: 1419–21). In other words, the consumer credit market is observed as a total social fact (Mauss 2002). From this perspective the National Credit Act was a meeting point of the political system, law and economy, and it is analysed following the recommendation of Marcel Mauss (2002: 103) not to abstract from the empirical completeness of the phenomenon too much.

The economically most striking characteristic of the NCA was that it granted the right to apply for credit to every citizen, with the requirement of credit providers to justify a rejection of an application for economic reasons alone. It reacted to a market situation in which 75 per cent of all private credit products were used by high-income groups, which represented only 15 per cent of the population, and distributed only 25 per cent of the loans among the remaining 85 per cent of the population ((DTI 2003: 6). In terms of the responsible Ministry, this represented a wrong allocation of resources because surplus liquidity was not provided to those who needed it most (Hawkins 2003: 13).

This perception of a mal-distribution of financial resources was to be addressed by the civil right to apply for a loan. 'Every adult natural person, and every juristic person or association of persons, has a right to apply to a credit provider for credit. [A] credit provider has a right to refuse to enter into a credit agreement with any prospective consumer on reasonable *commercial* grounds that are *consistent with its customary risk management* and underwriting practices' (s 60(a), (b) NCA, own emphasis). This means that the credit relationship was no longer a purely private matter of two parties. A borrower applying for a loan made use of a political right, and lenders had to produce economic justifications in order to reject an application. By this legislation the government of South Africa turned private agreements into a politically constituted market that was of public concern. More precisely, it granted the political right to every citizen to be checked for their financial eligibility in order to become a trusted borrower (Otto 2010: 55).

Besides lending capital, a credit provider had to supply a risk management policy, i.e. the granting of loans had to be based on a kind of bureaucratically organized procedure, instead of being the result of a personal peer-to-peer negotiation. Furthermore, the provision of lending services to everybody was defined as a goal of the legislation. The NCA gave orders to the National Credit Regulator to actively develop the market and to control the servicing of 'historically disadvantaged persons', of 'low income persons and communities', and of 'remote, isolated or low density populations or communities' (s 13(a) NCA). Drawbacks in this regard had to be reported to the Ministry.

The transformation of personal loans from a morally deprecated, incidental solution to a private financial crisis into consumer credit as a freely available commodity, that citizens were encouraged to make use of, could not have been made more evident than by this Act. It signified the turning away from a traditional form of lending to financialized consumer credit (Burton 2008: 67).

The understanding of the Act was that such a market had to be transparent and observable in order to function properly. The Act arranged for a whole set of instruments to fulfil this precondition. The legal framework provided by the NCA created two additional governmental bodies as market players, the National Credit Regulator and the National Consumer Tribunal. Moreover, it demanded the registration from three other types of actors, namely credit providers, credit bureaux and debt counsellors. Additionally, it consisted of two main mechanisms of regulation, the 'reckless lending rule' and the treatment of 'over-indebtedness'. Also, it limited the costs of credit. Finally, it contained a few exceptions from its rules, which caused some public disputes.

Guards of the Market: The National Credit Regulator and the National Consumer Tribunal

After defining its purpose and the scope of credit that was affected, the architecture of the law established two new institutions to stand in front of the lending business, so to speak, as guardians of the market. The National Credit Regulator took on the functions of the warden of norms and of the prosecutor, whereas the National Consumer Tribunal fulfilled the role of a court and policing agency, which had to clean up the market.[1]

The National Credit Regulator developed from an earlier institution which aimed at a market regulation, the MFRC. The MFRC had not been a governmental body but only a kind of non-profit company with the purpose of steering the market. Contrary to this, the National Credit Regulator was created as a part of the judiciary, i.e. it was independent from the government and superior to the market actors. Its main tasks were to actively develop and to monitor the market, to perform registration of market participants, and to analyse the development with regard to the purpose of the NCA (s 13 NCA). However, the Regulator was meant to observe the market and to give 'guidance by issuing explanatory notices outlining its procedures, by issuing *non-binding opinions* on the interpretation of the Act' (Otto 2010: 35; own emphasis) but not to interfere. This is to say that in case of an infringement of the rules, the Regulator could refuse the registration of actors or de-register already registered ones, and it could appeal to the National Consumer Tribunal discussed hereafter, but it was explicitly called upon to 'enforce this Act by promoting *informal* resolution of disputes arising in terms of this Act ... *without intervening* in or adjudicating any such dispute' (s 15(a) NCA, own emphasis).

With regard to lenders, the main powers of the Regulator lay in a refusal or a suspension of prospected market participants, thereby depriving their business of the legal protection that the Act provided. Concerning borrowers, it could check the market practices of credit providers, but it could do so only by making use of the information the market actors had transferred to it according to the Act. In the case of suspicion of an infringement of rights combined with fraudulent provision of information, the National Credit Regulator required a High Court or magistrate's court judgement to enter the premises of a credit provider (s 153 NCA). The Regulator reported to the Department of Trade and Industry about the market development. A power it learned to nurture over time was its entitlement to perform research on the market, and to publish the results, as was illustrated in the review of its actions during the crisis of 2012–2014.

The National Consumer Tribunal was the executive authority built by the Act. It had the powers not only to check and negotiate conflicts and complaints brought to its attention, but also to fine market actors in case of a violation of the law. Its powers in this regard were equal to that of a High Court, i.e. in some respects it could even overrule a magistrate's court's judgement, and its rulings would bind the National Credit Regulator (Otto 2010: 37). 'The Tribunal fulfils functions which are not dissimilar to those associated with a court of law, but it is not a court. Indeed, certain orders of the Act may be given only by a court, including for example, one declaring an agreement unlawful' (Otto 2010: 36). This means that the Tribunal was able to influence credit contracts by making them more expensive and less profitable for the lender by issuing a fine, but it could not intervene by suspending loan contracts. The Tribunal had the powers to prohibit unregistered credit business or to impose administrative fines. It could be referred to by the National Credit Regulator, by a court or by a complainant (s 140-141 NCA). Similar functions to that of the National Consumer Tribunal may have been conducted by consumer courts established by provincial legislation (Otto 2010: 39–40).

To sum up, the National Credit Regulator and The National Consumer Tribunal were governmental bodies superior to the market actors, but with restricted powers regarding law enforcement. They were deliberately created as a kind of non-economic market actor, steering its development indirectly, interrupting the contracting parties as little as possible.

Beyond these two guardians, the NCA institutionalized more market actors by requiring most credit providers, all credit bureaux and all debt counsellors to register. Credit providers were obliged to register if they had more than 100 credit agreements or outstanding loans of more than ZAR 500,000 (s 40(1)(a) NCA read with s 42(1) NCA). Their market position is analysed in the following sections.

Data Collection and Risk Management: The Task of Credit Scoring

Of huge importance were the provisions regarding credit bureaux because only through their involvement could the development of personal lending into a consumer credit market take place. Their work was a precondition for the supply of a 'customary risk management' by credit providers.

Credit bureaux had a long history, but their business changed dramatically due to the dissemination of digital data processing from the mid-twentieth century onwards (Altman and Saunders 1998; Hunt 2006). The application of new technological options of data collecting, data storage and calculation resulted in a fundamental change of lending practices. Until the 1970s, credit providers had performed their risk measurement 'by meeting potential borrowers and assessing their creditworthiness and trustworthiness through face-to-face dialogue and evaluation' (Burton 2008: 49). The new technologies allowed the conduct of this rating to happen at a distance, and much faster. Yet, this changed the procedure in essential ways: 'Instead of trusting people, institutions develop technologies that seek to remove the uncertainties of human behaviour by calculating the risks to the point of almost complete control' (Burton 2008: 50).

In the NCA, this was displayed in the complex status of credit bureaux, as being defined by a business anybody was free to set up. This means, generally, that every citizen was allowed to start such a business by collecting information about economically relevant traces of individuals, but they were also subject to specific minimum requirements, governed by quality standards. The Act obliged them to deliver defined services and subdued them to confidentiality. They were only registered by the National Credit Regulator if they showed 'appropriate qualification, competence, knowledge and experience' in their business, and proved that they had sufficient resources to perform the task (s 43(3)(a) NCA). The reason for this demanding construction was that they were intended to perform a very crucial function, which had to take place within an intricate time frame. Credit bureaux had to deliver figures that allowed a calculation of the future ability of prospective borrowers to repay a loan, which were compiled from information from the past, and had to be applied by credit providers to finalize a contract in the present.

Even more interesting in this legal architecture was that there were no clear instructions about the kind of data to gather, and of how to calculate credit risks. Section 82(1) of the NCA explicitly allowed credit providers to use their own means of evaluation as long as they were of comparable quality (Otto 2010: 78). Nevertheless, the Act clearly outlined a norm that had to be followed.

Usually, relevant data were delivered to credit bureaux by credit providers and banking institutions, motivated by a mutual interest. Credit providers delivered the required data to credit bureaux in order to create risk assessment tools, which they sold to credit providers, who in turn used them to minimize their own business risks (Hunt 2006: 303–307).

Credit providers were obliged to inform their customers about adverse information they intended to pass on to credit bureaux, so customers were able to challenge the information (Otto 2010: 57). Especially if judgements containing the signal words 'delinquent', 'default', 'slow paying', 'absconded' or 'not contactable' were to be passed on, the customers had to be provided with twenty days to object to the classification (s 19(4)a Regulations of the NCA). According to the Act, additional data were collected from the judicial bodies, the institutions involved in the functioning of the NCA, providers of insurance, educational institutions, entities involved in fraud investigation, debt collectors hired by a credit provider, and other credit bureaux (s 18(7) Regulations of the NCA).

The NCA itself only demanded that credit bureaux meet some general quality standards. The only compulsory data to be stored were those used to identify and locate a borrower, and their working place or place of business. It was forbidden to collect or store information about 'race', 'political affiliation' and 'medical status or history'. With regard to all other data the Act and its regulations only said that they 'may' be collected or 'might' be used for calculation. However, this recommendation was complicated by the obligation to verify the accuracy of this information in a timely manner (s 70 NCA; s 17-9 Regulations of the NCA).

The basic assumption of the NCA was that a consumer credit market could only prosper and regulate itself based on appropriate figures delivered by credit bureaux, because only these allowed a credit provider to perform a rational, careful and fair risk assessment of customers. Interestingly, two sections of the NCA contained very detailed lists that defined what was to be understood as 'consumer credit information', but they did so without ordering anybody to collect them or compelling their application to credit risk assessment procedures.

This recommended pool of data included a complete financial diary not only of an individual, but of his family and professional relationships, too. It is worth taking a detailed look at the list, which contained

> a person's credit history, including applications for credit, credit agreements to which the person is or has been party, pattern of payment or default under any such credit agreements, debt re-arrangement in terms of this Act, incidence of enforcement actions with respect to any such credit agreement, the circumstances of determination of any such credit agreement, and related matters; a person's financial history, including the person's past and current income, assets and debts, and other matters within the scope of that person's financial means, prospects and obligations, [which include 'income, or any right to receive income, regardless of the source, frequency or regularity of that income, other than income

> that the consumer or prospective consumer receives, has a right to receive, or holds in trust for another person; the financial means, prospects and obligations *of any other adult person within the customer's immediate family or household*, to the extent that the consumer … and that other person customarily share their respective financial means; and mutually bear their respective financial obligations; and if the consumer has or had a commercial purpose for applying for or entering into a particular credit agreement, the reasonably estimated future revenue flow from that business purpose'], and related matters; a person's education, employment, career, professional or business history, including the circumstances of termination of any employment, career or business relationship, and related matters; [and] a person's identity, including the person's name, date of birth, identity number, marital status and family relationships, past and current addresses and other contact details, and related matters. (s 70(1) NCA, s 78(3) NCA, own emphasis)

This list of data would result in a complex map of the economic activities not only of a borrower, but of his family and anybody he is economically interacting with, too. The extent of the information to be gathered and stored represented a problem for the civil rights of individuals and their capacity to decide autonomously about their data. Storing these personal details was a step towards informational surveillance, a topic that was viewed very critically in a country in which former regimes had collected personal data for the purpose of systematically discriminating against groups of its own citizens (Breckenridge 2014).

Therefore, a retention period of all this information was defined in Section 17(1) of the Regulations of the NCA. These periods were heavily disputed between credit providers and representatives of the civil rights movements. The former questioned how they could assess the credit-worthiness of customers properly without knowing about payment defaults and bankruptcies of the past, whereas the latter claimed that finally settled debts had to be removed from the records because otherwise the cancellation would be incomplete and the customer punished indefinitely. Both arguments were rationally correct; this is why no final agreement could be achieved, and the dispute flared up again and again.

This debate was based on the underlying, even more crucial disagreement about the transformation of trust into control. Already the first credit rating agencies, formed in the US in the first quarter of the twentieth century, aimed at delivering those negative pieces of information to credit providers that the customers themselves preferred to conceal. The very nature of the business meant that these companies aimed at collecting embarrassing details about individuals. The crucial point here is that it was precisely the exposition of this negative information that enabled credit providers to transform a principally unknown uncertainty into a calculable risk. As long as those negative facts were unknown, a credit provider would be unable to assess probabilities of a repayment default, making lending decisions completely arbitrary with a high potential for disaster. The mathematical transformation of an unknown future into a realm of calculable probabilities required the combination of positive factors of economic prospects with negative factors like chances of repayment defaults. Only by this procedure a profitable business could be developed (Hunt 2006; Knight 1921: 22–48). Unsecured lending, that is the granting of credit to people with no assets but the prospect of income, was only possible due to investigations into the negative and unflattering facts of a customer's past. In terms of the NCA, it was the only way to allow for a provision of lending services to the victims of apartheid, most of whom had been prevented from accumulating any form of assets.

These calculations were not performed with regard to a single borrower in the first place. Instead, big data were analysed, and certain variables of this data – like income, profession, or area of living – were classified in relation to a probable credit default, derived from past experiences of this group of borrowers. Then, these classifications were calculated with regard to the specific profile of an individual borrower. In other words, it was not the borrower as himself but as a representative of a combination of specific statistical cohorts that he was being judged with regard to his trustworthiness. Of course, this judgement was independent of the actual trustworthiness of a customer – it was a statistical probability only.

At the same time, the knowledge collected by credit rating agencies contained the power of control to access to credit, which was reflected in the provisions of the NCA that required the regular clearance of some data.

The core problem of the legal framework, however, was to bring the criteria of a proper risk assessment into effect without any intervention from the governmental side into private businesses. This was achieved by combining the necessity of registration of credit bureaux with the power to regulate the tasks of the National Credit Regulator in direct ways. This means that the criteria of the NCA could not be imposed on the credit rating agencies, but they contributed to the rules according to which the Regulator checked the eligibility of a credit bureaux to be registered. This way, credit bureaux felt pressurized to collect exactly this kind of data because it would increase the probability of being assessed as eligible. This led to the curious but clever solution of having a very detailed description of 'consumer credit information' without defining its explicit purpose in the Act itself.

Nevertheless, these criteria resulted in a proper risk assessment only if credit providers asked their prospective clients for the necessary information, checked them, and subsequently delivered them to credit bureaux. Finally, they had to apply the resulting tools in their credit granting procedures accordingly. This requirement was handicapped by the opposing incentive to sell as many high-risk loans as possible to increase earnings. The rejection of loan applications diminished profits, of course.

Debt Counsellors and the Two Core Rules of the NCA

The final category of market actors obliged to register with the National Credit Regulator were debt counsellors. Their role is explained separately because their function can be explained only in reference to the two core rules of the NCA, namely 'reckless lending' and 'over-indebtedness'.

The important consideration is that 'over-indebtedness' was a precondition of 'reckless lending' from a legal point of view. This led to the economically irritating point that 'reckless lending' could not, by definition, happen to solvent borrowers. This, in turn, had a strongly limiting effect on the capacities of debt counsellors, because they had no chance of preventing a future case of over-indebtedness.

The new instrument of debt counselling aimed at a debt review, i.e. a rearrangement of loan repayments of already over-indebted borrowers. Debt counsellors were not allowed to take on multiple roles in the credit industry, especially not to receive payments from a credit provider. Any other engagement with market actors disqualified the individual for registration as a debt counsellor. This means they were designed to be a kind of neutral actor.

Debt review was conceptualized as a preliminary stage to the already existing debt enforcement procedures. Twenty days after a default of repayment had occurred, the creditor could give notice to his customer about his intention to enforce repayment, but explicitly had to inform him of the option of a debt review, and only after another ten days could he approach a court for further action (s 129, 130 NCA).

In the process of debt counselling, the two basic mechanisms of the NCA were applied: 'over-indebtedness' as the limitation of free market procedures, and 'reckless lending' as the limitation of freedom of contract. It is important to notice that in the legal understanding of the lending process 'over-indebtedness' came first, and 'reckless lending' happened subsequently. The reason for this was that the contracting parties were seen as autonomous private actors, guided but undisturbed by institutions. As long as no disorder such as an 'over-indebtedness' had been identified, the actors should be able to continue unimpeded. As a consequence, 'reckless lending' was defined as the result of a loan granted to an actor who had already been classified as 'over-indebted', and could only be determined afterwards. Any other credit agreement in terms of the NCA was legal as a private contract on behalf of lender and borrower. This seems to be at odds with a social understanding that perceives 'over-indebtedness' as the result rather than the precondition of 'reckless lending'. To make this point clear, the explanation has to begin with the assessment of over-indebtedness by a debt counsellor.

During the ten days after receiving a notice about the intention of a credit provider to enforce repayment, the customer was able to let his state of over-indebtedness be checked, i.e. if he 'is or will be unable to satisfy in a timely manner all the obligations under all the agreements to which the consumer is party' (s 79(1) NCA). The primary test a counsellor had to conduct was related to this definition of over-indebtedness. In case of the acceptance of an application, the accrual of further financial claims by credit providers were stopped and legal procedures could not be started for another sixty days (s 86(10) NCA).

Oddly, if a person considered himself over-indebted, the first step consisted in the payment of an application fee to a debt counsellor. This was the outcome of the decision to turn debt counselling into a workplace generator, which could only be successful if debt counselling generated income directly. However, it seems contradictory to let someone pay for a check of his insolvency (James 2015: 78).

The following explanation is complex because the state of 'recklessness' and of 'over-indebtedness' was to be checked in reference to each specific contract, and not in reference to the general financial situation of a person. A potentially irritating effect of this was that the same person could be classified as being over-indebted and not over-indebted in reference to different loan contracts in the same debt review process.

If a customer had or expected to have sufficient 'financial means, prospects and obligations' to serve his instalments, a debt counsellor was obliged to reject the application. This was compulsory even if the credit agreement was determined to be illegal and 'reckless'. This means that if a credit agreement was classified as 'reckless' because the borrower had been over-indebted at the time of the formation of the contract, but had financially recovered meanwhile, then the applicant was not to be declared as over-indebted; the particular contract, however, could be brought to the attention of a magistrate's court for the purpose of suspension (s 86(7)(a) NCA). However, a borrower who had obligations resulting from a reckless, i.e. an illegal loan contract, in the past could have accrued more debts afterwards, which were not illegal by definition because his income had increased meanwhile. The fact that the already existing debts of a reckless loan had generated the need to take up more credit in the first place did not matter.

The state of over-indebtedness was measured against the factors of 'financial means, prospects and obligations'. This term was defined in Section 78(3) of the NCA. It was identical to the definition of the term 'income' as part of the 'consumer credit information' of Section 70(1) of the NCA, which have been explained as data sources to be targeted by credit bureaux. With regard to over-indebtedness it was most important that family members with whom the debtor 'customarily' shared financial means and obligations were included in the check of over-indebtedness. This is of huge importance because in South Africa, with its extremely high levels of unemployment and underemployment, many households functioned as a realm of redistribution, with a single earner feeding a couple of mouths (James 2015: 35–59). As a matter of fact, if a debtor revealed and gave proof of being financially stressed, that is, of having 'difficulty' satisfying his obligations in the near future, the debt counsellor had to reject the application if there were family members with a considerable income (s 86(7)(b) NCA). Taking the expected financial means of household members into account contrasts strikingly with the option of credit providers to sell financial claims in the process of securitization. It means that the lending party was allowed to remove itself from the contract by passing it on to buyers, whereas the borrowing party was at risk of involving family and household members, with no option to escape.

If the indebtedness had been caused by secured loans or mortgages, a customer could be expected to sell the goods to alleviate his indebtedness (Otto 2010: 61). In that case, the counsellor had to make a proposal for rearranged debt repayments. If the contracting parties did not consent voluntarily, the case had to be passed on to a court which had the power to bind creditors and debtors to a reviewed repayment scheme (s 86(8) NCA).

However, neither the debt counsellor nor the court could resort to a moratorium on a further increase of interest, fees or of their compounding by a credit provider. Not to put too fine a point on it, as long as a debtor, or a household member he shared a livelihood with, had at least a prospect of financial means to serve his instalments, he had no chance of stopping the further increase of debts without the unforced willingness of his creditors. The only prospect was to stay indebted for a longer time, as a result of a rearrangement agreement with lenders or a court ruling. Customers, and debt counsellors, could not prevent a future over-indebtedness without the voluntary agreement of all credit providers affected.

If a debtor was accepted for debt counselling, every credit provider involved and all registered credit bureaux had to be informed about the ongoing counselling procedure (s 86(4)(b) NCA). This step fulfilled three functions. To begin with, all creditors had to stop charging further amounts on the account of the debtor. Secondly, all credit providers were informed not to grant further loans to the debtor.[2] Finally, the credit scoring could be updated.

The prevention of further lending was important because of the economic effects of a debt review. An over-indebted borrower was obliged to list the 'statutory deductions and other deductions made as a condition of employment' from his income, defined as 'inclusive of, but not limited to taxes, unemployment insurance fund, pension, medical aid, insurance, court orders' and others. Additionally, he had to produce a list of his living expenses, consisting of 'groceries, utility and continuous service, school fees, transport costs' and others that had to be specified. The sum of the deductions was to be subtracted from the earnings to calculate the net income, and the sum of living expenses was to be deducted from the net income to demonstrate if the debtor's 'total monthly payments exceed the balance' (s 24 Regulations of the NCA). Only in that case could a debtor be acknowledged as 'over-indebted'.

The consequence of this was that a financially stressed customer who had applied for debt counselling, or was ordered to do so by a court, would inevitably be limited to his very basic living expenses until the final settlement of his debts. He would receive the protection attached to the status of over-indebtedness only if there was nothing left from his income after subtracting mandatory deductions and living expenses. Facing the alternatives of conceding over-indebtedness with the consequence of living on the breadline on the one hand, and of delaying the acknowledgement of insolvency and worsening the situation by taking out another loan on the other hand, could motivate him to opt for the latter. In anticipation of an incalculable period of extreme financial restriction, the temptation to postpone the state of over-indebtedness is comprehensible because there is no prospect of relief anyway. That is to say that the rational incentives of the rules of 'over-indebtedness' and 'reckless lending' were not unambiguous.

As long as there was money left to pay at least parts of the instalments, the debt counsellor was limited to the option of recommending a voluntary rearrangement of the repayment by creditors and consumers, or to ask a magistrate's court to order such a reviewed scheme. Deborah James (James 2015: 77) reported, with regard to on the practice of debt counsellors, that 'both creditors and debtors showed extreme levels of recalcitrance: many of the latter simply used debt counselling as a delaying tactic'. This recalcitrance is not difficult to understand. Debtors would be reduced to the very minimum of living expenses from the moment of the finalization of their debt counselling application, and until a rearrangement order was issued no creditor could be kept from accruing further claims. Neither had any incentive to agree because the former would have to pay their debts anyway, and the latter would retain their demands under all circumstances.

If the assessment of the remaining net income of the consumer revealed a state of over-indebtedness, because the financial obligations exceeded the net income, the matter had to be handed over to a magistrate's court. A debt counsellor had to check the credit agreements for 'reckless lending' and had to bring the status of over-indebtedness to the attention of the court.

It would then come under the cognizance of a magistrate's court to decide if a credit provider had checked his customer's ability to repay a loan in a satisfactory manner. In the legal system, 'over-indebtedness' and 'reckless lending' were checked independently. As outlined before, recklessness depended on the state of over-indebtedness at the moment of the formation of a contract, but it did not automatically result in an assessment of over-indebtedness at the time of the proceedings. Only if the risk assessment measure, conducted with the assistance of credit bureaux data, had not been thorough enough, or if the result of this measure had revealed an already existing over-indebtedness of the borrower but the credit provider had ignored this, was a credit agreement then classified as being 'reckless' (s 80(1) NCA). If this was the case, the agreement could be 'set aside' or 'suspended' by the court.

In the case of setting aside a loan contract in whole or in part, a consumer was not bound to perform his obligations; the contract was unenforceable in that event. Contrary to many other provisions of the Act, this option was not outlined any further, and according to the experienced legal scholar Jannie Otto (2010: 79), this made its application in litigations less probable than better documented rulings: 'In absence of any criteria in the National Credit Act, one can expect that courts will set aside an agreement only in extreme cases'.

Anyway, a suspension would only result in an interruption of a further accumulation of interest and fees, and a postponement of repayments until the borrower was no longer over-indebted. Section 84(2) of the NCA explicitly ruled that after the 'suspension of the force and the effect of the credit agreement ends all the respective rights and obligations of the credit provider and the consumer under that credit agreement are revived and are fully enforceable except to the extent that the court may order otherwise'. This last exception referred to the same section of the NCA that ruled the tasks that could be carried out by a debt counsellor, which meant that a court could check if fees and interest had been calculated according to the rules. All court judgements were explicitly directed towards 'an order re-arranging the consumer's obligations' by way of

> extending the period of agreement and reducing the amount of each payment due accordingly; postponing during a specified period of which payments are due under the agreement; extending the period of the agreement and postponing during a specified period the dates on which payments are due under the agreement; or recalculating the consumer's obligations because of contraventions of [unlawful agreement and provisions, and disclosure, form and effect of credit agreements] or [collection and repayment practices]. (s 87(1) NCA read with s 86(7)(c)(ii) NCA)

In other words, the court could order a reduction of the instalments, and prolong the repayment period, and it could remove any unlawful interest and fees on the principal – but it was not entitled to remove any obligation that was in accordance with the Act. In this regard it is important to notice that longer repayment periods of the same principal with unchanged fees and interest resulted in higher costs for the borrower and higher earnings of the credit provider. The financial beneficiaries of over-indebtedness were lenders and not borrowers (Schraten 2014: 10).

The consequences of 'reckless lending' received their full meaning only in contrast with the judgements on 'unlawful credit agreements' according to Section 89 of the NCA. The former referred to loans which had been ruled on by the NCA but that had been provided irregularly, whereas the latter referred to loans outlawed by the Act, for instance, loans granted by an unregistered lender. In case of unlawful loans, a 'credit provider must refund to the consumer any money paid by the consumer … with interest', and a court could even deprive the credit provider of the principal (s 89(5)(c) NCA). In any case, the credit agreement would be void, and the court had no discretionary powers in this regard, even if there should exist a contrary practice of common law. In particular, according to Section 90(2) of the NCA, every attempt to circumvent the norms of the NCA by way of private agreements had to be interpreted as an infringement that would result in an agreement to be declared unlawful, and under its criteria of illicitness it listed those rough debt collection methods of the free market period of the 1990s (Otto 2010: 47–51).

To summarize, property that was lent under the rulings of the NCA was nearly untouchable in later court proceedings, even in cases of reckless lending or over-indebtedness, but any loan agreement outside the NCA would result in a loss of money. This, of course, presented a very strong incentive to credit providers to operate under the umbrella of the NCA.

Three further specifications were of importance. The assessment of recklessness could be applied only to the moment of formation of the contract (s 80(1) NCA). Secondly, there was no precisely defined procedure of risk assessment that could have been enforced because 'a guideline published by the National Credit Regulator is not binding to a credit provider' (s 82(3) NCA). The latter point had to be seen in connection with Section 81(4)(a) of the NCA, in which it was said that 'it is a complete defence to an allegation that a credit agreement is reckless if the credit provider establishes that the consumer failed to fully or truthfully answer any requests for information'. The consequence of these two rules was that a credit provider was in no danger of having his agreements assessed as being reckless as long as he used the application forms published by the National Credit Regulator, and made use of the tools of registered credit bureaux. In other words, the dangers of risk assessment procedures could be outsourced by buying the services of credit bureaux. Finally, the time frame for applying for a debt review was limited to ten days only. Thereafter, a credit provider was entitled to seek other debt enforcement measures, and even the limited options of relief for a borrower by debt counselling were no longer accessible (s 86(2) NCA).

One matter of public concern was the fact that the mechanisms of 'over-indebtedness' and 'reckless lending' could not be applied to school and student loans, emergency loans, public interest credit agreements, pawn transactions, incidental credit agreements or temporary increased limits of credit facilities (s 78(2) NCA).[3]

The exclusion of 'emergency loans' in particular removed an important source of over-indebtedness from the rulings. They had been defined in chapter 1 of the NCA as

> a credit agreement entered into by a consumer to finance costs arising from or associated with a death, illness or medical condition, unexpected loss or interruption of income, or catastrophic loss or damage of home property due to fire, theft, or natural disaster, affecting the consumer, a person who is dependent upon the consumer or a person for whom the consumer is financially responsible.

This means that the protection and legal claim for a rearrangement of debts was not available for loans made in situations of extreme uncertainty of the future – as in the case of school and student loans – or in situations of most urgent financial need – as in the case of emergency loans. Viewed the other way around, in case of emergencies credit providers were not subjugated to the pricing limitations of the NCA and could charge as much as they wanted. During negotiations of the NCA this had been criticized by COSATU (2005: 11), but in vain.

The Monitoring of the Market: Payment Systems

Completing the overview of the institutional setting of the South African consumer credit market requires the addition of an important and often overlooked component: the payment systems. It was not part of the NCA, but an indispensable precondition of the consumer credit market. The purpose of payment systems is to monitor all payment procedures, and to clear the records of finalized procedures. They complement the function of credit scoring, and they link every customer who uses electronic payment tools and credit products to the global financial markets, because these are the centres that depend on a reliable clearance of all payment procedures in the first place.

A simple scenario makes the necessity for the coordination of payments quite clear: imagine a customer who takes out a loan, pays a commodity with his credit card, and then approaches an ATM in order to withdraw some cash. How does the ATM know about the new credit line of the customer? This is where the payment system comes in.

Payment systems are quite old because wherever monetary transactions are authorized in a cash-free form, e.g. by using a cheque or a bill of exchange, the imperative to post the monetary figures and to clear the payments arises. However, through the accelerated and multiple options of a liberalized banking industry driven by telecommunications technology in the way it emerged from the 1970s onwards, the risks of errors and fraud increased and became a concern for central bankers. As a result, the extension of payment systems was promoted by the central bank of the central banks, i.e. the Bank for International Settlements

(South African Reserve Bank 2005: 1). 'Payment systems have moved from the *backroom* to the *boardroom* of all financial institutions due to the recognition of the critical node that a well functioning payment system plays in supporting the financial and real economies' (BIS 2006: v; emphasis in original). In this process, payment systems grew from peer-to-peer channels, in which a transfer of value was confirmed and finally settled, into complex networks, which were made workable by a multitude of financial tools.

The South African Reserve Bank (2005: 3), as the national maintainer of such a system, described it as 'the infrastructure that provides the economy with the highways for processing the payments resulting from various economic activities'. Although this appraisal may have been coloured by the pride of the proprietor, the magnitude of change in the monetary system of South Africa caused by its payment system should not be underestimated. These 'highways' were an important part of the ruling relations of the consumer credit market because they multiplied and accelerated the financial social interactions inside the market as an infrastructure.

A precondition of the NPS (National Payment System) was the re-entering of the world market by the South African banking business from 1990 onwards, and the construction works began in February 1994, even before the final turn to democracy (South African Reserve Bank 2005: 1). On 9 March 1998 the new NPS was basically instituted by implementing a national payment settlement system (BIS 2006: 151, 2012, 2013; South African Reserve Bank 2005: 7). In its structural effect on the monetary system, this date is just as important as the abandonment of gold coins in December 1932, although it happened almost unnoticed. From this day onwards, South Africans were able to buy and pay cash-free and electronically nation-wide. It made a financialization of the everyday life possible in the first place.

The architecture of the NPS consisted of two networks that were interposed for payments from their initial point to their destination. The first of them was the payment network. If a customer instructed a payment to be made at a bank counter, or the bank disbursed money to a customer at an ATM, or if a broker made a deal, these events were gathered at the bank as the central hub of a payment network. The bank was connected to the second one, the settlement network. Here, all data from different payment networks were transferred to the centre of the NPS, called SAMOS (South African Multiple Option Settlement). At this point, all payments were cleared, which means that at this centre it could be observed if each input of money was matched by an output of the same amount. The necessity for two networks instead of one arose from the desire to spread the system geographically.

Connecting a fundamentally unlimited number of payment networks to a single network of settlement allowed for the simultaneous processing of payments at different places, which nonetheless were all finally cleared on the same day. Payment networks were responsible for the final coordination of all their own payments. However, this did not necessarily have to take place on the same day, and a crisis like that of African Bank in August 2014 represented a case in which the imbalance inside a single payment network had grown to such an extent that it had become unbearable for the settlement network. On a material level, these networks consisted of a complex infrastructure of components, and SAMOS was updated quite a few times after 1998 to improve its features (South African Reserve Bank 2005: 4–8).

The strategic importance of the NPS derived from two of its functions. To begin with, it represented the level of continuous cooperation of commercial banks which otherwise competed with each other. Their common interest was to avoid double or non-matching payments. Secondly, it connected the South African circuit of money to the world economy because all payments performed in South Africa were registered in an internationally standardized form (and, most importantly, at an internationally standardized point of time) so that they could be compared. This second function enabled the performance of transnational payments.

From a sociological point of view, two other effects attract attention. On the one hand, the establishment of the NPS extended the monetary system of South Africa in time and space. Participating in the economy no longer required cash or a point of sale.

On the other hand, it complemented the replacement of direct social interaction and trust by institutional control. Negotiation between human beings was replaced by the digital feedback of an electronic system that could be neither tricked nor persuaded. In the existing literature, credit granting is very often directly linked with the notion of trust, which seems to be of unquestionable evidence, like here: 'To extend credit, the creditor must trust that debtors will repay' (Carruthers 2005: 362). However, trust involves repeated social interaction between participants of the interaction (Sztompka 2003). This means that the basic assumption of trust is fundamentally at odds with the concept of a competitive market, in which sellers and buyers connect with each other in reference to price signals. 'The point that needs to be borne in mind is that the agents enter and leave the exchange like strangers' (Callon 1998b: 3). From the institutional analysis, culminating in the description of transnationally interconnected payment systems, the basic insight of Dawn Burton (2008: 50) is confirmed: 'Instead of trusting people, institutions develop technologies that seek to remove the uncertainties of human behaviour by calculating the risks to the point of almost complete control'.

Following this analysis of the different market actors established by the NCA and the banking industry, the intended logic of the social construction shall now be exposed.

The Price of Loans as a Signal for Rational Action

The requirement to register and the basic mechanisms of the NCA revealed an information flow in the form of 'consumer credit information' from the borrower towards credit providers and credit bureaux for the purpose of risk assessment. A corridor was built between the legal barriers of 'reckless lending' and 'over-indebtedness'. It was characterized by the guarantee that credit providers who comply need not fear the loss of their property, even if they lent to high-risk costumers, which formed the majority of the population of South Africa.

In the worst case, a debtor and his household would stop repaying during the contract period, but only if their income sufficed for no more than the basic living expenses. To make such an event foreseeable, the lender was encouraged to gather detailed knowledge about the economic conditions of the customer's household, and to apply collected and pre-processed data delivered by credit bureaux.

A second piece of important knowledge had to be passed on from credit providers to the customers. This information had to reveal the consequences of a loan contract to a customer, motivating him to apply for credit only if he could afford it. Basically, this flow of information was divided into three parts: the legal limitation of the cost of credit, the pre-agreements disclosure of the details of the contract, and the legal provisions of loan advertisements.

The limitation of the cost of credit and the minimum requirements of information, which had to be revealed to the borrower, fulfilled barrier functions similar to the rules of 'over-indebtedness' and 'reckless lending', because the first functioned as a limitation of free market procedures, and the latter as a limitation of the freedom of contract.

Contrary to many recommendations by the micro-lending industry during the negotiations of the NCA, ceilings of maximum interest rates had been implemented, and the fees were limited in the Regulations of the NCA. Loans were categorized into seven divisions, which were differentiated by a maximum addition that could be added to the basic formula of interest. The foundation of this calculation was based on the Repurchase Rate of the central bank, multiplied by the factor 2.2.[4] During the crisis period from 2012 to 2014, the additions allowed ranged from 5 per cent in the case of a mortgage to 20 per cent in the case of unsecured loans and developmental credit agreements. For the period of the crisis this meant that the maximum interest rate for unsecured loans was at 32.1 per cent per annum in January 2011 and February 2014, and was lowered to 31 per cent between 19 July 2012 and 29 January 2014. In comparison with the free market period, this was a massive reduction of the maximum price of a loan.

However, the interest rates had to be seen against the background of the possibility of compounding. Compounding designated the practice of levying interest on interest. The option was part of Section 40(1) of the Regulations of the NCA where it said that interest 'may be calculated daily and may be added to the deferred amount monthly, at the end of the month'. The 'deferred amount' included other loan components and, more importantly, the increase of the principal debt by the interest added to it during the months before (s 39(1) Regulations of the NCA). This amount became even higher with the option of payment holidays, offered by some credit providers at the beginning of a loan contract or at times where consumers found it difficult to make payments, e.g. after the festive season. During this period the loan would accumulate interest and capitalized fees, of course (NCR 2012g: 68–69). So, the option of compounding had a disguising effect on the disclosure of credit costs on the side of the borrower.

Furthermore, a loan could – and usually would – comprise an initiation fee, a service fee, and the cost of credit life insurance. Apart from credit life insurance they were limited by the Act.[5] The main problem with these fees was that low-income borrowers in particular would not have the money for them in advance. After all, they applied for a loan because they were in need of money. As part of the compounded additional costs of a loan, they could easily extend the loan by significant amounts (Campbell 2007: 260).

These factors were complemented by credit life insurance. Credit providers were allowed to demand insurance but the consumer could choose his own policy. At a first glance the three components looked small and negligible, but a research report on behalf of the NCR revealed that the initiation fees contributed 11.2 per cent to the total revenue from unsecured loans, the service fees added 9.7 per cent and, finally, the credit life insurance contributed another 11.2 per cent (NCR 2012g: 63). Soon after the introduction of the NCA, Jonathan Campbell (2007: 263–64) posed the question of whether these fees were not a way of obscuring the real costs of a loan. This question did not lose its relevance.

The second ruling concerning the flow of information from lender to borrower referred to the pre-agreement disclosure of costs. Important in this regard was the provision to deliver every document in one of the eleven official languages of South Africa according to Section 63 of the NCA. Additionally, Section 64 of the NCA required the documents to be in 'plain and understandable' language, so that it would be 'reasonable to conclude that an ordinary consumer of the class of persons for whom the document was intended, with average literary skills and minimal credit experience, could be expected to understand the content, significance, and import of the document without undue effort'. This regulation translated the 'imbalances in negotiating power' into an unequal distribution of knowledge on the cognitive level of language. It deliberately targeted the 'style of the document', 'the vocabulary, usage and sentence structure of the text', and the utilization of illustrations and examples (s 64(2) NCA).

The risks of these conditions could be seen in the regulations of the disclosure of credit costs. Section 92(2)(b) of the NCA demanded that 'the principal debt, the proposed distribution of that amount, the interest rate and other credit costs, the total cost of the proposed agreement' be set out, together with any handling fees that would be retained in case of a resignation by the customer after the reflection period of the contract proposal. Sections 28 and 29 of the Regulations explained these requirements, first extending them to thirteen elements in case of intermediate loans, and reducing them to only three figures at the end: these consisted of the total amount of credit advanced, the monthly instalment, and the total amount of repayment.

Without taking into account any intricacies of actual repayment procedures, the disclosure of credit costs had to present every contributing factor, and the way it was calculated, but it had to simplify the outcome of the calculation at the same time. These requirements were complex, but they had to be made 'plain and understandable' at the same time, resulting in prescribed forms that listed difficult financial calculations first, and three plain figures last – an order that was irritating and complex in itself. The information disclosed had to be comprehensive in order to inform consumers about as many consequences of a loan contract as possible, but it had to be concise enough to make reading and understanding probable (Otto 2010: 46).

The most important aspect of this construction was the idea of a calculability of reason: the idea behind the disclosure of credit costs was that every customer would draw the same conclusions from the same figures, regardless of the individual social situation and the specific motivation to apply for a loan. In other words, the economic rationality of the consumer credit market was conceptualized as an objective entity, and as an insight every citizen could arrive at as soon as the information was available.

The Conceptualization of 'Imbalances in Negotiation Power'

To summarize the functions of the NCA, it could be said that it defined a corridor of private exchange between credit providers and their customers. Inside this corridor, the property rights of lenders were protected, whereas every lending procedure beyond the legal barriers was declared unlawful (s 40(4), 89 NCA; Otto 2010: 42). The boundaries of the corridor were built by norms and by assisting and observing institutions. The norms were spelled out in detail, which was unusual for South African legislation (Otto 2010: 3). This could be explained by the new character of the legislation, the necessity of applying these rules to an already existing consumer credit market, and the difficulty of 'imbalances in negotiation power', which was acknowledged by the act itself (s 3(e) NCA) and had driven many borrowers into indebtedness during the 1990s. The contrast between the protection of property rights inside the corridor and the deprecation of any lending business outside of the framework was intended to serve as an incentive to compliance.

The legal character was framed by the political intentions of the legislator, which had been outlined in policy frameworks. A main peculiarity was the translation of asymmetries of negotiation power into an uneven distribution of knowledge. A disclosure of information and additional consumer education were conceptualized as remedies for the 'imbalances in negotiation power'. In debates on the Consumer Protection Act 68 of 2008, which took place parallel to the discussion and implementation of the Consumer Credit Bill, the imbalance was explained more thoroughly:

> The imbalance between consumer and businesses is of special concern in South Africa because the majority of consumers are poor and many consumers have low levels of literacy and reside in rural areas with no easy access to complaints assistance. The legacy of systemic dispossession and

> under investment [*sic*] in education for black South Africans has a fundamental impact on the current market place and exacerbates existing imbalances. Whatever consumer protection was in existence prior to 1994 responded in large part to the problems of white consumers. Since 1994, there have been significant changes in income distribution, with a large increase in black spending power and many new entrants into the consumer market. However, many of the new entrants to the marketplace are still vulnerable, with limited life-skills, high levels of illiteracy and poverty. This exacerbates the conventional information asymmetries and imbalances in bargaining power, and must be addressed. (DTI 2004b: 11)

This explanation of social distortions was then boiled down to the following list of consumer nuisances: 'unfair advertising and predatory selling mechanisms; lack of access to concise and balanced sale and purchase information; unfavourable deals and contract terms; post-purchase harassment and denial of fair settlement terms; and unfriendly customer service' (DTI 2004b: 12).

This was in line with the interpretation of imbalances in negotiation power in the National Credit Act. The policy framework for the consumer credit market confirmed this point of view, though not without highlighting the specific problem of social inequality: 'There is greater need to balance the access to credit [than to the access of water, healthcare and electricity] with protection for consumers, especially the vulnerable' (DTI 2004c: 7). From the perspective of creditors, this danger was translated into a cost factor. 'Effective debt recovery procedures would assist credit providers by reducing bad debts write-offs, and assist consumers by ensuring that high bad debts of a minority of consumers do not feed through into higher interest rates for the rest' (DTI 2004c: 7). Nevertheless, the notion of possible irrationalities in the market remained present: 'Even with competitive markets and well-informed consumers, transactions can go wrong' (DTI 2004c: 9).

In a first version of the policy framework for the consumer credit market, the specific circumstances under which borrowers might ask for credit was explicitly reflected: 'When applying for credit, consumers are frequently desperate and not in a position or frame of mind to contest the contents of the contract' (DTI 2003: 12). This refers to the character of the commodity, that is, money itself, which is not a commodity like any other. It does not represent the satisfaction of a specific need that can be neglected, replaced or suppressed. Applicants for a loan fear nothing more than being rejected, which would deprive them of the option of satisfying any need in a market in general. But this insight was downplayed to contractual terms being 'not well explained' or 'misleading', i.e. to a problem of information disclosure (DTI 2003: 12). The special character of the commodity at stake was neglected.

The basic contradiction to which the market exposed the actors consisted of, on the one hand, the eagerness to extend credit to those citizens most urgently in need of it as a result of historical discrimination, and, on the other hand, 'to restrict the South African consumer from borrowing in excess of his or her financial capability' (DTI 2003: 11). This means that the intention of the law was to extend the supply of consumer credit as far as possible, and to restrict its sale to capable borrowers at the same time. In the final version of the NCA all concerns about the effects of customers pressed by their social needs were put aside. It claimed instead: 'Confident customers are one of the important drivers of competitiveness' (DTI 2004b: 3).

Finally, the National Credit Act created a channel of interaction in which credit providers and borrowers were granted the basic privileges of law and the privilege to regulate their concrete relation through a private contract. Additionally, they were granted the privilege of freedom, which was understood as protection against the interference from a third party, especially from the state. This was the legal part of the regulation, and from a theoretical point of view it designated the turn from a literally free and unregulated market of uncontrolled actors to 'the emergence of certain economic relations which may be either a certain order of economic control or a certain agreement based on economic expectations' (Weber 1978: 667).

However, this channel of interaction was obviously confronted with a problem inherent in credit markets, because a market demands the interaction of strangers with no continuous relationships, whereas credit requires the continuation of interaction until the contract is fulfilled. The alienation of actors into strangers is a necessary precondition for the instrumental rationality of markets, because any social bond between actors and/ or commodities consisting of sympathy, obligation, tradition or affect would prevent the rigorous pursuit of individual interest. The repayment of credit money, by contrast, requires the establishment of a lasting bond. The crucial characteristic of a financialized consumer credit market is to achieve this bond by institutional control instead of trust, as has been shown by the detailed review of the institutional framework.

This social setting does not function without friction, though, as can be explained by using the terms 'framing' and 'overflow', as suggested by Michael Callon. 'Framing' designates the operation of identifying and isolating actors and commodities, and of disentangling them from their former contexts: workers lose access to their produce, engineers the claims to their ideas and organizational power, commodities become single items that can change hands. In the process of framing, the formerly existing links are 'externalized'; this means that they are no longer part of contracts, accounts and calculations. However, this process can be confrontational, the most prominent analysis of resulting conflicts surely being the alienation of labour power as provided by Karl Marx. In these conflicts, the term 'overflowing' comes in, designating those persons or things that resist a complete externalization by literally 'overflowing' the boundaries into the current contract, deal or calculation. 'There are always relations which defy framing. [Framing] mobilizes or concerns objects or beings endowed with an irreducible autonomy, [this] is a source of overflowing. Complete framing is a contradiction in terms, whereas complete externalization is possible' (Callon 1998b: 18). In a financialized consumer credit market, we can identify a complete framing on the part of the credit provider, because after the delivery of the principal, he has no lasting obligations towards the borrower, and he is entitled to sell on his claims and get rid of the contract, whereas the borrower, with his 'irreducible autonomy', is a source of overflowing. Not only are his circumstances of living constantly overflowing into the contract in the form of his ability to make repayments in time, but also his obligations deriving from the contract may overflow into the lives of his family and household members. 'If the thing remains entangled, the one who receives it is never quit and cannot escape from the web of relations. This frame is never over. The debt cannot be settled' (Callon 1998b: 19).

The 'imbalances in negotiation power between consumers and credit providers' do not consist of an uneven distribution of information and knowledge, but of the unequal status of contracting parties with regard to externalization and overflowing, which means their different capacity to finalize the credit contract. The option of a credit provider to leave the contract is limited only by the market demand, and even in these cases political interventions may help him to get out. This is what happened in the course of the split of African Bank into a 'good' and a 'bad bank' in 2014. Thereafter, the persons responsible for the bank were disentangled again, and the 'bad bank' had overflown into the obligations of South African taxpayers. As shown in this chapter, the single option of a credit provider not to get disentangled is contrasted by only one option to leave the credit contract unharmed on the side of the borrower: it consists of a repayment of the loan in time. In any other case, overflowing will take place continually. Against the background of this imbalance in power, the debate between credit providers and consumers about the clearance of negative credit records, which seemed to be insoluble at first, results in a clear judgement: the options of borrowers to disentangle themselves from credit contracts of the past is very limited, and the credit providers have a lot of tools and options to extract profits and enforce their claims. Therefore, the clearance of negative credit information after a loan has been cancelled or repaid is necessary in order to restore the democratic autonomy of citizens. The options of an improvement of credit scoring calculations can only be of subordinate importance here.

With regard to the understanding of the consumer credit market as it can be derived from the NCA itself and from the reports that document the discussion of its establishment, we are facing a contradictory construction: the establishment of a complex and detailed regulatory framework that claims to provide a realm of free market interaction. In fact, the purpose of the institutions was to prevent the actors from pursuing their own interest unimpeded. Yet, the extent of limitations regarding the contracting parties was distributed very unevenly, stabilizing the 'imbalances in negotiation power' rather than eliminating them.

The next chapter will discuss the implemented and envisaged changes to the basic frame outlined here.

NOTES

1. Otto (2010: 12) argued that the National Credit Regulator was the 'police' of the market, but the Regulator could not fine or arrest actors.
2. At this point it should be noted that the finding of over-indebtedness resulted in a prohibition of further lending. However, as outlined before, if over-indebtedness remained undiscovered, and the borrower took up more loans, these contracts remained valid if the income situation had improved meanwhile.
3. Otto (2010: 6, 20–21) points out that 'incidental credit agreements' is 'rather meaningless' as a phrase, almost equal to that of a 'discount transaction' in South African law.
4. The Repurchase Rate is the rate at which the Reserve Bank repurchased government securities from commercial banks in exchange for money supply.
5. The initiation fee (s 101 (1)(b) NCA) was limited to ZAR 1,000 or 15 per cent of the principal debt; the service fees were limited to ZAR 50 per month (s 42(2), 43(3), 44 Regulations of the NCA).

CHAPTER 4

Legislators' Reactions to the Consumer Credit Market Crisis

As we have already seen in the first chapter, governmental actors and banking business representatives were keen to leave this basic market construction untouched after the National Credit Regulator had raised concerns in March 2012. However, they could not abstain from any reaction, and strived to alleviate the causes of the grievances.

This section will review the further development, beginning with the agreement between the Ministry of Finance and the business representatives from 19 October 2012 (Treasury 2012a). It continues with the debates surrounding a new policy framework that was published in the Government Gazette, and finally led to a reform of the NCA in 2015.

The Amendment of 2017: Affordability Measurement

The consent that was reached between the government and the banking business, which was published on 1 November 2012, recognized over-indebtedness as a serious concern, but defended the principles of the NCA. The further developments after this agreement revealed the difficulty of the task of canalizing the practices of actors in a market that was seen as a realm of voluntarily acting, contracted partners. Without limiting freedom of action by legal regulations, governmental bodies relied on the establishment of norms that would encourage credit providers not to exploit every economic opportunity and customers to behave cautiously.

On 26 November 2012 a number of 'Codes of Good Practice on Broad-Based Black Economic Empowerment' were published in the Government Gazette as another step of the implementation of the Financial Sector Charter, a policy paper geared towards a reform of the financial sector, which had been agreed upon in August 2002, immediately after the bank crash. It encouraged the banking industry 'to enhance, improve, and grow financial access' to the previously disadvantaged. The Code declared the access to loan products, and explicitly to unsecured lending, a 'national imperative'. It said nothing about risk measurements and affordability but only about consumer education. It confirmed the perception of the consumer credit market as a place of rational action once more. 'Consumer Education is the process of transferring knowledge and skills to consumers, future consumers and potential consumers for individual well-being and the public good' (Government Gazette No. 35914: 125). To enhance this kind of education, though, it suggested nothing more than the provision of educational material and information campaigns (Government Gazette No. 35914: 110-15).

On 29 May 2013, the Department of Trade and Industry published a 'draft National Credit Act Policy Review Framework for broader public comments' in the Government Gazette (No. 36504: 3). In contrast to the uniformly positive connotation of other publications on the matter, this one juxtaposed the possibilities of the consumer credit market with its dangers. According to the framework, the market 'not only has the potential to create opportunities for individuals to access goods and services, start businesses, obtain education or improve living standards, but also serves as a shock-absorber during periods of financial hardship. However, while credit can have positive implications for the person accessing it, it also can destroy a person's financial security' (Government Gazette No. 36504: 6). The document was designed to review the existing NCA because 'its intended outcomes have not always materialized as anticipated' (Government Gazette No. 36504: 7).

Yet, it contained very positive statements about the situation of the consumer credit market, too. The report claimed that the consumer credit market had an impact 'in tempering the effect of the global financial crisis [of 2007-2009] in South Africa' (Government Gazette No. 36504: 4). With regard to the problem of 'addressing over-indebtedness', it kept this positive tone: 'While the affordability assessments do not necessarily meet all the ideals of the policy, it is true to say that virtually every credit provider has improved on its evaluation processes and at least attempts such an evaluation prior to granting credit' (Government Gazette No. 36504: 5). The success of the NCA was measured in the extension of the industry.

These figures were judged as 'economic progress' and celebrated a 'steadily growing gross debtors book' (Government Gazette No. 36504: 6–7). With regard to the problems indicated by the National Credit Regulator, the policy framework began unambiguously: 'The policy of prevention of over-indebtedness and reckless lending is sound' (Government Gazette No. 36504: 20). The perspective on options of

Table 4.1. Market growth, 2002–2012.

Year	Amount of credit in ZAR	Number of credit accounts
2002	360 billion	19.8 million
September 2012	1.39 trillion	68.28 million

Source: Government Gazette No. 36504: 6.

discharge for over-indebted borrowers was addressed equally clearly: 'The policy regarding debt relief is sound and should be retained' (Government Gazette No. 36504: 33).

Most important, there was a dramatic discrepancy between the acknowledgement of existing problems with the NCA on the one hand, and the suggestions of remedies on the other.

The governmental authors recognized that there was a sizeable number of credit providers who 'operate under the radar of the enforcement bodies'. Further on, it named 'Payment Distribution Agencies' as actors who regularly betrayed debtors. It acknowledged a 'lack of enforcement and redress', insufficient affordability measurement procedures and a continuation of profiting even after reckless lending had been identified. The report understood that the 'NCA has not succeeded in addressing the issue of lack of consumer knowledge or low financial literacy', and especially that the accessibility of information did not necessarily result in an understanding of the consequences by a customer. Moreover, credit life insurance was named as a prominent way of increasing the cost of credit multiple times (Government Gazette No. 36504: 19, 21, 24, 26, 28).

The policy framework outlined the futility of the debt counselling approach because it worked 'only for a limited few'. The reason for this was explicitly named: 'A consumer is subject to the restraints of debt review until all the debts subject to the debt review have been paid', which means that a debtor was downscaled to a minimum of living expenses until the final settlement of his financial obligations (Government Gazette No. 36504: 38, 41). This did not motivate individuals to enrol in a debt review process nor to increase their earnings.

Despite these critical insights, only a few improvements were envisaged. It was suggested that the powers of the National Credit Regulator and the National Consumer Tribunal should be outlined more clearly in order to allow them a faster and more efficient reaction to misbehaviour. It was proposed that the registration of credit providers be extended to every lender doing business on a regular basis regardless of the size of his business. Another step in the direction of making the consumer credit market more visible was the intention to finally implement the National Credit Register, which had already been conceptualized in the NCA, but had never been realized (s 72 NCA; Government Gazette No. 36504: 27). This register would function as a kind of nation-wide monitor of running loan contracts.

The governmental reactions to some malfunctions of the NCA that had been explicitly identified were restrained. Although Payment Distribution Services charged fees and, therefore, presented additional costs to already financially stressed customers, their future existence was still on the table (Government Gazette No. 36504: 22). With regard to reckless lending, it was considered 'to lower priority in terms of restructured payments and applying an interest and fee reduction in the case of credit providers who provided credit recklessly', but a reduction of the principal of such loans was not taken into view (Government Gazette No.36504: 24).

Most interesting was the helplessness in reference to the crucial approach of consumer education. Though the scope of the problem was recognized, by designating financial illiteracy, by acknowledging the difference between information disclosure and the understanding of the consequences thereof, and finally by recognizing 'that consumers do not feel adequately informed on the actual cost of credit', no proper idea for a solution was brought forward. 'Consumer education needs to be improved. The participation of stakeholders that interact with consumers is needed to improve consumer education as it relates to more than just the provision of information. Legislative provisions, Government and industry participation is necessary' (Government Gazette No. 36504: 26). That was all.

The firm defence of the basic principles of the NCA was remarkable. The policy framework did so by ignoring its own statements. It clearly outlined that debt counselling 'is not a feasible option for all consumers particularly consumers with no income and no assets or low income and limited assets' (Government Gazette No. 36504: 42). Notwithstanding this, the report encouraged education and voluntary agreements as a solution: 'Consumers need to be educated on their rights and the remedies available' (Government Gazette No. 36504: 27). It considered a 'rehabilitation of a consumer at a determined point in time where a debt counsellor can provide a clearance certificate at a stage prior to satisfying all the debts' but supported the approach 'that the purpose of debt review remains to assist the consumer to repay his or her debts' and concluded from this: 'The policy regarding the eventual satisfaction of all proper debt obligations is an important measure to retain and ensure responsibility and sustainability in the credit market. In this regard, any financial debt relief such as a reduction of obligations towards credit providers should be allowed on a consensual basis' (Government Gazette No. 36504: 41–42). So, voluntary waiver by a lender was conceptualized as the only option of debt relief for an over-indebted borrower. It remained unclear how such a voluntary relinquishment should come about, though.

The government, as the responsible author of the policy framework, clearly understood that the NCA may prevent reckless lending only after over-indebtedness had been diagnosed, and that it did not offer a solution especially to the impoverished over-indebted citizens:

> The different forms of debt relief have effective entry thresholds, which determine whether a consumer can access a particular option or not. Under certain circumstances, this may have the effect that none of the options or more than one option may be available to a consumer. … Some consumers will not qualify for any of these processes and hence will be indebted indefinitely. (Government Gazette No. 36504: 34)

This insight was clearly extended to debt counselling as the main remedy contemplated in the NCA (Government Gazette No. 36504: 35). Nevertheless, the government came to the unequivocal conclusion not to offer any help: 'It is recommended that the purpose of debt review remains to assist the consumer to repay his or her debts. The consumer further has to be in the financial position to repay all the debts within a reasonable period of time as negotiated by the industry' (Government Gazette No. 36504: 42).

Despite a more thorough analysis of the outcomes of the NCA, the new policy framework resembled in its recommendations all previous documents due to a indecision between appreciation of negative market results and a continuation of market extension.

The next step by the government to reform the NCA 34 of 2005 was the suggestion to remove adverse information of credit customers from the credit bureaux records after their debts had been cleared. Initially, this step was motivated by the widespread existence of adverse credit information that derived from a legal state prior to the implementation of the NCA. For instance, before the reckless lending rule became effective on 1 June 2007, many consumers 'were bombarded with invitations from financial institutions offering pre-approved credit cards and loans' (Kelly-Louw 2009: 189), resulting in negative credit records that now kept these citizens from getting access to the credit market again.

In addition, the removal of adverse information was a matter of justice from the perspective of consumers who finally had settled their debts. There were three models of credit information amnesty under consideration by the legislators, differing in the range of information on delayed repayment of debts that should be cleared. In February 2013, representatives of the banking business rejected the plan in general, as *Business Day* reported under the title 'Banks tell parliament no to credit amnesty' (28 February). Remarkably, instead of labelling it a 'credit information amnesty', the mass media took up the misleading term of a 'credit amnesty' from this positioning of credit providers.

As a consequence, the DTI had to intervene once more after an official notice on the 'Removal of Adverse Consumer Credit Information and Information Relating to Paid Up Judgements' had been published for public comment by the Minister of Finance (Government Gazette No. 36889). On 27 November 2013, the DTI felt compelled to clarify in a media statement that the regulations did not intend 'to cancel the debts of consumers', and that the measures affected only the recording of repayment defaults (DTI 2013a). It had to repeat this step on 27 February 2014. It was characteristic of the public debate that the Ministry repeatedly referred to economic growth rates as a motivation for this piece of legislation, instead of defending it as a measure of fairness or justice: 'It will also remove barriers to employment, stimulate economic growth … Credit spurs consumer spending which is a key driver to economic growth. Therefore, inaccessible or expensive credit hinders growth' (DTI 2014a).

The opponents of the reform argued that the expunction of negative credit information would make risk assessment more difficult, but without success. On 1 April 2014 the new regulations came into effect (Government Gazette No. 37386: 5). Adverse information on consumers who had repaid their debts had to be removed after two months. This step documented the centrality of the idea of credit-induced economic growth in the ideology of the government that was willing to oppose business interest if only it facilitated the access to consumer credit.

Already a few months earlier, in December 2013, the Ministry of Finance and the Department of Trade and Industry had come back to the initial problem of over-indebtedness and declared that they had been mandated by the government 'to take measures to assist over-indebted households and also prevent them from becoming over-indebted in future', showing concern 'about the very high levels of household debt and over-indebtedness'. It listed several goals, ranging from establishing affordability and suitability criteria in the process of risk assessment to setting 'norms and standards' with regard to the treatment of reckless lending and emolument attachment orders. It promised in particular 'to provide appropriate relief to qualifying distressed borrowers by reducing their instalment burden, without additional cost to the borrower' (DTI 2013b). The roots of these problems were in many cases ascribed to illegal or reckless practices. According to this point of view the problems resulted from a lack of enforcement, thereby supporting the government's perception that no legislative changes were required.

The recommendations for changes remained at the level of voluntary agreements and informal changes of the business:

> Treating customers fairly should be instilled into the corporate culture of lenders. ... Government will continue to engage with major lenders to consider steps they may take to assist currently over-indebted households. [And] major lenders are encouraged to offer debt relief measures without charge to distressed borrowers, which will be a welcome addition to the menu of options available to borrowers who are overwhelmed by their debt. (DTI 2013b)

The Ministry refused to take any political steps to solve the identified problems and retreated to the position of a counsellor of the lending business.

In another media release from May 2014, referring to the still to come National Credit Act Amendment Bill, the then President Zuma supported the matter once again. Explicitly referring to the fact that more than 50 per cent of credit customers showed impaired records, he and Minister Rob Davies confirmed their intention 'to protect vulnerable consumers against unscrupulous practices'. They even referred to the police killings of striking miners in Marikana in August 2012 – a topic the government usually avoided – to support their claim: 'Our investigation in Marikana found that 100% of the lenders looked at, did not adhere to the Act, thus leading to reckless credit. The National Credit Amendment Bill (NCAB) therefore empowered the Minister to prescribe affordability assessment regulations to achieve uniformity and consistency in this area' (DTI 2014b). Once again, this statement ascribed these undesirable developments to the contraventions of the NCA, and hence defended its principles. Nevertheless, it presented the prospect of help to the over-indebted, but without suggesting concrete measures.

After the collapse of African Bank Ltd in August 2014, the concern for financial stability took centre stage in public attention. Public debates focussed on the soundness of banks, and over-indebtedness disappeared from the public agenda for a longer time. The reform of the NCA received no more public attention.

Finally, on 13 March 2015 the first Amendment of the NCA was published in the Government Gazette. It did not change the principles of the NCA but added some regulations to the law.

The dispute on Payment Distribution Agents, who facilitated the recollection of debts for credit providers but posed additional costs to borrowers and acted fraudulently in some cases, was solved by including them in the list of market actors that had to register, i.e. they also became public actors in the credit market (s 10A Regulations of the NCA).

The core of the reform consisted of the final establishment of prescribed limitations of risk assessment procedures. Credit providers were still free to choose their method of calculation, but the terms were more clearly defined now. A norm of minimum living expenses was introduced into the Regulations of the NCA which had to be set aside from the net income, as suggested by the policy framework: 'Provision needs to be made for minimum standards relating to affordability assessment mechanisms' (Government Gazette No. 36504: 25). In full accordance with the basic ideology of the NCA, which required economically rational calculation as a precondition of a self-regulating consumer credit market, this was translated into forms and figures in chapter 3 of the Amendment of the Regulations of the NCA. Section 8 demanded that a 'credit provider must make a calculation of the consumer's existing financial means, prospects and obligations' and provided a mathematical methodology for doing this in section 10. A table defined the 'minimum expense norms', which demanded that credit providers should approve a credit application only if the form outlined a sufficient amount of remaining income.

Table 4.2. Affordability measurement thresholds.

Minimum income in ZAR	**Maximum income in ZAR**	**Fixed expenses factor in ZAR**	**Additional factor of income that has to remain freely available in per cent**
0.00	800.00	0.00	100
800.01	6,250.00	800.00	6.75
6,250.01	25,000.00	1,167.88	9.00
25,000.01	50,000.00	2,855.33	8.20
50,000.01	Unlimited	4,905.38	6.75

Source: Chapter 3, section 10, Amendment of the Regulations of the NCA.

This table stipulates that only persons earning above an average monthly income of ZAR 800 during the past three months were eligible for a consumer loan. A person with a monthly income of ZAR 15,000 would have to set aside 1,167.88, plus 9 per cent of the income above this figure, i.e. ZAR 1,244.89. From the remaining income, all regular expenses of a customer had to be subtracted. The 'consumer declaration', whose form was appended to the Amendment of the Regulations, listed expenses for accommodation, transport, food, education, medical items, water and electricity, and the general category 'maintenance'. The sum of these figures would further reduce the available income of ZAR 12,587. All the rest could be charged as monthly instalments by the credit provider without lending recklessly. This means that this formula provided a new and very clearly defined margin of profit a credit provider was allowed to take. However, at the same time it encouraged credit providers to do exactly this by protecting their claims due to their compliance to the NCA and giving them the notion that a borrower had calculated his financial capacities precisely.

Accordingly, a minimum income of ZAR 800 per month was necessary to apply for credit, and above this bottom line a share of the income between 6.75 per cent and 9 per cent had to be reserved for the customer. If the remaining disposable income was sufficient to afford the instalments of the loan, the contracting parties could proceed. In the case of a customer who claimed to be satisfied with a smaller amount than outlined by the Regulations, he had to calculate his minimum expenses explicitly and in detail (Government Gazette No. 38557: 17–22, 32–35). The information from credit bureaux used to calculate the affordability had to be of recent date.

The debate on improving the disclosure of the costs of credit to the customer resulted in the provision that a credit provider had to direct the attention of a customer to the ratio of his total repayments to the principal. The intention of this measure was to explain to customers that the affordability of monthly instalments was important, but also that the rationality of taking out a loan depended on the proportion between the money they received immediately as principal on the one hand, and the total amount they would have to repay until the finalization of the contract on the other hand. Still, the customers had to draw the conclusions from the figures themselves.

Beyond this, the Amendment demanded more professional skills from credit providers, credit bureau clerks and debt counsellors, all of whom needed some skills in financial management and accounting from then on. The procedures of the National Consumer Tribunal were formalized to speed up the proceedings.

The National Credit Amendment Act was an important step towards preventing irresponsible lending to the lowest ranks of income. Another important part of the reform was that customers gained an increased awareness of their financial management by being forced to outline their basic monthly expenses. This would obviously facilitate the understanding of the effects of a loan. Moreover, it made it clear that the availability of a loan came at a monetary cost.

On the other hand, the new regulations still excluded emergency loans, school and student loans. It did not discount financial inexperience or motivations different from economic rationality on the side of customers. The effect of disclosed information was conceptualized as a fixed mechanism.

In another step, the government brought in a new interest rate ceiling, which, however, was only of minor importance. From 6 May 2016 on, the interest rate on unsecured loans increased and was now limited to 21 per cent plus the repurchase rate of the central bank, which had stood at 7 per cent since 17 March 2016 (Government Gazette No. 39379: 109). With effect from 10 August 2017, the cost of credit life insurance was capped at ZAR 4.50 per ZAR 1000 for unsecured loans (Government Gazette No. 40606: 7). These two steps fixed the maximum costs of consumer loans at a certain limit, but these products still remained very expensive.

The Draft Amendment of 2017: Debt Discharge on the Horizon?

With a remarkable degree of delay, the South African legislators finally thought about the possibility of debt discharge. Although the debate on this legislative piece started together with the other Amendment bills, no measures had actually been implemented by the time of writing. On 7 September 2018 the parliamentary Committee on Trade and Industry adopted the National Credit Amendment Bill, and the Parliament passed it on 12 September 2018. Yet, it still has to be debated by the National Council of Provinces and was intended to be sent to the presidency some time (Parliament of South Africa 2018a, 2018b; Tshwane 2018).

Despite not having been launched yet, the basic character of the National Credit Amendment Bill, 2018 (Government Gazette No. 41274) is clear enough for its intentions to be described here, and to be able to compare the reform with current tendencies in international legislations concerning consumer bankruptcies.

The debt relief bill will probably provide the option for a debt discharge for the first time, but this option will only be accessible to a very restricted set of persons following a time-consuming procedure. Greater impact should be expected from other details of the bill, which is planned to make the NCR and the NCT more effective.

The Consumer Tribunal in particular might be granted the right to declare in a more efficient way that loans are reckless with the proposed section 88C(2)(d) of the Bill. In future, it could be sufficient that a single member of the Tribunal judges a loan under consideration to be a violation of the NCA.

Most public debates, however, have referred to the possibility of debt discharge, and a widespread discomfort became obvious from a parliamentary presentation on the matter by the Ministry of Finance, in which it remarked that 'South Africa has never before gone this route' (Treasury 2017).

The Amendment Bill suggests a completely new procedure called 'debt intervention', which, according to its section 88F, will be closely monitored by the Minister of Trade and Industry personally, who will have to consult with the Minister of Finance, the Minister of Justice, the representatives of the credit industry and parliament in each case in which he or she intends to grant debt relief.

Only persons earning below ZAR 7,500 will be eligible, after they have reduced their possessions, and debts must not exceed ZAR 50,000.[1] They will be allowed to keep 'necessary tools and implements of trade stock and agricultural implements up to a maximum of [ZA]R 10,000; professional books, documents or instruments used … in his or her profession up to a maximum of [ZA]R 10,000; necessary household furniture and household utensils up to a maximum of [ZA]R 10,000; necessary beds, bedding and wearing apparel' of the applicant and his immediate household members, and 'the supply of food and drink in the residence … for a period of one month' (s 88A(1)(b)(i)-(v) National Credit Act Amendment Bill). Pension funds and retirement annuities will remain untouched. These preconditions demand that the applicant voluntarily agrees to become impoverished, if he has not already become so.

But that is not all. A debt intervention will require an 'exogenous' economic shock that has caused unemployment, or a 'regional natural disaster', or similar unavoidable events coming from the outside. Domestic unemployment, for instance, only justifies a debt intervention procedure if the labour market sector has been officially identified through a public announcement in the Government Gazette by the Minister as being in a crisis (s 88F(2), (3) National Credit Act Amendment Bill). This makes it clear how extraordinary circumstances must be cited by the applicant to justify any debt intervention. The regular accumulation of debts without mishaps does not qualify a debtor for a debt intervention procedure.

There are even more preconditions, such as the necessity to provide a letter of acknowledgement from every affected credit provider by the debt intervention applicant (s 88E(3) National Credit Act Amendment Bill). The bill makes no arrangements for the case whereby a credit provider refuses to produce such a letter. All the financial obligations of the applicant also have to be scrutinized carefully, excluding every contract that does not fulfil the preconditions, or that might be reckless.

After all preconditions have been fulfilled, the National Consumer Tribunal has two basic options other than rejecting the application. It can refer the applicant to a debt counsellor for a re-arrangement of the repayment – a suggestion that once more depends on the willingness of creditors. Or it can reduce the fees, interest and charges – but, again, not the principal – for a period of up to twenty-four months. If the financial situation of the applicant does not improve during this period then 'the Tribunal must declare the debt under the qualifying credit agreements as extinguished' (s 88D(4) National Credit Act Amendment Bill). This means that the Tribunal has no margin of discretion left, and extinguishing means a final annulment of debts.

As part of the preconditions of the procedure, a debtor must have completed a 'financial literacy or budgeting skills programme' and can be compelled to undertake 'any matter that in the view of the tribunal will aid the debt intervention applicant to manage or improve his or her financial position and become a productive member of society' (s 88D(4) (d), (e) National Credit Act Amendment Bill). A productive member of society repays his debts.

Overall, the reform will probably affect only a small number of debtors. More importantly, it does not change the basic approach towards consumer credit and the 'imbalances of negotiation power'.

The NCA itself, as well as the Amendment Bill 2018 have been conceptualized after international legislations have been studied. And the final assessment of the NCA and its Amendments will be based on a summary of these laws.

The DTI (Department of Trade and Industry) is reported to have developed the NCA after reviewing the legislations of Australia, New Zealand, England, Canada, the USA and the European Union (DTI 2003: 7, 23). The Amendment Bill of 2017 was drafted in reference to more recent developments in Croatia, India, England and Wales. This selection seemed strange only at a first glance: these legislations had in common that the credit industry did not have to bear the costs of debt relief. The following paragraphs will provide an overview of the consumer bankruptcy and insolvency legislations in these countries at the time of the drafting of the South African NCA and the Amendment of 2018.

All these legislations were in a state of constant reform as a consequence of the negotiation of two contradictory principles of democratic market societies: on the one hand, the principle of the sanctity of contracts (*pacta sunt servanda*) should enforce the fulfilment of mutual obligations in cases in which a voluntary agreement appeared to be insufficient. This principle was essential in risky economic procedures, because differentiated societies lacked the social sanctions of communities to impose the fulfilment of promises. On the other hand, democracies are compelled to include all their citizens into a society. Over-indebted citizens not only lack the financial means to participate in social life, they are also unable to develop an economic future for themselves and their families. Therefore, long-term over-indebtedness represents a limitation of the democratic promise and hampers its legitimization.

The European reform process of consumer insolvency legislations, which started in 1984 in Denmark and was followed by a number of laws in rapid succession, was triggered by the insight that in financialized consumer societies most attempts at debt collection from over-indebted borrowers were to no avail. Creditors did not receive significant repayments due to the insolvency of their clients. Borrowers were turned into hardship cases for the welfare state and lacked any motivation to earn money because all income would be distributed among creditors. And, finally, the state had to cover the costs of fruitless debt enforcement procedures (Hiilamo 2018; Kilborn 2007; Niemi, Ramsay and Whitford 2009; Niemi-Kiesiläinen, Ramsay and Whitford 2003). As a result, solutions for relieving borrowers from the debt trap by simultaneously satisfying the claims of creditors to a maximum amount were developed.

Historically, the oldest ruling of bankruptcy that could be applied to consumers was that of the US Bankruptcy Act of 1898. Obviously, its intention was not to serve over-indebted consumers, because the lending business originated in the United States only after World War I (Calder 1999: 109–208). Instead, the law resulted from the economic necessities of a territorially expanding country with rapidly moving entrepreneurs. It addressed venturesome businessmen in an unstable social environment. The purpose of the Bankruptcy Act of 1898 was to secure the claims of creditors against debtors, who might leave the local spot quickly after their operating plan had failed. Therefore, the Bankruptcy Act of 1898 provided the possibility of seizing all belongings of a debtor, apart from a social minimum, for the disposition of a creditor. This allowed the debtor a fresh start afterwards – a term that stuck to this policy, which seemed appropriate to a literally free market economy, in which risk-prone economic endeavours could fail and creditors were in danger of losing sight of their constantly migrating clients. However, it should be noticed that the intention of the law was not the relief of debtors, but the securing of the property rights of creditors as far as possible (Skeel Jr. 2001: 3–4).

The 'fresh start' rule was complemented by the Chandler Act of 1938, i.e. after the establishment of regular wage labour in the US. The new procedure was practised in the aftermath of the Great Depression in 1933 for the first time. The Chandler Act provided a payment plan, according to which a debtor could keep his possessions after delivering his earnings beyond a social minimum for distribution among his creditors for three to five years (Skeel Jr. 2001: 7). This was an appropriate solution for a consumer society, in which wage earners possessed expensive durables like houses, cars or domestic appliances. Payment plans offer debtors a way of keeping essential possessions in the process of debt relief. A precondition for the agreement of creditors to a payment plan was the possibility of a promising economic future income on the part of the debtor.

Both principles, immediate debt relief and a payment plan, were resumed in the US Bankruptcy Code of 1978, i.e. after the financialized consumer credit gained momentum in the 1970s and the levels of over-indebted citizens increased (Krippner 2011; Schraten 2015). The principle of 'discharge-for-current-assets' was coded in Chapter 7, and the payment plan, lasting three to five years, was fixed in Chapter 13 of the Bankruptcy Code of 1978 (Kilborn 2007: 54–55).

Both options represented a restriction of the property rights of creditors. After debtors had successfully passed the legal procedures, a creditor was deprived of his options of legal enforcement of his claims. It means that debts were turned into natural obligations, i.e. they still existed but could no longer be enforced by the legal system.

The historical origins of these rulings show that in both cases the main intention of legislators was to keep the economy running. The fresh start policy aimed at risk-taking entrepreneurs, who could consequently fail with their plans, and their creditors. A smoothly operating growth-oriented economy required a quick solution of their conflict. The payment plan procedure was intended to secure the general standard of living of over-indebted wage earners. The importance of this approach became obvious after the Great Depression had revealed the economically devastating consequences of an impoverishment of large parts of the population. It originated in a political climate in which the standard of living of citizens had been identified as a crucial factor of the economy. Poor citizens do not generate a consumer demand for expensive goods, and they block the expansion of manufacturing and commercial trade.

At the time of the preparation of the South African National Credit Act, the US legislation was undergoing a process of reform too. The reason lay in repeated complaints of the credit industry about too many debtors choosing the fresh start option. Concurrent with the NCA, an amendment of the Bankruptcy Code of 1978 became effective on 17 October 2005, which restricted the access of over-indebted citizens to debt relief due to a procedure called 'means testing' (Kilborn 2007: 55–62). This reform adjusted the US legislation to continental European legislations. Many of them required attempts at extra-judicial negotiations between creditors and debtors before granting access to legal debt relief solutions. The 'means testing' procedure removed the freedom of choice between Chapter 7 and Chapter 13; those debtors with a prospect of income were limited to the option of a payment plan. The intention of the US reform was to encourage debtors to fulfil their financial obligations as far as possible. This reform rested on the political expectation that unemployed citizens could find a job again.

In the European Union, there was no uniform consumer bankruptcy and insolvency legislation, as the wording of the report of the DTI might have suggested. Instead, a number of countries introduced national solutions to the increasing problem of over-indebtedness, beginning with Denmark in 1984. The rulings differed, but all continental legislations had in common the fact that they aimed at disciplining consumers, in contrast to the common law approach of settling the claims of creditors quickly. This means that payment plans served an educational rather than economic purpose with regard to consumers.

In Denmark, candidates of an insolvency procedure had to propose a payment plan, lasting for five years. During this period, the debtor was limited to the social minimum income of the welfare state. Additional earnings had to be delivered to a trustee for distribution among his creditors. After successfully following this strict budget, the debtor would have his remaining debts cancelled by a court (Ziegel 2003: 139–40).

This Danish model was further developed in the German insolvency legislation, which was passed in 1994 and came into effect in 1999. Kilborn (2004: 257) praised it as a 'role model' for the continent. Before the legal procedure could begin, the German insolvency law required a final attempt at out-of-court arrangements between creditors and debtors. Initially, the official procedure had included another attempt at a re-negotiated payment plan, mediated by a court this time, but this practice was soon reduced to a mere legal option due to a lack of success. This demonstrated that administrative help was seen as a means of last resort. After opening the insolvency process, all the remaining assets of debtors beyond the social minimum were liquidated. In contrast to the US payment plan, expensive items which were deemed to be 'luxurious' could be replaced by cheaper alternatives. The debtor then entered a 'period of good conduct' usually lasting six years. During this period, a debtor had to look for employment actively, in order to earn money that could be distributed among his creditors. He himself was obliged to live on a social minimum income of the welfare state.[2] At the end of the period, a court decided on the application to cancel the remaining debts. Although there was no automatic authorization of debt relief, it was granted in almost every case (Kilborn 2004, 2007: 39–42, 77–81).

France enacted the *Loi Neierz* in 1989 and amended it in 1995. It took a different approach than Denmark and Germany, granting the central bank the main position in the procedure. Of particular importance for the South African legislation was the establishment of a nation-wide credit reporting system, which gathered negative incidents of the financial life of prospective borrowers. This way, creditors were given the opportunity to conduct a better risk assessment. This was complemented by a system of debt renegotiation. In every *départment*, there existed a debt commission which mediated a rescheduling of payment obligations of debtors. The goal was to draft payments plans which were feasible for the debtor, and to collect enough money to motivate creditors to consent to the plan. These plans lasted up to ten years. Due to the failure of many payment plans, the legislation was amended by a two-step coercive procedure in the mid-1990s. If a payment plan turned out to be too demanding for the debtors, the commission was entitled to order a payment moratorium of up to two years. During this period, the debtor could recover financially, and would be redirected to the ordinary procedure in the case of success. However, if no significant recovery took place, the commission had the option to discharge debtors from part or all of their financial obligations (Kilborn 2007: 27–29, 63–67; Ziegel 2003: 140). The role of the central bank was of particular interest. It documented the French understanding that the final cancellation of payments was at the heart of the monetary system. In other words, creditors finally negotiated with their own lenders of last resort.

The French model resembled the legal solutions in Belgium and Luxembourg, whereas the Austrian system was akin to the German approach. In 1998 the Netherlands set up a two-tier system of amicable and enforced renegotiations of debts, which was basically similar to the German model. The subsequent statutory debt settlement procedure could end with a debt discharge after three years. However, according to Jungmann and Huls (2009: 419–20), the main intention of the Dutch statutory system was to encourage creditors to reach an agreement with regard to voluntary debt arrangements in the first stage of the legal procedure. This means that the Dutch system attempted to discipline debtors and creditors, because the careless unwillingness of a creditor to agree to a voluntary payment plan could end in an administrative cancellation of his claims.

The continental European legislations differed significantly from the common law rulings of Australia, New Zealand, Canada, England and Wales.

The Australian Bankruptcy Act 1966 offered over-indebted citizens a solution which was very similar to the fresh start policy of the United States. Without paying a fee, a debtor could present a petition for bankruptcy, together with a statement of his financial affairs documenting his inability to pay, to the ITSA (Insolvency and Trustee Service Australia). An 'Official Receiver', or a privately engaged registered trustee, would then take administration of the estates and assets of the debtor beyond some exempt basic property. After accepting the petition, the debtor was declared bankrupt. For the next three years, the 'Official Receiver' or trustee would strive to utilize the sequestrated property, and after this period the debtor would be discharged from his debts. There were options to reduce the waiting period, and in 2002 an Amendment Bill aimed at impeding the access to bankruptcy by demanding more thorough checks of the insolvency of debtors. Additionally, debtors were encouraged to seek extra-court agreements (Mason and Duns 2003).

The rulings as well as the developments in New Zealand were similar to those in the United States, too. The Insolvency Act 1967 provided the option of debt discharge after a three-year period against the utilization of assets and estates. Additionally, there were two options for entering into a payment plan, one for trading or business people, and another one for wage earners. At the time the South African DTI was conducting its research, New Zealand's politicians were discussing reforms similar to those carried out in the United States and Australia in order to increase the share of debtors that would prefer repayment plans over bankruptcy (Telfer 2003).

In Canada, bankruptcy was ruled partly by federal and partly by provincial law. From 1919, there was a state-wide option to file for bankruptcy by assigning the assets of a debtor to the creditors, and from 1949 this included the automatic application of a debt discharge after nine months, which could be opposed by a trustee or the 'Superintendent'. The amendment of 1997 introduced the obligations of debtors to pay their surplus income to creditors (Ziegel 2003: 13–51). This means that Canada entered on the same path as in the US, which reduced the option of debt discharge to borrowers without prospect of future income.

With regard to the options of debt discharge, the bankruptcy rulings of England and Wales were at the opposite pole to legislations of other common law systems for a long time, because until 2007 the voluntary agreement of creditors and debtors was implemented as the standard procedure. The very limited options of statutory debt settlement resembled the situation in South Africa before the NCA, because there was no specific procedure for consumer debtors, but only the general bankruptcy options of the Insolvency Act 1986, which were reformed in the Enterprise Act of 2002.

Obviously, the traditional approach to indebtedness in England and Wales differed significantly from that in other common law systems and from the European continent. Although the first options of bankruptcy, strictly limited to commercial traders, were introduced in England as early as 1705, it was quite common to imprison debtors until the mid-twentieth century (Tabb 1991). In the early 1960s, debtors constituted 14 per cent of all prisoners in England and Wales (Ramsay 2003: 212).

The Insolvency Act of 1986 created the option of filing for bankruptcy, but it required the initial payment of £250 for administration costs, and another £120 for court fees. In cases involving debts up to £20,000, borrowers could be discharged after two or three years, a period that was shortened to twelve months by the Enterprise Act of 2002. This was, however, an expensive solution and not available to penniless debtors. Some welfare organizations supported debtors to file for bankruptcy, but this cannot be viewed at as a systematic approach.

The first alternative to bankruptcy consisted of individual voluntary agreements, which required the approval of creditors. Due to the inaccessibility of the legal bankruptcy procedure, many debtors had to resort to this solution, and ask for the help of private debt counsellors. The second alternative consisted in county court administration orders, which mandated a payment plan feasible for the debtor. However, this solution contained no debt discharge, and some courts did not even prevent compounding of interest during the period of repayment.

In 2007, England and Wales introduced the option of a 'Debt Relief Order', which became publicly known as 'No Income, No Assets Debt Relief' or 'NINA Debt Relief' (Netshitenzhe 2017: 7). The Tribunals, Courts and Enforcement Act 2007 addressed the extremely poor citizens of England and Wales, who could not repay debts up to a threshold of £20,000. 'Poor' meant that they had no assets worth more than £300, and a disposable monthly income of up to £50. Astonishingly, despite these quite harsh preconditions, the application required the payment of a fee, which stood at £90 at the time of writing. Consequently, the poor had to save the equivalent of nearly two months of disposable income before they could apply – a clear sign that the Debt Relief Order was meant to be a measure of last resort. The effect of a Debt Relief Order took the form of a twelve months' moratorium on debt repayment. During this period the debtor was to try to recover financially. If this was not successful, the debts could then be discharged (Tribunals, Courts and Enforcement Act 2007 Part 5).

Some of the political justifications of the Enterprise Act 2002 were remarkable because they explicitly stated the desire to copy the fresh start advantages of the United States for enterprises as much as possible, but warned of the promotion of recklessness if these options were made available to ordinary citizens (Kilborn 2007: 88–89; Ramsay 2003: 219–22). In other words, legislators in England and Wales wanted to promote risky economic endeavours but to discourage debtors from over-borrowing by presenting the consequence of inevitable over-indebtedness to them. With regard to companies, they adopted the liberal ideology, according to which an entrepreneur should be able to get rid of the obligations of his failed business attempt, but concerning individual borrowers, they followed the ideology of moral hazard. 'Moral hazard' expected irresponsible behaviour as a consequence of a prospect on debt relief due to a subsequent recklessness of social actors (Baker 1996).

A further two pieces of legislation were consulted by South African politicians during the drafting of the Amendment Bill 2018, namely that of Croatia and of India. Croatia had introduced a fresh start scheme in 2015. Those eligible had to have debts of up to ZAR 76,000, a monthly income of not more than ZAR 2,770, no property and no savings. The programme was applied to 60,000 citizens, i.e. 2 per cent of the adult population, at an approximate cost of ZAR 467 million.

India introduced a debt relief scheme in 2008 that addressed small farmers in rural areas, after high levels of over-indebtedness had been caused by unpredictable rainfall and high interest rates. The measure affected 36 to 40 million farmers and covered an outstanding debt of

ZAR 156 billion. Borrowers who pledged less than 2 hectares of their own land as collateral received unconditional full debt relief while borrowers who pledged more than 2 hectares received 25 per cent conditional debt relief. The government had re-capitalized the loans written off for the full amount. In both cases the costs had to be paid by the taxpayers.

This overview of international legislations reveals that the South African NCA of 2005 was mostly influenced by the approach of England and Wales. This confirmed a long-term tendency of South African legislation, which had been strongly shaped by English law since the early nineteenth century (Hahlo and Kahn 1960; Meyerhenrich 2008). This was especially true in all economic matters which rested on a shared common law tradition that was barely affected by the turn to political democracy in 1994 (Glenn 2010: 237–87). Although the South African constitution was heralded for its inclusion of socio-economic rights, courts soon made it clear that these did not extend into matters of economic policies (Klug 2010: 133–34).

In the NCA, another suggestion was taken from French legislation: the central importance of credit scoring. However, the legal options of debt discharge that had been integrated into French law since the mid-1990s emphasized a better risk assessment of creditors, which meant that the failure to perform proper risk assessments incurred the danger of a loss of property on the part of creditors. In South Africa, in contrast, all measures focus on the responsibility and financial literacy of borrowers.

Obviously, another reason for South African politicians to take Croatia as a role model was that it represented a transitory political system with high levels of poverty and unemployment, too. Croatia had adopted the famous term 'fresh start' for its policy, which signalled the hope for a new beginning for citizens in a relatively young democracy. Yet, the genuine fresh start model had been implemented in the fast growing and economically expanding United States of the nineteenth century and was modelled for the benefit of creditors. In Croatia and South Africa, however, the law aimed at supporting vulnerable debtors, who had mainly borrowed due to a lack of money from their daily livelihood. Unfortunately, South African policymakers ignored the background of the US Chandler Act from 1938, whose payment plan had deliberately addressed the protection of a new middle class. After the Great Depression it had been important to prevent this group from becoming impoverished again. The South African National Credit Act Amendment Bill urged debtors to sell many durables above the ZAR 10,000 threshold instead, a move which would lower the general standard of living of these persons. In the short run, this may reduce the costs for credit providers – but in the long run it regrouped previously middle-class citizens into the lower social strata of society.

In contrast to Croatia, South Africa planned to introduce an income threshold three times higher, which suggested a more realistic idea of the scope of the problem on the one hand, but which would necessitate much higher costs on the other hand. Furthermore, these costs should be restrained by the limitation of the debt intervention to applicants who had been hit by exogenous or extraordinary economic shocks, natural or personal disasters – a suggestion obviously taken from India.

Finally, the creators of the NCA and its Amendments had been influenced by the continental European idea of disciplining and educating consumers. The debt relief bill explicitly demanded that a failing debtor 'become a productive member of society' (s 88D(4)(e) National Credit Act Amendment Bill). This ignored – in European countries as well as in South Africa – the main reasons for over-indebtedness, which resided in a lack of income, hence in unemployment and illness. The idea of disciplining over-indebtedness that was caused by borrowers being too generous did not make sense in the South African case, as such persons by definition would be excluded from debt intervention. In any case, this idea conflicted with the political goal of a constantly growing consumer credit market.

To summarize: the drafted South African debt relief scheme excluded too many over-indebted citizens in need of help. It sentenced eligible candidates to long-term impoverishment. It increased the accountability of credit providers to a small extent but did so reluctantly. And, most importantly of all, the core principle of the South African consumer credit market remained untouched. It provided a realm of private negotiation about loan contracts with a maximum protection of private property and a minimum outlook of relief to over-indebted customers. This channel of negotiation was now restricted by a defined minimum of living expenses, and within this channel a customer was more clearly confronted with the total cost of credit. The relinquishment of interventions into existing contracts reflected the split discourse on the consumer credit market, in which supply side and demand side were discussed separately.

The description of the financialized consumer credit market, the historical reconstruction of its development and the sociological analysis of its legal framework have all showed the firm adherence of the government to the idea of a self-regulating consumer credit market.

The next chapter will offer a theoretical explanation of this idea, as well as the historical roots of this kind of thinking. The core argument is that the economy is performative to a huge degree, which means that economic ideas are not a simple illustration of an economy but an integral part thereof. Economic ideas shape the formation of markets (Appadurai 2012; Callon 1998a; Hart 2012).

NOTES

1. The threshold amount of income, and all other amounts, will become adjustable by the Minister of Trade and Industry in accordance with the inflation rate.
2. To be more precise, the level was defined by the threshold at which durables were exempt from execution.

CHAPTER 5

The Model of Rational Action in the South African Consumer Credit Market

This chapter will analyse the results of the empirically oriented chapters. So far we have been able to identify a deeply rooted adherence to the idea of a self-regulating market in South Africa. This idea is based on the image of an equilibrium of supply and demand. However, the empirical findings showed a stable hierarchy between a minority benefiting from the earnings of the consumer credit market on the one hand, and a large and socially relevant group of financially stretched and long-term indebted citizens. Accordingly, the task of this chapter is to analyse the roots of power and the legitimacy of such a societal setting.

The first section of the chapter aims at providing a plain model of the market. Images illustrate the identified mechanisms. From this it will become clear that the establishment of the South African consumer credit market was shaped by a specific idea of self-governing markets and economic rationality.

Consequently, the second section will analyse the attempts of various classical theorists to grasp the paradigmatic rationality that was established in industrialized market economies. Adam Smith promoted the public prominence of the idea of a selfish interest that benefits society. The unique characteristics of the writings of Georg Simmel and Max Weber are to be found in the fact that they analysed the expanding market economies of their times without presupposing a governing idea, and both identified monetary relations as the core of such an autonomously developing social order. The writings of Weber deserve special attention here because he roots the hidden core of a self-regulating economy in the founding relations of law, and of property law in particular. He develops a pessimistic outlook regarding the long-term stability of rational market economies from this.

The last section draws conclusions with regard to the normative quality of the NCA.

The Image of Lending Action in the NCA

The NCA, its regulations, amendments and revised versions were all built around a specific understanding of action. To be more precise, it was modelled as economic action consisting of an instrumental rationality framed by legal restrictions and institutional modifications (Weber 1978: 24).

In the following passages, the NCA is interpreted as an institutional arrangement that is experienced by actors as objective reality in the sense that its existence cannot be suspended by individual will, and in that it is shared with others. The consumer credit market represents an infrastructural environment that exposes social actors to a set of ruling relations. Accordingly, action takes place within this reality.[1] The NCA offered the option of interaction, without legitimate interference from outside, to those who complied. Institutions of a diverse kind secured the accomplishment of legal action in this way. That is to say, action in this context was conducted within 'institutionally set channels' (Berger and Luckmann 1991: 80). These kinds of channelled proceedings, which were bordered by legal restrictions, are visualized in what follows.

Two images will illustrate the expectations of the legislators with regard to a self-regulating and frictionless consumer credit market. Two further images will illustrate the supposed deviations from rationality in the forms of reckless lending and over-indebtedness.

The first illustration in this chapter shows the channel of negotiation which was supposed to result in the mutual exchange of money (Figure 5.1). The borders of the channel were framed by illegality, and beyond these borders neither lender nor borrower could claim the support of society in the case of conflict. For a lender, this would potentially result in the loss of his property, and a borrower would be without legal protection and at the mercy of direct social power relations.

Reckless lending on the part of the credit provider, and false information about income on the part of the customer, represented those modes of behaviour which would turn negotiations into an illegal procedure. However, both kinds of illegal action would be treated as a deviation from the basic norm of the NCA, in contrast to ignoring the NCA altogether. They would therefore be dealt with inside the legal framework. This will be further explained by the second and third images below.

Inside the channel of action two parties were expected to negotiate a double exchange of money, consisting of a payment and repayment. The negotiation was performed by equals. The flows of money surrounding this agreement, however, differed from each other because the repayment was expected to exceed the amount of the initial payment. That is to say that legal equality was accompanied by an economic disequilibrium from the onset of the lending procedure; this derived from the right of the credit provider to claim interest and fees. This disequilibrium was nowhere explained in the NCA because it was assumed as a given economic rationality, according to which seller and buyer were attracted to each other by exactly this imbalance. A more detailed suggestion was made in the policy framework of the Department of Trade and Industry.

> Credit transactions are necessary where a person seeks to obtain a product or service for which the person cannot, or chooses not to pay in cash or by way of exchange in kind or barter. Credit enables people to have use of a product or service, at a cost represented by an interest rate, prior to their having paid for that product or service or, where an item cannot be afforded from a single month's salary, to spread the payments over a number of months. (DTI 2004c: 6)

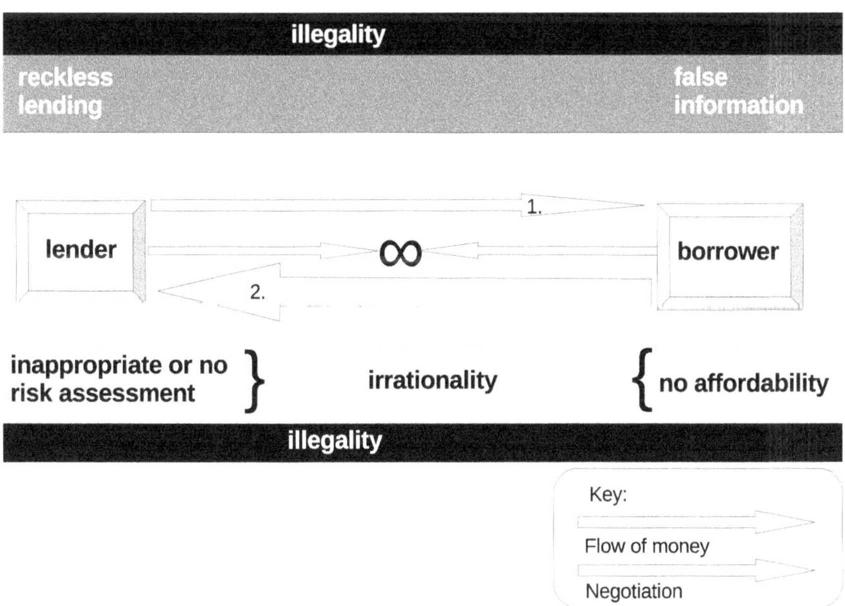

Figure 5.1. Channel of lending interaction. Created by the author.

The policy framework listed, among incentives to take out a loan, the purchase of houses, cars, fridges, beds, radios or televisions, university or school fees, school uniforms, or the wish to buy trading stock for a small business.[2] The surplus amount of money in return was justified by the 'cost represented by an interest rate'. Figure 5.1 represents the incentive for credit providers to offer credit in the form of the wider second vector representing money, including the cost of credit, consisting of principal, fees and interest. As the policy framework made clear, the borrower was conceptualized as being motivated by the option of consuming now and paying later.

At the bottom of the channel of negotiation, though, there existed two dangers that had to be avoided to make the model of action work. A risk assessment by the lender and an affordability assessment by the borrower were seen as those requirements of economic action which posed a precondition for a frictionless market development. Any neglect of them was interpreted as a deviation from rationality that had to be eschewed.

The necessities were to be fulfilled with the help of credit bureaux. Their crucial function is introduced in another, more complex illustration. Credit bureaux received information from two directions. On the one hand, credit providers delivered information about past economic relationships with their customers. On the other hand, various sources like other financial institutions, state agencies or insurance companies, which had dealt economically with the borrower in the past, would be checked for prior economic failures and deficiencies on the demand side of the deal. Basically, this second tier of facts was seen as a counterbalance, eliminating those pieces of 'false information' a borrower could use in order to deceive a credit provider. Credit bureaux were conceptualized as a provision against fraud on the side of a credit customer. This pool of information was conveyed to the credit provider again and served his risk assessment procedures.

Figure 5.2 shows how the potential realm of irrationality should be dissolved through the services of credit bureaux. It also visualizes that the governance of this behaviour addresses the supply side of the market only, and it reveals the affordability assessment of the borrower to be a reaction to the procedures of the credit providers' arrangements, because the price of a loan derives from the result of the risk assessment.

According to this model the danger of irrationality was counteracted by the pursuit of rational interests. A nexus of actors aspiring towards the best ends for themselves should bring about a dissolution of unwanted behaviour. This reminds one of a philosophical idea of Paul Thiry

Baron d'Holbach (1889: 158), a contemporary of Adam Smith, about the origins of rational interests of humans:

> Passions are the true counterpoise to passions ... Reason, the fruit of experience, is only the art of choosing those passions to which, for his own peculiar happiness, [man] ought to listen. Education is the true art of disseminating, the proper method of cultivating advantageous passions in the heart of man. Legislation is the art of restraining dangerous passions, and exciting those which may be conducive to the public welfare.

This idea was referenced by Albert O. Hirschman as he outlined a broad philosophical movement, which had lifted religiously condemned passions to the status of selfish but rational interests that would accommodate if they were carefully balanced (Hirschman 2013: 20–42). In this development of ideas, interest emerged as an autonomously managed impetus that was stripped of the irrationality of passions.

The further narrowing down of the meaning of 'interest' as a term referring to economic rationality was presumed by Hirschman (2013: 39) to be rooted in the origins of credit: 'Possibly, too, the special affinity to rational calculation implicit in the concept of interest [in the meaning of a return of money lending] with the nature of economic activities

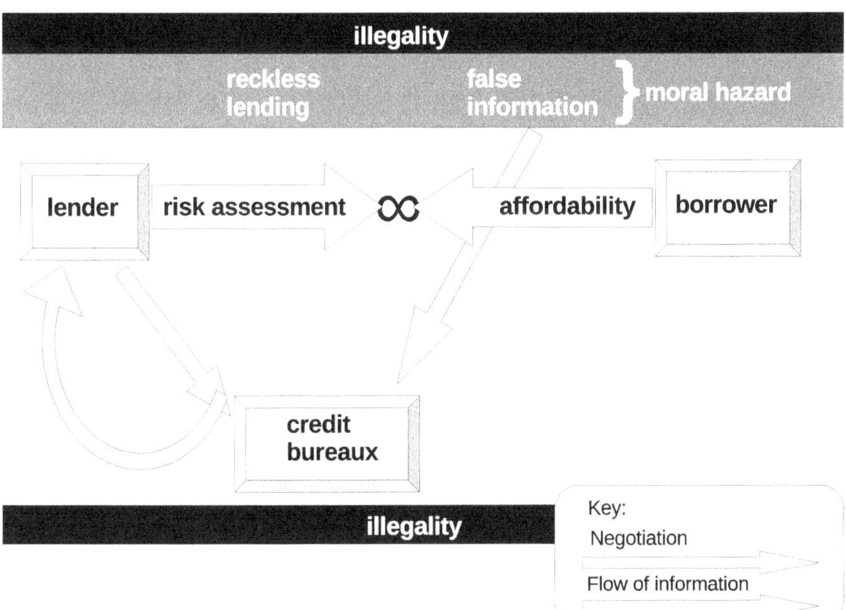

Figure 5.2. Risk assessment and affordability measurement. Created by the author.

accounts for these activities eventually monopolizing the contents of the concept'. Whatever the historical development may have been, the NCA conceptualized the establishment of economic rationality in the South African consumer credit market in exactly this way.

The implicit model runs as follows: credit bureaux and money lending institutions pursued their interest in earning money and served each other in this capacity. Both benefited from the passion of the borrower to consume now and pay later. In this regard, credit bureaux functioned as controllers of irrational excesses by collecting details of economic misbehaviour. The risk assessment procedures of credit providers deriving from this, flanked by the legal obligation to clearly disclose the cost of credit, presented the price of a loan to a borrower in such a way that he would inevitably check the reasonableness of his desire to consume. Finally, credit providers would only offer loans with a manageable risk attached, and customers would only take up loans they could afford. The individual passions were downscaled to rationalized and balanced interests that way.

A remarkable parallel between the implicit model of the NCA and d'Holbach's quotation lay in the idea of education as simply disseminating the familiarization with economic behaviour, and of legislation possessing the double function of motivating and controlling the corresponding actions.

This control, of course, had to deal with the threat of deliberate fraud; the NCA was not naïve in this regard. In Figure 5.2 the deviations from law into illegality are represented by reckless lending on the part of credit providers, and misleading or missing information about their economic conditions on the part of borrowers.

Another detail of the NCA attracts attention in this context. The possible forms of misconduct by lenders, and the prevention thereof, were outlined in a number of sections of the law. However, the breach of regulations by borrowers was only mentioned in a single sentence.

On the supply side, reckless lending was defined in section 80 of the NCA; section 81 outlined how credit providers could make sure they would not come under suspicion for having sold loans recklessly; section 83 laid out the requirements for the court process of reckless lending in detail; and section 84 explained the effects of court rulings. Additionally, section 89 and 90 explained the consequences of illegal credit agreements, as distinguished from reckless lending, in detail.

On the demand side the misdeed of 'false information' by the customer was regulated in section 81(4)(a) of the NCA alone, in which a single sentence defined how a lack of 'fully or truthfully' answered requests for information prevented a judgement of over-indebtedness and reckless lending. In that case the consequences consisted in the formal execution of the loan contract, including all options of debt enforcement by the credit provider. This striking disparity in the specificity of legal regulation was the consequence of the characterizing of one part – that of 'false information' – as moral hazard.

Moral hazard is a liberal concept which complements the assumptions of rational choice and economic rationality. Its basic expectation is that attempts to insure against losses would be unreasonable because it would reduce the cautiousness of the persons concerned. This means that any kind of social insurance would pose a threat to the rational action of individuals because the anticipation of a safety net would cause hazardous and irrational behaviour. Therefore, moral hazard is applied in order to argue against social protection and welfare mechanisms. Or, expressed more simply, Tom Baker (1996: 238) summarized the basic lesson of moral hazard as 'less is more'.

In the case of the NCA this meant that the best precautionary measure to prevent any over-indebtedness of a consumer would be to let him face the full consequences of over-borrowing. In reference to English legislation, which had a strong influence on South African policy makers, Ian Ramsay confirmed that the deterrent effect of indebtedness on borrowers was a recurring motive in debates about over-indebtedness (DTI 2003: 7; Ramsay 2003: 18). The difference in the effort to safeguard credit providers against reckless lending was remarkable. For a borrower, the difference between defying and violating the NCA was almost insignificant, whereas for a credit provider it consisted of the contrast between a full protection of the principal and a potential loss of his property. This difference is illustrated in the next two graphs.

In the case of reckless lending, illegality derived from the conscious and willing application of irrationality. Not performing risk assessment procedures, or ignoring their negative outcomes, could result in a seizure of the earnings of the loan contract if the borrower was over-indebted. Figure 5.3 shows the result of lender and borrower still being on an equal level as contracting parties, with the borrower settling the legal part of the contract after having taken legal action. That is to say that legal equality was complemented by an economic disequilibrium because the borrower was still obliged to pay back his principal.

Figure 5.3 acquires its full significance only in comparison with Figure 5.4, which depicts the situation of over-indebtedness. In this case, legal equality is turned into hierarchy. The borrower who ran into over-indebtedness due to an irrational affordability assessment or because of

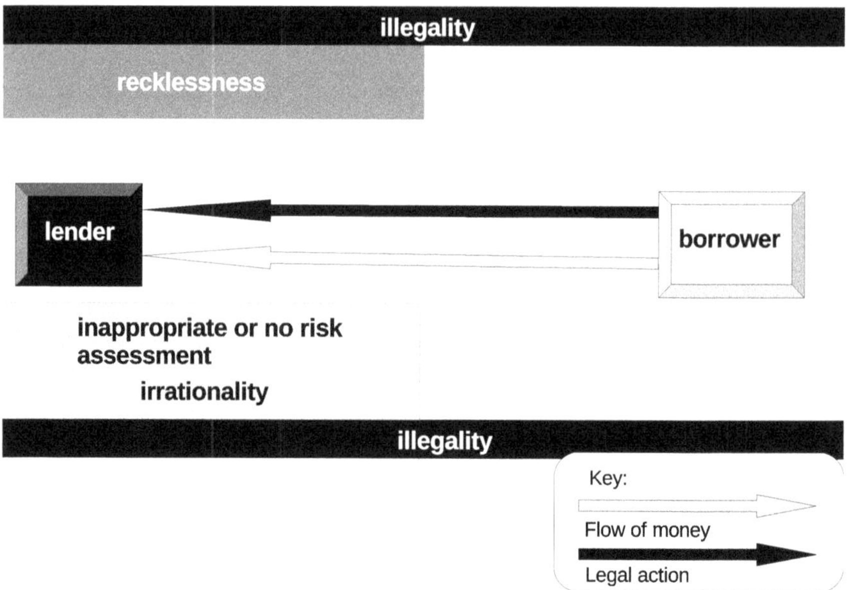

Figure 5.3. Conflict resolution for borrowers. Created by the author.

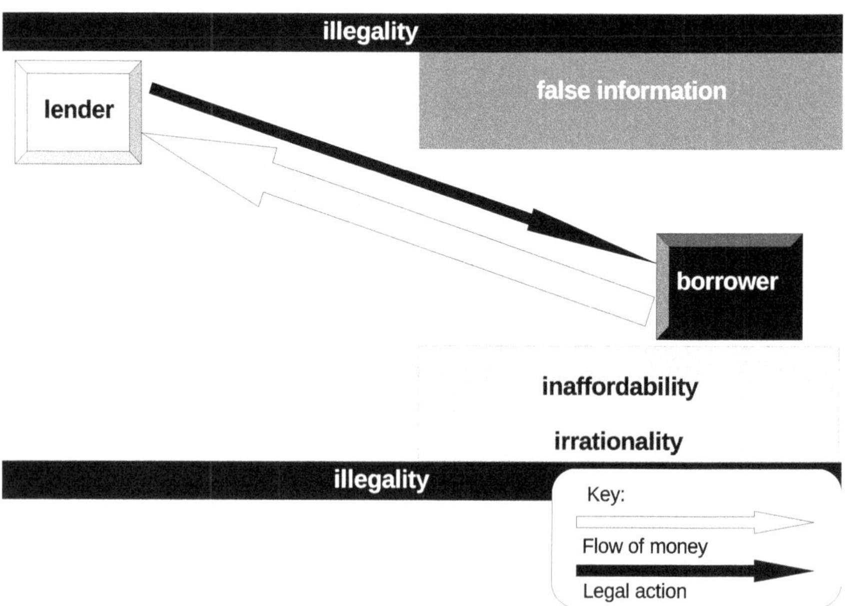

Figure 5.4. Conflict resolution for lenders. Created by the author.

deliberately providing false information would receive his legal equality only once he had repaid all his debts. On the other side, the credit provider was entitled to change the treatment of his customer by applying financial penalties, and might even earn more than initially agreed upon due to the effects of the compounding of interest and extending the repayment period.

The main purpose of Figures 5.3 and 5.4 is to present the idea that 'imbalances in negotiating power' (NCA s 3(e)) did not derive from unequal access to information in the first place but from the capacity to mobilize social institutions in the case of a conflict. A borrower would be able to invoke the legal system only in the case of existing over-indebtedness, i.e. after the fulfilment of a contract was objectively no longer possible. Such a breach of contract would make him inferior to the lender, but the law offered him the option of being elevated onto an equal footing again. In the course of the same proceedings, the lender could still refer to the legal protection of the money he had lent, and was only threatened by a reduction or loss of his additional earnings.

Then again, in the case of the self-inflicted over-indebtedness of borrowers, according to the NCA definition, a lender received the right to enforce increased repayments under all circumstances. There was nothing the borrower could do about this, and he would remain in an inferior position until the final settlement of all his debts.

The whole arrangement of the NCA aimed at eliminating uncertainty in favour of certainty and risk as an opportunity to make profit. It did so by expecting a clear and unambiguous interest from the actors of the market within this framework. Market participants should be deterred from ignoring the Act by tough punishments – more on the side of lenders than on the side of borrowers – and from illegal practice in terms of the Act by the threat of financial loss – more on the side of borrowers than on the side of lenders.

The counterbalance of self-interest was intended to eliminate the dangers of irrational behaviour. But everything was based on an orthodox concept of a rationality that seemed inescapable in the view of an outside reality.

However, a reality that poses neither alternatives nor a multitude of rationalities is an extremely artificial construction because it depends on the provision of a whole range of preconditions (March and Simon 2004). Such a reality would require unambiguously rational behaviour from all actors, unbounded self-interest and infinite willpower. Instrumental rationality, though, seems to be hampered by limited computational skills and individually shaped memories of human beings, who in return often act according to rules of thumb. More importantly, there are more forms of rationality, for instance, because there is a realistic likelihood of actors caring about others and having a sense of fairness which encourages them to bind their instrumental self-interest. Additionally, willpower will usually be modified by preferences which will vary over time, sometimes dominated by impulsive desires and sometimes by careful planning. Still, even if bounded rationality, bounded self-interest and bounded willpower could be neutralized, it had to be admitted that a 'majority of bankruptcies occur because of unanticipated events' like unemployment, illness or divorce (Schwartz 2003: 67). The implicit model of a self-governing rationality of the South African consumer credit market, as outlined in the NCA, was unrealistic.

The Instrumental Rationality of Consumer Credit Markets

The previous section has offered an institutional analysis of the South African consumer credit market from a reflexive level of observation. It revealed a specific understanding of rationality, according to which freely interacting individuals would generate, as far as possible, a self-regulating consumer credit market. The consumer's pursuit of his own interests, framed by institutionally set restrictions, should bring about competition for the best loan offers, which would result in a selection of successful products and a rejection of malformed ones. It was hoped that a growing, solid, transparent and fair market would emerge, offering investment opportunities for the better-off and financial resources to borrow for those in need.

Although the crisis of 2014 showed an increased resilience in comparison to the unregulated market prior to 2005, the hopes of the legislators were disappointed, as the attempts to reform the NCA showed. The South African consumer credit market did not generate an economic equilibrium. On the contrary, social inequality was increased because a growing share of the population became medium-term and long-term indebted. Many borrowers worked and generated value, but they had to transfer a huge proportion of their earnings to their creditors, meaning that economic actors with surplus amounts of money received interest, whereas productive citizens accumulated less wealth than they actually earned. Borrowers with insufficient income only piled up more debts, of course. As a result of this, the financialized consumer credit market contributed to the growing increase in social inequality in South Africa, instead of alleviating it (Makgetla 2018).

The assumption of South African legislators rested on a popular argument for the justification of competitive markets. This argument basically consists of a specific form of rationality, and a model of markets comprising two components, which support each other. The specific form of economic rationality suggests that actors strive for the maximization of their gains and apply every means to achieve it. Although this kind of instrumental rationality is contested in everyday life due to its socially destructive effects, it appears to be without any alternative in economic contexts, as will be shown in this section.

The first part of the argument presents the counter-intuitive idea that instrumentally and self-interested social action of individuals would not result in chaos and conflict, but in economically growing societies. The second part is built upon the assumption of an equilibrium of markets, which expects freely enacted demand and supply to level each other out harmoniously, a result that could be disturbed only by interference in the (supra-)natural course of things from the outside.

This means that the first part of the argument presents the conundrum that social action, which disregards the competing or conflicting interests of other actors, would nevertheless serve the requirements of the whole community, and hence of these others, best. If, politically speaking, this were to be questioned, the common response is that free markets contain the mechanism of supply and demand, which would always tend towards an equilibrium.

A request for the first part of the argument is usually referred to the second part of the argument, which maintains exactly this axiomatic claim of an automatic self-regulation of imbalances in markets. It is rarely explained. Instead, if the assertion of a theoretical equation of interests is confronted with the fact of actually existing social inequality, apologists of the competitive market idea refer to the first part of the argument again, and blame restrictions on the exertion of free interests, which would prevent the harmonious balancing of conflicting aims to take place. However, this is circular reasoning and not an explanation.

Therefore, the next subsections intend to outline some important stages of the career of this argument in order to understand its impact on contemporary economic thought and politics, of which the institutionalization of the South African consumer credit market is an example. They explain the origin of the idea of self-regulating markets, and how and why it captured the centre stage of market economies.

The first subsection refers to the origin of the counter-intuitive idea that a multitude of selfish interests could result in an overall harmonious economy. The writings of Adam Smith are reviewed because they popularized this thought and they are still referenced today when a justification of free market economies is required. However, a close reading of Smith's writings reveals the argument to be a rhetorical trick without explanatory power. Nevertheless, the famous arguments of Adam Smith mark an important watershed of economic thought because they transformed hitherto detrimental passions into advantageous interests.

The second subsection recounts the arguments of Georg Simmel. Instead of focussing on the capacity of money to represent value or utility, Simmel starts from the monetary quality as a tool of measurement and shows how a closely woven fabric of economic relations may derive from this. These are important because they identify money itself as the reason for a possible equilibrium of market economies. Simmel's reasoning is quite complex but possesses a remarkable logic. The important insight is that a self-balancing of supply and demand depends on the equal access of all economic actors to money and commodities – a precondition that conflicts with the popular argument that money has to be scarce in order to keep its value.

The argument regarding an indispensable scarcity of money rests on the insight that only instrumentally rational economic behaviour results in a growth-oriented and profit-generating economy. Simmel expects such a specific kind of rationality of economic actors, but without an explanation of its possible origins. The proper reference in order to close this gap is Max Weber. His insights are so important that two subsections are devoted to his reasoning. The first explains the reduction of the multiple rationalities, which can be applied in social action, to the single economic rationality of market economies. However, this economic reasoning rests on a legal precondition, which is discussed in the ensuing subsection: exclusive property rights build the foundation of an economic rationality that seems to be without any alternative. An indispensable part of this reasoning is the pessimistic outlook reached by Max Weber. His intention was not to de-legitimize the market economy. On the contrary, his analysis started from the impression of a mighty capitalistic world economy which was expanding before his very eyes. However, he was forced to reach a pessimistic outlook by the strengths of his own arguments. For this very reason his understanding of the socially distorting effects of market economies is of importance.

Origins of the Idea of an 'Invisible Hand'

As mentioned before, Albert O. Hirschman (2013) has analysed the development from the state of a total condemnation of human passions in early Christianity towards the idea of acceptable individual interests, which would, enigmatically, serve the whole of society. He identified Machiavelli and Spinoza as crucial protagonists who argued in favour of an analysis of existing passionate actions of human beings as opposed to speculative considerations of an ideal society, in which people would be free of vices. So, the first step of the development consisted of a positivist recognition of effectively existing passions.

According to Hirschman, the decreasing influence of Christianity encouraged philosophers to search for different ways of keeping humans from self-destructive and socially deleterious practices. Basically, there were three options available. First, passions could be contained by the power of the state, an idea that was fully developed by Thomas Hobbes. It failed because it required the guarantee of a morally good sovereign and conflicted with the demands for freedom by individuals in increasingly differentiating societies. The second option was to be found in a transformation of harmful passions into useful virtues. Although this was a compelling idea, its protagonists failed to explain how such a transformation could be intentionally induced. The third option eventually became the dominating one. It suggested the countervailing of passions with other passions. In most versions, which were reviewed by Hirschman, this required some kind of political organization. In the course of the development of the idea, the damaging passions were often confronted with the more beneficial interests. The basic mechanism of turning passions into interests consisted in a removal of affective lust from a more rational core of the desire.

In the course of this development, avarice turned into rational economic interest.[3] However, Hirschman emphasizes the importance of a political organization in such a balance of harmful desires, an idea he first found fully developed in the writings of Giambattista Vico in 1725 (Hirschman 2013: 17). In the course of less than a century it was transformed into the idea of common economic – instead of political – benefits of the individual pursuit of interests in the work of Adam Smith (Hirschman 2013: 100–13).

Therefore, it is worthwhile reviewing Smith's writings in detail. In his version, the equilibrium of markets is attributed to a divine intervention, which became famous in the metaphor of the 'invisible hand'. This term had first appeared in the work of Montesquieu in reference to the political benefits of individual aspirations for glory (Hirschman 2013: 10). Yet, a careful reading of Smith's work unravels the invisible hand to be a simple trick of argumentation. Smith (1981: 454) starts from the equation that the pursuit of individual self-interest would be to the best advantage of the society: 'Every individual is continually exerting himself to find out the most advantageous employment for whatever capital he can command. It is his own advantage, indeed, and not that of society, which he has in view. But the study of his own advantage naturally, or rather necessarily leads him to prefer that employment which is most advantageous to society'.

Hereafter, Smith introduces two criteria for the investment of capital: first, 'nearly equal profits' and, second, a preference for domestic application. With these two parts of the argument Smith claims that economic actors prefer to invest their capital near home, so long as the profits are acceptable. Smith roots this preference in the better knowledge of the local environment, which would increase control over the outcomes. Only unsatisfactory profits at home would motivate economic actors to take the greater risk of distant or widely dispersed business. He understands discomfort with the economic prospects as the main reason for this risk-averse attitude.

In the next step, Smith parallels the individual preference of domestic business with the higher social profitability of domestic investments, which he had introduced at an earlier stage of his analysis. It is justified by two factors. His first assumption is that the business cycle at home would be faster, simply because of the geographic proximity and reduced transportation costs. The second argument states that foreign trade would always require the emission of an equal supply of domestic goods in exchange, which, alternatively, could be accumulated in local businesses. From this he deduces the collective tendency of merchants to direct as much as possible of their foreign trade to domestic shores (A. Smith 1981: 368–69). He concludes that capital invested in local businesses would employ more people and move more resources than foreign trade.

He supports this higher social profitability of domestic business with the argument of lower individual uncertainty. 'He [the domestic investor] can know better the character and the situation of the persons whom he trusts, and if he should happen to be deceived, he knows better the laws of the country from which he must seek redress' (A. Smith 1981: 454). Here, Smith claims a complex social framework to be responsible for the preference for domestic business. On the one hand, an actor can extend his business more easily at home, simply because he knows the people, their capacities and trustworthiness better. On the other hand, a legal system supports his interests in case of conflict and fraud. To sum up, trust and confidence, which must have been established by previous social interaction, and legal protection deriving from the political organization of the community, induce the economic actor to prefer domestic over foreign trade.

This means that the individual preference for domestic business is caused by the expectation of higher certainty at home, and that the general factor of higher benefits for the society is derived from a comparison with a lower profitability from foreign trade. The latter is caused by slower business cycles, higher expenses and higher levels of uncertainty.

In the next stage of his argumentation, Smith (1981: 456) simply contracts this complex construction into two factors, that of individual choice and that of common social benefit:

> By the support of domestick [*sic*] to that of foreign industry, he intends only his security; and by directing that security in such a manner that its produce may be of the greatest value, he intends only his own gain, and he is in this, as in many other cases, led by an invisible hand to promote an end which was not part of his intention. Nor is it always the worse for the society that it was not part of it. By pursuing his own interest he frequently promotes that of the society more effectually than when he really intends to promote it.

Carefully interpreted, the miracle of the invisible hand turns out to be quite rational. To begin with, in distinction from the first quotation, individual actors are not mostly interested in profits but in security. Quite simply, Smith combined the individual preference of security with the economic profitability of domestic trade in comparison to foreign trade, and therefore the individual choice of domestic security is tantamount to higher profitability.

Then, he reduces these three factors to two, and generalizes them by removing the middle part of his argument. Now, the individual self-interest meets the highest benefits of society, and this surprising effect is assigned to the intervention of an 'invisible hand'.

So, the trick of Smith lies in attributing two different primary self-interests to an individual. In the beginning, individuals strive for the highest profits, and in the later statement they prefer the highest security of returns. In the middle part, Smith argued that domestic trade is more profitable than foreign trade – a historically appropriate argument, but without universal validity. Then, he returns to his point of departure, but replaces the preference for profits with the preference for security. Yet, due to his intermediate step, this security is synonymous with growth in the domestic economy – voilá.

The magic of the 'invisible hand' is dissolved into nothingness. The benefits of society rest on the safeguarding existence of this society as their very precondition.

Adam Smith applied the idea of an invisible hand in an economic context for the first time seventeen years prior to *The Wealth of Nations*. In *The Theory of Moral Sentiments* his trick is even simpler to figure out. His argument is that in an unequal society the pursuit of their own happiness by the rich would benefit even the poor, and that this effect would come about by the deeds of the 'invisible hand'.

However, in this case he simply claims a trickle-down effect, which would be caused by the limitation of the consumption capacities of the rich. Smith (1984: 184) defines how the rich 'consume little more than the poor', so that most of the surplus of their goods would be applied and distributed to the rest of the society. In reality this would happen only if, first, the consumption of the rich were indeed limited and, second, the surplus was distributed. With his argument, Smith removes the possibility of the accumulated or wasted fortunes of the rich, and he silently adds the willingness and political organization of social redistribution. Again, the invisible hand requires the existence of a well-organized society, which allegedly benefits from selfish economic actions in order to function.

This review reveals that the origins of the idea of a self-regulating market have no argumentative foundations in the work of Adam Smith. A careful reading of his texts is sufficient to dispel the magic. This, however, cannot invalidate the social effectiveness of the idea of self-regulating markets. Actually, the idea was practically implemented in the South African consumer credit market. The intention of the following is not to fully cover the path of this theorem in social theory, but to demonstrate how the classics of social theory have reflected an idea that has been present in economic thinking and in politics since the times of Adam Smith.

The Monetary Equilibrium of Georg Simmel

Two classics of social theory are important in this regard, Georg Simmel and Max Weber. What these two have in common, and what distinguishes them from other theorists, is their general understanding of society as a realm of communication and interaction that is not stabilized by a metaphysical order or an identifiable single principle.

Additionally, both place a strong focus on money and the economy. The connection of these two factors – the imagining of society as an autonomous realm of human beings, and the importance of the economy – is no coincidence. As has become clear from the reconstruction of ideas by Albert Hirschman, economic exchange took a prominent role as a replacement for the traditional ideas of social order deriving from cosmos, God or nature. Simmel and Weber acknowledged the importance of economic exchange as a central way of communication and interaction in society, without defining it as the sole or determining mechanism in advance, as Marx did. This turns Simmel and Weber into the proper points of reference for addressing the question about how the ideas of an economic equilibrium and of economic rationality spread through modern and decentralized societies (Taylor 2002: 101).

After Karl Marx had thrown out ideas of self-regulation, equality and balance in his analysis of capital-oriented market economies as realms of social command, the idea of the economic equilibrium returned to social theory with Georg Simmel's *Philosophy of Money*, which was first published in 1901. Simmel does not reference an 'invisible hand', though. Instead, it is money in the form of a price itself which is ascribed the function of balancing the relation of the sum of money on the one hand, and the sum of purchasable commodities on the other.

Simmel starts from the logical conclusion that two incommensurable objects may become comparable in relation to a third entity, which is affected in the same way by both. His example is the branch of a tree, which may be bent by the force of the wind just as it may be by the force of a human hand. Although the wind and a human hand are not directly comparable, they become so with regard to their capacity to bend a branch.

On a more abstract level, this means that two incommensurable objects become comparable as soon as proportions of them change in analogue directions or related amounts. In such a case, the third entity can be founded by relating the total sums of the objects to each other, regardless of their qualities. For instance, if a given amount of money and a given amount of a specific commodity are juxtaposed, proportions of them become comparable as soon as the growth or reduction of the portion of money can be related to a growth or reduction of pieces of the commodities. Then, the change of monetary value of these objects becomes comparable.

A precondition for a calculation of the exchange value is knowledge about the total amount of available money, and of the relation of a single commodity to the total amount of all commodities on purchase. Then, a third relation can be founded by referring the total amounts to each other. This mechanism is shown in Figure 5.5.

If such a foundational relation is given, the precise quantitative relation between parts of the total amounts becomes the result of a simple mathematical operation. The fact that this relation can be calculated in equations is of crucial importance here because it explains the basic kinship between the economy and mathematics. It also shows how mathematical calculations invade the realm of social negotiations:

> Every single commodity is now a definite part of the available sum of commodities ... Its price is the corresponding part of the total quantity of money ... If we knew the quantity of [commodities] and [money], and the proportion of all saleable goods which a specific object represents, then we should also know its price in terms of money, and vice-versa. A definite amount of money can thus determine or measure the value of an object, regardless of whether money and the valuable object possess any identical quality, and so regardless of whether money itself is valuable. (Simmel 1990: 131)

Here, Simmel concludes that the knowledge of the relation of a single commodity to the total amount of available commodities represents sufficient knowledge for determining the price as soon as there exists a defined relation between the total amount of money and the total amount of this specific commodity. In this case the money-value in form of the price simply derives from the equation of all available commodities to the total amount of money that could be spent. This is also the reason why Simmel can switch the terminology of 'value' and 'price' here. The total value of commodities is by definition set as equal to the total amount of money, and other ways of commodity exchange are not taken into consideration, therefore there exists no difference between an 'exchange value' and a 'price'.

Up to this point, there is nothing magical in Simmel's considerations. However, this changes as soon as he comes to the question of concrete

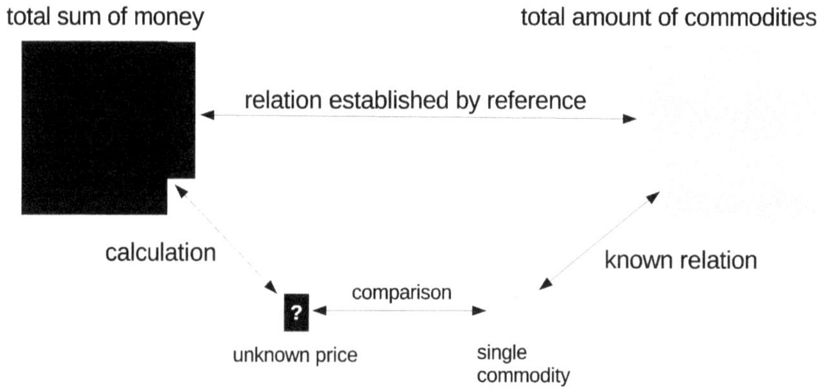

Figure 5.5. Price calculation according to Simmel. Created by the author.

knowledge about the a priori given absolute amounts of objects. He stresses how important it is 'to keep in mind the complete relativity of measurement. … [The defined quantities of money and commodities] are set in relation of equivalence only through the relationship that both have to the valuing person and his practical purposes' (Simmel 1990: 131–32). He explains this in a superficial reference to some anthropological observations of economic exchanges between non-monetary and monetary societies. In these cases, the main tool of non-monetary exchange, i.e. its commodity money, would have been equal to the currency of the monetary society.[4] Without any detailed analysis, Simmel (1990: 132) derives a generalization of his principle of quantitative measurement from this:

> If the equivalence of these total amounts [of commodity money and of money] exists as an effective, though unconscious a priori, there emerges an objective proportion between the partial quantities apart from that of their subjective fortuitousness. For now there really exists something that is exactly the same on both sides; namely, the division between each of the two partial quantities and the total quantity to which it belongs.

Simmel's argument here is that each actor of such an economic exchange takes his experience about the relative value of his special form of money as a starting point of the negotiation of a price. Without knowing about the absolute amount of money or commodity money of the other side, both participants would enact a relation of these total amounts by referring to the relative value of their own exchange good. Therefore, the sum of all monetary resources on both sides would represent the 'unconscious' points of reference, which would enable the final definition of a price of exchange between monetary currency and commodity money. Repetition of exchanges would actually establish the third relation between the total amount of money on the one side, and the total amount of commodity money on the other side. This is depicted in Figure 5.6.

Repeated exchanges of the participants establish a mutual understanding of the relative value of the specific form of money of the other side. After the relative value of the other's special form of money has become known, a calculable exchange rate appears. The idea of Simmel is that a relative value of the exchange good is used by both participants as a measuring device of their own willingness to perform the exchange in relation to the absolute value of the goods of exchange. Each party has an idea about the relation of the exchange value to the total sum of value. In a single act of exchange they establish an initial relation of

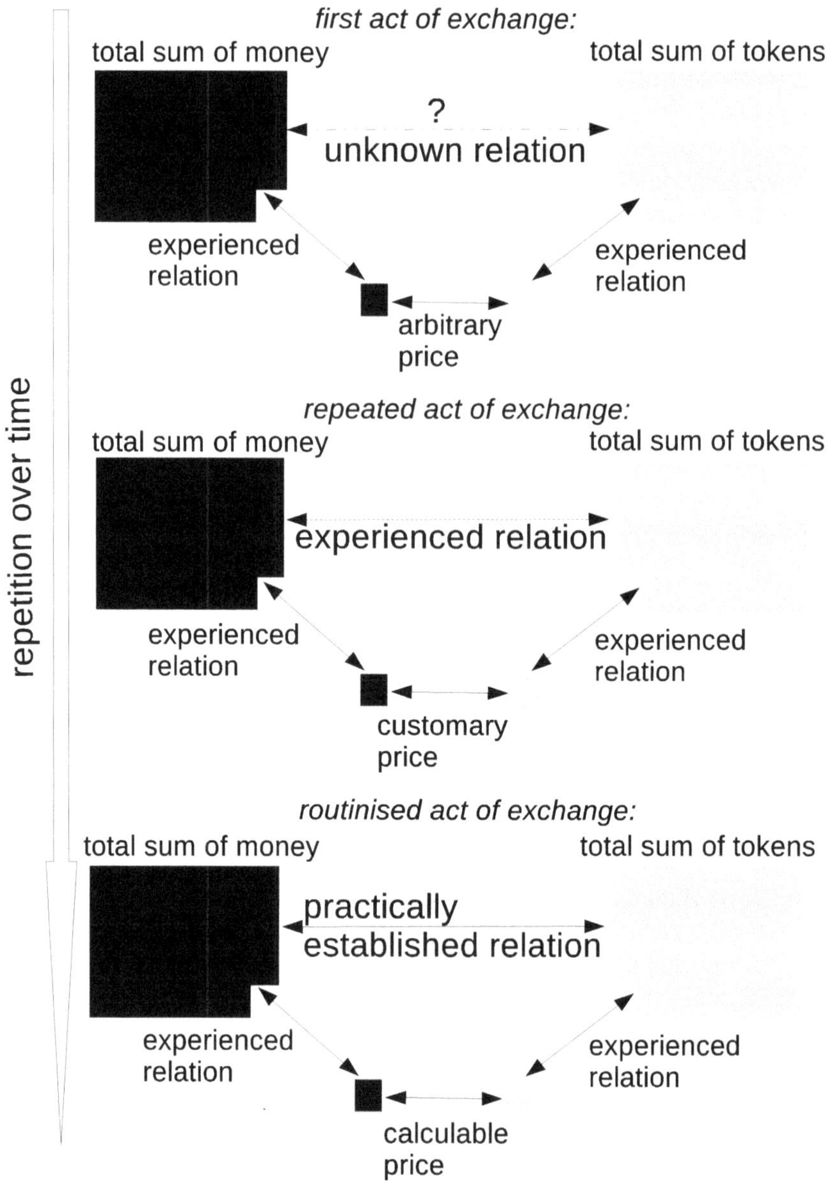

Figure 5.6. Familiarization with price negotiation according to Simmel. Created by the author.

these total amounts, and by repetition both parties develop an idea of the relative value of the other party's exchange value, too.

Simmel continues by showing how economically acting persons would get used to the relative value of their exchange goods – be it money or commodity money or bullion – over time, and almost forget about the relation to the total amount. The necessity of deliberately thinking about the exact relation of a price to the total sum of available money would vanish when actors become familiarized with the relative value of money. Simmel outlines how the foundational and accustomed knowledge about the absolute value functions as a kind of contrast foil of countless relative value measurements. He develops a theory of differentiation as the foundation of his *Philosophy of Money* here, in which every value appears only as a difference against the background of accustomed relations. The price becomes a relation of relations, fully flexible but limited by the relative stability of those factors in the background:

> The equation between the value of a commodity and the value of a definite amount of money does not signify an equation between simple factors but a proportion, that is an equation between two fractions, the denominator of which, within a given economic area, is on one side the sum total of all commodities and on the other the total amount of money. These two quantities, of course, have to be more strictly determined. The equation is established by the fact that, for practical reasons, these two sums are posed a priori as equivalents; or, to state the matter more precisely, the practical circumstances in which we handle both categories are reflected in our theoretical consciousness as an equation. However, since this is the general basis of all equations between specific commodities and specific prices, it does not enter our consciousness, but provides the unconsciously operating factor without which the individual instances, which alone are interesting and thus enter into consciousness, could not possibly form a relationship. (Simmel 1990: 134)

As we see, the equilibrium of two relative factors enters the stage of market operations 'unconsciously' through a rear door. The measurement of the sum of all available money on the one side, and the total value of all commodities of a specific kind on the other side, is never actually really performed. Instead, it exists only as 'unconscious' knowledge because human beings in a market economy are socialized by daily practices of value measurement from their childhood onwards, and they interact with others performing value assessments all the time – often in competition. Additionally, Simmel claims that members of non-monetary societies can become accustomed to this practice very quickly.

However, Simmel has to acknowledge some problems with his equation. Let us recall how his definition starts from the basic assumption of a missing commonality between money and commodities. This, of course, means that any amount of money could represent the exchange value of a commodity as long as the changes of value happen proportionally. There are no logical limits. Therefore, very small amounts of money could represent relatively large portions of commodities and, hence, the total sum of money could be very small. This, in turn, would mean that there would be very fierce competition for money in society. Secondly, the circulation of money is faster in exchange with some commodities than with others, e.g. we buy bread more often than cars. This means that the same money can buy commodities of lower durability more often than long-lasting commodities. Hence, less money is able to represent the value of the former in comparison to the latter. This problem is aggravated by the assumption that commodities need not be available for purchase but may be stored, and consequently the amount of circulating commodities may change very suddenly. All these considerations demonstrate the difficulty of establishing a relation between the total sum of available money and the total value of all commodities.

Simmel's attempts to solve these theoretical problems demonstrate the close link between calculative thinking and the economy on a deeper level, because it shows that some relations between money and commodities can be established only on an abstract level. This means that they do not appear as a simple relation of coins and things, but only as an effect of calculative thought. This is important because it illustrates an inherent tendency of economics: abstract concepts gain dominance over the material exchange of goods and services and real-world interactions of human beings due to the importance of calculation. Economic thinking starts from concepts.

Simmel's attempt to solve the aforementioned problems begins with the simple equation that the total sum of money represents the total value of all purchasable commodities. Based on the (unrealistic) precondition that monetary payments form the only option of exchange, this statement is true in an autological sense. If commodities can be exchanged for money alone, then the total amount of money inevitably represents the total value of commodities on purchase. In this calculation, credit money has to be included because it is able to buy commodities, too.

However, the different pace of circulation of money with regard to different commodities requires the observation of this equation over a certain period of time.

> Thus it is possible to assert, *with reference to a specific period but not to a single moment*, that the total amount of money in circulation corresponds with the total amount of objects saleable during this period. ... In our equation, the money fraction may attain equality with the commodity fraction through the fact that its denominator is not the money available as a substance, but is a multiple of this amount determined by the circulation of money during a given period. From this point of view, the antinomy between the stock of available commodities and those commodities that are the value counterparts of money can be solved; and the assertion that *no basic disproportion can arise between the total amount of commodities and of money in an autonomous economic area* may be upheld. This is true in spite of disagreements about the proper relation between a particular commodity and its price, in spite of the fluctuations and discrepancies that may develop if some definite size of the fractions concerned has become psychologically established while a different one has become more appropriate by reason of objective changes, and in spite of temporary shortages in the means of exchange resulting from a rapid increase in the number of transactions. (Simmel 1990: 137; my own emphasis)

This longer quotation shows how the definition of an equilibrium is maintained against all odds. In contrast to Simmel's initial examples, the equation now represents nothing that could actually be precisely calculated. Nevertheless, Simmel claims to arrive at a point where he asserts the existence of an 'answer to the question whether a given price is appropriate or not', because it could 'be derived *directly* from the two previous questions: first, what is the amount of money and the sum total of objects for sale at the present time; and, second, what proportion does the object under consideration form of the total quantity of commodities available?' He unhesitatingly adds that his definition would be 'a matter of expediency, not one of truth in the sense that it can be logically established' (Simmel 1990: 137–38; my own emphasis).

In other words, Simmel claims to have established a mechanism of unconscious economic custom here, and not a theory consisting of testable scientific logic. He compares it to the experiences of appropriate amounts of pleasure and pain in human life. Despite the fact that not every pleasure is represented by a compensatory pain or vice versa, people would develop a sense of adequate amounts of lust and of impositions in life. The notion of time – the relatively fast or slow passing of time – is introduced as another example of this kind. Notwithstanding his start from absolute relativity, Simmel (1990: 139) arrives at definite judgements here: 'In so far as, in individual cases, the elements repeat the proportions that occur in the total quantities, then the elements have a *correct*, i.e. normal, average or typical relation, and deviations appear as a *preponderance* or *disproportion* of one element' (emphasis in original). It is important to acknowledge that a tension remains between the mathematical equations, with their indisputable logic in the beginning, and the assertion of 'unconsciously' established 'correct' proportions in the end. The latter reminds one of an 'invisible hand', and it gives us an example of how calculative thought, which might be based on precise empirical experiences, is abstracted and generalized and turned into codes of economic conduct.

Simmel transposes this thought to individual budgeting, too. Individuals would measure the amount of money they are willing to pay according to the mid-range disposable income. Again, an equilibrium appears out of a couple of relativities.

> If everybody regulates his private expenditures in such a way that the payment for every type of commodity is proportionate to his total income, this means that his expenditure for the single object is related to his total expenses just as the importance of the single object is related to the totality of desired and available objects. This scheme of the private economy of an individual is obviously not only an analogy of the general economy; its general application determines the average prices. (Simmel 1990: 139)

That is to say that every single economic actor could contribute to a functioning monetary economy by adjusting his expenses rationally in relation to the total income, which has to be related to the total value of commodities. This reminds us of the logic of the South African National Credit Act, which expected the rational decision of individual actors after certain crucial factors had become known. Like Simmel, the legislators of the NCA encouraged lenders and borrowers to take responsible decisions about their budgets.

Simmel's own intention to perform this chain of thought was to justify the assumption that money does not require an intrinsic value (like gold) in order to measure the value of commodities in an economy in appropriate ways. This means that Simmel makes use of the term 'appropriate' only in regard to money's capacity to measure exchange values and does not intend to make any statements about fairness or justice with this word. Nevertheless, an almost indestructible equilibrium appears from a set of relations of relations. Simmel (1990: 145) develops it into a general theorem of differentiation, with the case of economic exchange as its core: 'Money, as a product of this fundamental power or form of our mind, is not only its most extreme example, but is, as it were, its pure embodiment'. This means that money is not only an important tool of payment, exchange and storage of value, but also the foundation of a specific kind of thought because monetary thinking opens up new realms of social relations on an abstract level that influence real-world social interaction as an effect.

To summarize, Simmel starts from the idea that two objects without a common quality can be compared as soon as a shared relation with regard to a third entity is established. From this he develops the abstraction according to which the comparison of two equal changes of proportions of objects may serve as such a point of reference. Simmel then outlines the dissemination and establishment of such a kind of measurement: in the course of its social distribution, the precise knowledge of the reference quantity vanishes, and is replaced by the experience of different values of different objects. The foundational relation between absolute values thereby disappears into the background. What remains is the common capacity to measure appropriate prices based on experiences of relative values. Fundamentally, Simmel arrives at a state of stability that can guide individual actors towards rational economic action, which is developed from the accumulation of such rational actions. The option of rational relations of a different kind and of power-dominated relations between economic actors, prices and commodities evaporates in his line of argument.

What both the logical reasoning of Simmel and the economic expectations of the South African legislators miss is the discrepancy between the financial capacities of households and the prices of the overall economy. Even if we assume that in a given society the price level of commodities will adjust according to the relation of all commodities on purchase and all the money available by a common pattern of behaviour, and we then add the assumption that households establish a rational management of their own resources, this would not exclude the possibility of a fundamental social inequality in this society because of an uneven distribution of monetary capacities. The South African consumer credit market demonstrated exactly this fact. Certain income strata were predestined to take out loans, whereas others benefited from the profits of credit providers – and the financialized South African consumer credit market stabilized this pattern of distribution instead of undermining it.

This reasoning was referenced here because it demonstrates two tendencies incorporated in the monetary economy, one on the empirical level of personal economic interaction in society, and another one on the theoretical level of economic thinking. The important insight on the empirical level is that the capacity of money to serve as a means of measurement between hitherto incomparable entities motivates the users of money to calculate and to perform abstract comparisons. This means that Simmel shows how a society that develops a monetized economy gets used to performing abstract calculations as well. At the same time, however, this means that the competence to interact in economically beneficial ways depends on experience, and experience is something different to cognitive knowledge. On the theoretical level, though, Simmel himself conducts a generalization of principles, which rest on a shaky foundation because precise calculations are turned into theorems and economic guidance despite significant deviations from the basic facts. However, these abstract rules of thumb that are often presented as relentless laws of the market economies are met with a general trust due to the propensity to calculate economic relations in market societies.

The hidden kernel of Simmel's argument is to be found in the sharing of a multiplicity of value measurements in society. An individual actor is not capable of performing the learning process outlined by Simmel, but individuals are able to as part of a monetary society. All members of society, constantly swapping money and commodities, develop a notion of the value of each of the commodities without the necessity of referring to an absolute denominator. And for the South African case we should add: those who are excluded from participation will not develop comparable capacities.

However, the application of abstract mathematical calculations for solving problems of economic supply and provision is a demanding precondition. It requires a special form of rationality. Georg Simmel (1990: 140) seems to acknowledge this when he states with regard to monetary exchanges: 'Nobody will be stupid enough to exchange a value against something that is valueless, unless he is sure of being able to convert the latter into values again'. Here, he establishes a binary alternative – to act stupidly or not – but in fact countless gradual alternatives do exist. The possibility that someone may be urged, or even forced, to exchange valuable items against something valueless is denied. Value-oriented generosity or conspicuous consumption are excluded by definition, too. Additionally, the choice of not acting stupidly requires an overview of the logic of the whole process on the part of the calculating actor. Without knowledge about the values to expect in future exchanges, or without anticipation of the desires and wishes to come, or without prospects of the development of their own income, such a calculation could not produce satisfying results. In any case, the functioning of the calculation depends on linear and expectable developments and will not work in an environment of surprising changes. However, in market societies economic turmoil is quite common.

The proper reference for inspecting the specific kind of rationality that is suggested by Simmel as a requirement of monetary market economies is Max Weber. The interesting thing about Weber's statements concerning rationality in economic markets is that his solution, which consists of a clear preference for instrumental rationality, leads him to a pessimistic outlook about the stability of market economies. In other words, his definition of the mode of action, which would be required by self-interested economic actors to generate benefits, leaves him no alternative but to dispense with the idea of a conflict-free equilibrium.

Markets as a Peaceful Conflict in the Work of Max Weber

Weber offers a sociological explanation of the special type of rationality which would turn markets into self-regulating social institutions. This section reconstructs the economic rationality as it is conceptualized in different sections of his work.

For the interpretation of society in general, Weber (1978: 24–25) has developed four 'ideal types' of social action: 'instrumentally rational action', which consequently prioritizes ends over means as a way to achieve the first; 'value-oriented action', which emphasizes the normative acceptability of means as a way to realize legitimate ends; 'affectual action', which is governed by emotions rather than by thought and can be equated with the passions Hirschman started his analysis from; and 'traditional action', which is oriented towards the preferences of the past and/or the community instead of individual desires. 'Ideal type' means that these modes represent intellectually constructed poles of interpretation of actual, ongoing social action, and should not be mistaken for conscious orientations of social actors.

A second important precondition for interpreting Weber is to acknowledge his conceptualizations of 'legal orders' and 'economic orders' as autonomous realms which penetrate society. In this regard, he characterizes the economy more precisely as an 'autocephalous' realm, which means that actors are submitted to rules and mechanisms which derive from their own actions (Weber 1978: 63). Regardless of the compatible or conflicting adjustment of law and economy in a given society, these social systems refer to fundamentally different orientations of action. 'Legal orders' define social realms in which action is predefined according to norms, i.e. action is justified and judged in respect of collective expectations. 'Economic orders', in contrast, gauge social action in reference to the realization of opportunities (Weber 1978: 311–12). This means that legal orders and economic orders demand different timely orientations of actors. On the one hand, they have to respect norms transmitted to them from the past in order to act legitimately, on the other they are also expected to take future opportunities for social improvement.

This notion of legal and economic orders as independently developing but interacting social realms makes the work of Max Weber a qualified resource for the analysis of consumer credit markets. As has been visualized in the first sections of this chapter, the South African NCA established exactly this: a framework of normative demands to be fulfilled, constituting a realm of free economic action in which citizens were expected to take risks and realize opportunities.

After defining economic action as 'any peaceful exercise of an actor's control over resources', Weber (1978: 63) clearly states that this would require 'instrumental rationality in its orientation, that is, deliberate planning'. Two important aspects characterize Weber's definition, as he explains himself. To begin with, economic interaction can be identified only on a symbolic level because it is distinguished from non-economic action by the 'meaning' addressed to it by actors.[5] As we will see below, the exchange of items itself is not characterized as economic action by Weber. Secondly, economic actions always include the reference to a future stretch of time because it makes 'provision' for the necessities to come (Weber 1978: 64).

In reference to the previous section of this chapter, it is important to notice a congruence between Weber and Simmel on these two points. Both locate the monetary economy on a different level than the exchange of goods. Simmel (1990: 204–11), too, places monetary exchanges on a symbolic level because money only represents a tool, i.e. a means to achieve an end, and the very idea of applying means for an end requires abstract thinking about a 'sequence of purposes'. This sequence is time consuming, and planning is tantamount to the 'creation of higher supra-individual formations' in which the economic action actually takes place (Simmel 1990: 173).

In Weber's (1978: 64) account, the symbolic quality of economic action generates the paradoxical formulation of the 'peaceful exercise of … control', which deliberately excludes every action that 'makes use of physical force as a means'. On the one hand, Weber assigns to economic action the capacity of powerful control but, on the other hand, he definitely qualifies this power as being non-violent. The reason for this is that for Weber (1978: 65) economic action derives from two freedoms: the option of the creative application of means in regard to their 'scarcity', and choosing prudently between different ends. These flexible choices between alternatives are incompatible with non-peaceful practices. 'The use of force is unquestionably very strongly opposed to the spirit of economic acquisition in the usual sense. Hence the term economic action will not be applied to the direct appropriation of goods by force or the direct coercion of the other party by threats of force' (Weber 1978: 64). Of course, Weber is aware of the common enforcement of agreements in economic life, but he decisively excludes this from his definition of 'economic action' and addresses it to the state. He acknowledges this as a kind of secondary back-up of agreements and part of the legal order, not of the economy. However, at the same time Weber defines the power of disposal over resources and labour as essential for any economy, regardless of its political constitution. This means that economic action inevitably requires the application of enforceable power (Weber 1978: 67–68).

This relation of economic and legal action is important in the context of the analysis of a consumer credit market. The commonality between the conceptualizations of Weber and of the South African legislators lies in the creation of an economic realm of freely interacting lenders and borrowers, but one which is institutionally embedded in a legal order that possesses the capacity to enforce contracts. The quite paradoxical consequence of this understanding is that a loan contract belongs to the economic realm as long as a borrower is able to serve his instalments of his own accord, but that it becomes a part of the legal system as soon as he would have to be forced into repayments. It is important to recognize that this distinction between 'the economy' and 'the law' is not an intellectual game but actual social practice in financialized consumer credit markets: as soon as a borrower becomes unable to repay his debts as agreed upon the whole procedure is handed over to the legal branch. Limiting the understanding of 'the economy' to a realm of free-will interaction is misleading due to the inseparable mingling of monetary and legal elements in it.

Proceeding with Weber's reasoning, we must furthermore note that he does not equate rational economic action with the exchange of goods and services. He claims 'utility' to be an additional necessity for commendable economic action, whereas compensatory exchanges may be 'not economically rational', e.g. if they are performed in traditional or conventional ways (Weber 1978: 68–69, 72). In other words, in economic contexts he reduces his ideal types of rationality from four to one, and a completely harmonious exchange would not qualify for rational economic action in the sense of Weber (1978: 72) if there was no utility involved: 'Every case of a rationally oriented exchange is the resolution of a previously open or latent conflict of interests by means of a compromise'. This means that Weber only talks of an 'economy' if a conflict is present. The price battle and the competition with rivals are seen as typical conflicts to be solved by rational exchanges. 'Rational exchange is only possible when both parts expect to profit from it, or when one is under compulsion because of his own need or the other's economic power' (Weber 1978: 73). From this Weber concludes that rational economic action is limited to markets. His emphasis on conflict distinguishes him from Simmel. Yet we have to note that Weber adds social interaction 'under compulsion' as still belonging to the economy and as being in accordance with his demand of the double freedom. The demarcation to enforcement, which would belong to the legal realm, remains unclear at this point.

The link between Weber's insistence on advantageous exchanges and market situations as preconditions of an economic rationality becomes clearer after the introduction of the concept of money.[6] As formal consequences of monetization, Weber lists the possible interruption of the direct contact of actors in exchanges, accompanied by the option to extend trade over time and space. It would also entail the translation of economic relations into monetary terms as their common ground. The individuation of consumption, the tendency of capital procurement towards marginal utility and the dissemination of all kinds of acquisitive action are adduced, too. Finally, Weber (1978: 81) comes to the most important consequence of the generalization of the monetary economy in his view, namely

> the possibility of monetary calculation; that is, the possibility of assigning money values to all goods and services which in any way might enter into transaction of purchase or sale. In substantive as distinguished from formal terms, monetary calculation means that goods are not evaluated merely in their immediate importance as utilities at the given time and place and for the given person only. Rather, goods are more or less systematically compared, whether for consumption or for production, with all potential future opportunities of utilization or of gaining a return, including their possible utility to an indefinite number of other persons who can be brought into the comparison insofar as they are potential buyers of the powers of control and disposal of the present owner. Where money calculations have become typical, this defines the market situation of the good in question.

The distinction between the substantive and the formal rationality refers to the two addressees of free action. Substantively rational action focusses on the economic end of an action, whereas formally rational economic action applies means in beneficial ways to this end. In other words, substantive rationality refers to the purpose, and formal rationality to the social technique of the economy. Only both rationalities together result in an economic meaning of an action, and both secure the future continuance of economic action, but the first refers to the goal attainment and the latter to the function (Weber 1978: 85).

However, it is the separate application of the formal from the substantive rationality by focussing on the future gains instead of the individual utility that turns monetary markets into capitalistic endeavours, in which the prospect of profits can be used to urge other people into collaboration.

On the formal level, the quantitative extractions of economic items communicate in the language of mathematics with each other. The way this happens was the topic of the previous section. What becomes possible now is rational economic accounting. Values can be compared, in unlimited amounts and without timely restrictions, advantages can be considered and consequences can be extrapolated – and all of this can be done without affecting reality (Weber 1978: 86–90).

However, the results of this accounting can be applied to reality, of course. To clarify still further: this kind of application of resources in reality only becomes a likely process by taking the detour on the symbolic level. Without calculating possible profits in advance, the acquisition of resources, the provision of machinery and labour, the time-consuming and error-prone process of production and the uncertain sale of commodities would probably not be performed. The calculative processes of accounting create the imaginary realm in which capitalism can be realized.

Market societies, in which the general calculation of future economic gains is a common formal pattern of social behaviour, can only emerge as a consequence of many market places, in which this procedure is applied in substantive ways. This historical development in medieval Europe has been analysed by Braudel (1992).

The procedure of calculation enables economic actors to optimize future economic actions by symbolically forecasting the outcomes of specific constellations. Weber outlines the economic motivation of the possibility of ever increasing profits. He makes it clear that the accounting procedure which accompanies the business process finally turns money into capital: money is a social tool that allows the individual to defer the settlement of exchanges, a socially flexible procedure that can take multiple forms, but capital contains the social power that makes someone pay money. So, calculative action turns out to be a precondition of capital because it enables actors to compare between initial expectations and final results. Only by this comparison do certain amounts of money appear as gains of a longer and always precarious process of planning, production and sale, and can be identified as a starting point of another business cycle, which contains the ability to increase the amount once again. Capital, this ever increasing resource of market economies, is something that can only be adequately expressed in the quantitative figures which usually refer to money (Weber 1978: 90–94).

When we arrive at the question of utility, the importance of Weber's conceptualizations of the interpenetrating realms of economy and law becomes obvious. Utility and scarcity derive from the social fact of exclusive, and therefore competitive, legitimate powers of control and disposal. In the quotation above Weber outlined how the conflict, which motivates the struggle for rational solutions, derives from the fact that both actors attempt to seize an economic item due to the expectation of profit. The conflict emanates from the exclusiveness of property. Market economies, with their time-consuming planning and complex processes, develop property rights into 'a complete network of exchange contracts' and this represents 'the principle source of the relation of economic action to the law' (Weber 1978: 67). Weber (1978: 67–68) emphasizes the fact that any political organization of the economy in his sense, i.e. the symbolic planning and optimization of provision of commodities, 'must be able to count on some kind of control over the necessary services of labour and of the means of production', and he explicitly includes socialism and anarchism in this definition. The economy as a collective purpose would require regulations about the utilization of individual capacities and resources, regardless of the political constitution. This is the point at which social relations and norms inevitably re-enter the realm of economy: a society that organizes itself as a market economy has to demand from its members the application of an economic rationality in their daily affairs, and this, of course, is a norm.

In the context of this line of argument Weber introduces the concept of credit, and not by chance. Credit refers to the capability of optimizing the process of profit making for two parties at the same time: the lender can apply his money by passing it on for interest, and the borrower is able to apply money according to his economic plans. In other words, credit is a temporary transformation of the property right of the lender, who postpones his claims according to the agreement. It is remarkable that Weber (1978: 81) was already introducing as early as 1919–1920 the concept of 'probability', i.e. at a time when consumer credit and credit scoring are still part of an unknown future.

> The granting of credit means in the first instance that action is oriented to the probability that this future transfer of disposal will actually take place. In this sense the primary significance of credit lies in the fact that it makes it possible for an economic unit to exchange an expected future surplus of control over goods or money against the present control of some other unit over goods which the latter does not now intend to use.

This sounds very much like the exemplary hopes of the South African legislators with regard to the NCA. However, as shown in the previous chapters, the South African parliament had anticipated 'imbalances in negotiation power', and Max Weber is much clearer in this regard. This will be outlined in the following review of Weber's expectations of the societal consequences of his own concepts.

The Temporary Limitation of Rational Markets

We have seen that Simmel and Weber, as contemporaries at the turn of the twentieth century, refer to arguments which are in part mutually replaceable. This documents the fact that both were devoted to the task of understanding an economic dynamic which had received an impressive momentum in their times. The purpose of the previous sections was not to cover again the development of these arguments completely, but to document a shared interpretation of these phenomena, which promoted a widespread prominence for the ideas of market equilibrium and economic rationality.

However, there exists a fundamental disagreement between Simmel's concept of a stable realm of exchange values, which would only require satisfying the access of all actors to money and commodities, and Weber's concept of a competitive economy based upon a peaceful power of disposal. It has been shown that the establishment of functioning exchange values in Simmel's concept requires a specific form of rationality. Weber is able to explain why economic exchanges foster such an instrumental rationality, optimally performed in calculations of quantities, but his conception of markets sees economic actors who are always on the brink of a violent conflict.

For the analysis of the disequilibrium of the South African consumer credit market, this is of great importance. To begin with, both Simmel and Weber make it clear that a socially distributed rationality of credit can only be brought about by the establishment of a market. The difference between the age-old practice of personal money lending and a consumer credit market is very clear now. The first refers to the direct negotiation of social and economic power between two actors, and its outcome is fully dependent on their capacities. No standard of procedure or comparable prices could be derived from this. In contrast, a consumer credit market generalizes the beneficial options of money lending and generates a specific rationality by enabling market participants to calculate costs and advantages.

Yet a market constitutes very unstable social relations because actors enter into and leave a deal as strangers. This can only be overcome by the provision of a legal framework, as Weber (1978: 635) points out in a fragment on the ethic of markets:

> From a sociological point of view, the market represents a coexistence and sequence of rational consociations, each of which is specifically ephemeral insofar as it ceases to exist with the act of exchanging the goods, unless a norm has been promulgated which imposes upon the transfers of the exchangeable goods the guaranty of their lawful acquisition as warranty of title, or of quiet enjoyment.

The social interconnection is provided by the common practice of economic calculation, and Weber explicitly notes that it represents a socially shared capacity linking different bipartisan deals. In other words, rational economic action is comprehensible only as a generalized social practice, but not as occasional single exchanges.

The same is true for the use of money, because it only functions as a common tool of society. Weber (1978: 73) stresses the socializing effect of economic action because of the symbolic inclusion of all possible market participants into society. Subjectively estimating the value of a commodity, or the possible advantage deriving from a deal, is tantamount to thinking of the rest of society. 'The market community as such is the most impersonal relationship of practical life into which humans can enter with one another' (Weber 1978: 636). This consociation is an impersonal one because it is focussed on the commodity as the cause of the relationship, and by a mutual expectation of instrumental rationality applied by all actors.

Weber proceeds to argue that this expectation would usually be fixed and institutionally distributed by the legal order, which means that actors inevitably have to expect economically rational behaviour of their counterparts even if they individually would prefer a different form of interaction. In other words, instrumentally rational economic interaction is imposed as a norm, which means that legally framed markets are urging actors into economic rationality. Constitutionally established market economies represent normative orders because they demand instrumentally rational, economic interaction of their citizens despite the fact that there exist potential alternatives of interaction.

As we have shown above, Weber is forced to exclude the harmonious exchange between equals from this concept due to the logic of his own considerations, because an exchange without a struggle about maximized benefits would block the generalized demand for continually optimized economic processes, which are based on an ever increasing acquisition of resources at lower costs. The bipartisan agreement on a good-natured exchange without defrauding the other represents a denial of the normative demand of a rational market. Or to put it the other way around: the existence of a non-violent conflict is a precondition for the limitation of rational options. The possibilities of solidary, affectual or traditional social action lose their rationality due to the general expectation of competitive materialization of exclusive advantages.

The call for an advantageous performance of exchange is in full accordance with Simmel's line of argument. As he implicitly stated, a non-instrumental deal would have to be characterized as 'stupid' (Simmel 1990: 140) because it would undermine the possibility of others to estimate exchange values on a reliable basis.

Max Weber (1978: 636) is very explicit in expecting a destructive effect from solidary economic interaction, because in a market economy 'there are no obligations of brotherliness or reverence, and none of those spontaneous human relations that are sustained by personal unions. They all would just obstruct the free development of the bare market relationship, and its specific interests serve, in their turn, to weaken the sentiments on which these obstructions rest'.

Despite being interested in advantageous exchanges and increasing control of resources, and not in the well-being of other persons, the emerging order is not conceptualized as being free of norms. The social bond is established by the tendency of contractual relationships, because in a network of interrelated and future-oriented enterprises it is essential 'to respect the formal inviolability of a promise once given. … Violations of agreements, even though they may be concluded by mere signs, entirely unrecorded, and devoid of evidence, are almost unheard of in the annals of the stock exchange' (Weber 1978: 636–37). This means that the impersonality of markets causes its own ethic that rests on the necessity of the continuity of the economy.

Nevertheless, 'the market is fundamentally alien to any fraternal relationship'. Under the precondition of a shared interest of continuous economic market relationships, all actors would avoid 'infringements of the rules of good faith and fair dealing' (Weber 1978: 637).

At this point, a new normative equilibrium appears out of purely instrumental relationships. It could be seen as an ironic inversion of Adam Smith's idea of an invisible hand. Instead of a divine intervention, which orders the egoistic actions of individuals into a generally beneficial social order, at this stage of Weber's thinking a new, stable and normative order appears out of a consequent pursuit of instrumental rationality by all actors. Yet, this is only an intermediary result, which collapses in consequence of Weber's reasoning. Weber continues by outlining the differences between automatic mechanisms (like the standardized application of machinery or calculations) and social interaction of an economy.

In contrast to the term 'technology', he emphasizes that economic action consists of an optimal application of means to achieve freely chosen ends (Weber 1978: 65–67). In economic action the optimization – i.e. the technological part of economic action – serves the specific purpose of achieving ever increasing power of control over resources. There exists no prior definition of what these increased ends may be – this represents the freedom of economic choice – but they inevitably require a desire for growth. The market ethic, yielded by economic rationality, is a favourable way of achieving this end, but only to a certain point, as Weber (1978: 638) makes clear:

> Capitalistic interests thus favour the continuous extension of the free market, but only up to the point at which some of them succeed, through the purchase of privileges from the political authority or simply through the power of capital, in obtaining for themselves a monopoly for the sale of their products or the acquisition of their means of production, and in thus closing the market on their own part.

As soon as the achievement of beneficial ends did not require the maintenance of impersonal relationships, which justify confidence in the progress of economic interaction, the motivation to support the normative requirements of free markets would vanish. This means that Weber finally agrees with Marx with regard to the tendency of capitalistic competition to abandon itself due to its inherent dynamic. However, Weber focusses on the planning and calculation of economic processes, whereas Marx had put the social hierarchy of the production process at the centre of his analysis. More precisely than Marx, Weber identifies the interpenetration of legal and economic orders as autonomous realms of society as the reason for this: on the one hand, monetary profits can be secured only by applying the norm of exclusive individual property, and on the other hand, this protection of the power of control sets market competition in motion. Weber (1978: 639) identifies the logical limitation of this tendency: 'This state of affairs, which we call free competition, lasts until it is replaced by new, this time capitalistic, monopolies which are acquired in the market through the power of property'.

As outlined at the beginning of this section, the legal order refers to the fulfilment of expectations which derive from the past. The economic principle of realizing future chances is restricted by the acknowledgement of property rights, which have been identified as indispensable resources of economic rationality by Max Weber. The importance of this theoretical reconstruction is that it defines the demarcation between free-will compulsion and violent enforcement in the concept of Max Weber, and, hence, explains when and why the execution of loan contracts is moved from economic to legal interaction.

With regard to the 'imbalances in negotiation power' in credit agreements, this means that the party which possesses property rights, i.e. the lender, remains interested in a maintenance of the economic relation only as long as he can expect an increase in benefits from it. In other words, economically rational behaviour in the sense of Weber means that credit providers waive the reclamation of their property as long as they expect profits from the borrower's management of credit money. As soon as the prospect of further increasing the profits by adding fees and interest vanishes, because a service of instalments becomes improbable, they should begin to enforce their claims with the help of the legal system. Such an option for retreat from the market mechanism exists only on the supply side of the deal – and this is the root of 'imbalances in negotiation power'.

Summary

This chapter started from illustrations of the institutional model of the South African consumer credit market, which aimed at creating a channel of private interaction that was framed by the boundaries of illegality. Those practices, which had been identified as reasons for the failure of the free consumer credit market of the 1990s, had been banished beyond this boundary: reckless lending and covert inability to repay. Violation would be corrected by the institutions of the law. Lending or borrowing in disregard of the NCA deprived actors of any legal entitlement, though.

Inside the channel of interaction, the problem of imbalances in negotiation power of market actors was conceptualized as a consequence of non-transparency and missing information but turned out to derive from different capacities to mobilize social institutions in the case of conflict. Despite the claim of the NCA to provide vulnerable consumers with protection, the institutional arrangement of the credit market actually safeguarded the property of lenders and endowed them with options of legal enforcement of contracts, whereas borrowers faced the obligation to repay their loans under nearly all circumstances. The equality of actors was limited to the moment of the conclusion of a loan contract, and borrowers were turned into a subordinate party until the final settlement after the formation of the contract.

The sections of theoretical reflections revealed this institutional setting to be more than a political mis-configuration. Instead, it was constructed in accordance with a popular ideological motive, which claims that general benefits of markets result from the self-interested rational action of all participants. The specific rationality, though, could only be achieved by the maintenance of a constant peaceful conflict of the actors, which would be brought about by competition for the option of exclusive disposal over resources. This was accomplished by the protection of property. In other words, the privileged treatment of the capital of lenders was established as a means to force borrowers into economically rational behaviour.

The attempts of Georg Simmel and Max Weber to grasp the rationale of the dynamically expanding capitalism at the beginning of the twentieth century revealed the confusing paradox of this idea of economic rationality. On the one hand, Georg Simmel was able to show how money, as a tool of economic action, could develop into a powerful resource which allowed individuals to bargain incommensurable wants, goods and services. According to his work, actors in monetized markets learn to estimate the proper value of any commodity by experience. The distribution of wealth in society can therefore be negotiated peacefully, and a broad network of economic relationships can be established as a core of modern societies. However, he had to presuppose a self-interested rationality in order to make his equilibrium of a common satisfaction of needs workable. On the other hand, Max Weber was able to provide a theoretical model that explained the establishment of an instrumental rationality from the conflict about exclusive disposal over resources, but he had to draw the conclusion of an ultimate instability of the social order deriving from it. The paradox that appeared from these considerations was that the equilibrium could be established by enabling all actors to calculate the value of money and commodities in an unconstrained fashion, but that it required the maintenance of a conflict, which rested on the strict limitation of access to resources. Max Weber came to the pessimistic conclusion that the freedom of choice in market societies would come to an end when some economic actors had accumulated enough capital and power to enforce their interests, without recognizing the boundaries of the freedom of competitors.

The popularity of the argument about a generally beneficial market economy that is allegedly based on self-interested economic action emerged from the economic opportunities that resulted from the symbolic transformation of the economy. Simmel and Weber agreed on the evolutionary progress that was achieved by the ability to calculate the prospected outcomes of economic action. For one thing, the transformation of qualities into quantitative amounts allowed every good, service and person to be included in economic negotiations. Apart from that, quantitative expressions, i.e. numbers, could be calculated, which means that an extrapolation of future outcomes was possible, provided that the figures represented the qualitative figurations adequately. Finally, the optimal tool for performing these economic procedures was money, which allowed economic transactions to be stretched out in time and space: the accumulation of money has no limits. These three factors together caused a massive expansion of economic action – with regard to the commodities and people included, the intricacies and amounts that could be handled, and the geographic and temporal expansion of the economy. The presupposed inherent rationality of market oriented economic action seemed to be evident on the basis of the growth rates since the eighteenth century, and a final equilibrium to the benefit of the whole of society could be calculated for a point of time in the never ending future of economic progress.

However, the social outcome of extended market economies usually increased inequality, as in the case of the South African consumer credit market. Two factors were identified as being of crucial importance for the economic capacities developed on the symbolic level of communication: property and mathematics. The first stirred the latent conflict of competition, and the latter allowed for a calculation of advantages.

Exclusive private property generated social scarcity through the exclusion of others, and this served a basic constellation of conflict in rational economic interaction. Only the normatively demanded struggle for exclusive disposal over resources forced individual actors to optimize their economic procedures. This revealed the crossing of the border between the economic and the legal realm of society to be crucial: the imbalances of power become obvious when economic partners change their roles into that of plaintiff and culprit.

Together, the specific South African property right and the role of mathematically performed economics in the consumer credit market resulted in a consumer credit market that turned out to be very profitable for lenders, and resilient in face of high levels of mid-term and long-term indebted consumers. However, it was a normative order and not without alternatives. Therefore, the last chapter will consider where the humanitarian potential of consumer credit gets lost.

NOTES

1. This is true even in the case when actors decide to ignore the NCA. In such circumstances, the objective reality of the NCA makes itself felt exactly by the potential interference of law enforcement agencies.
2. Interestingly, the policy framework lists school and student loans as incentives despite their exclusion from the main mechanisms of the NCA according to s 78(2) NCA.
3. We come across this difficult distinction of passions from interests in every financial crisis, when public media, politicians and scientists suddenly transform the much praised economic rationality into greed and avarice as being allegedly roots of the crisis. The crucial point is that there is no difference in the rationality of action of economic actors in both cases – only the circumstances of their interpretation have changed in retrospective.
4. Simmel refers to historical and anthropological examples, in which animals or common tools like iron hoes become the common currency of exchange, i.e. 'special purpose money' in the sense of Polanyi (1977: 98). Simmel's reference to a swift adjustment even of the non-monetary economies of Africa, Asia and the Americas to the European custom of monetary exchange suffers from its ignorance of historically existing power relations. In fact, most of these societies had to be forced into market economies. The exchange rates did not result from practically established experiences but were imposed by the force of power.
5. Weber also acknowledges economically oriented action, which addresses economic issues but is governed by non-economic ends in the first place.
6. In *Economy and Society*, Weber contents himself mostly with a formal definition of money, and only refers very briefly to his preference for the money theory of Ludwig von Mises over that of Georg Friedrich Knapp. *Economy and Society* is an unfinished work: Weber planned to develop an economic sociology, a task he was not able to fulfil. *Economy and Society* was meant to be merely the introduction to an unknown opus.

Conclusion

The Missed Options of the South African Consumer Credit Market

This study has been especially interested in the political establishment of a consumer credit market in South Africa. Therefore, it has not focussed primarily on offering a general examination of credit and debt (Gelpi and Julien-Labruyère 2000; Graeber 2011; Peebles 2010), but rather on the contemporary construction of such a market. The crucial lesson to be learned from Karl Polanyi (2001) was that the extension of market mechanisms had to take into account social counter movements, which aimed at containing any resulting conflicts and repairing a destroyed social fabric. Consequently, the historical parts of the study were not intended to provide ideas about any general character of money and credit, but rather to reveal institutional trajectories in the conflict between access to credit on the one hand, and limitations on resulting social distortions on the other.

The establishment of a consumer credit market in South Africa caused a fundamental change in money lending. Traditional money lending depended on the interaction of lenders and borrowers; it could be understood by examining their social ties and following the movements of money. This changes in a market economy, because lenders and borrowers now turn into participants of a complex and stabilized infrastructure that continues to exist even during their own individual absence. As long as the demand for credit seems likely, the market will exist. The provision of credit, the calculative devices for risk assessment, the legal bureaucracies of conflict resolution, the monitoring and clearance procedures of the financial system as well as the mediating and enforcing capacities of the political system, are perpetuated. Additionally, without a central bank that provides a currency and takes responsibility for the monitoring of incomplete payment procedures, a credit market would be unimaginable (Burton 2008: 50–53; historically see Wennerlind 2011: 2–4).

The first attempt to build a consumer credit market in South Africa failed. The results had endangered not only the stability of the political system but also that of the economy. The operational enactment of the consumer credit market had been shown to be profitable, but it generated over-indebtedness and violent debt collection methods. At first, this destroyed the general social legitimacy and, then, it endangered the banking business due to the expectation of widespread repayment defaults. The dissolution of the legitimacy led to political attempts to re-regulate between 1999 and 2002, and the malfunctioning of the economic institutions in 2002 generated the general willingness to accept a complete overhaul of the consumer credit market by establishing the National Credit Act 34 of 2005.

The crucial point about the NCA was that policy makers deliberately decided to undertake a second attempt at establishing a consumer credit market, instead of returning to previous policies of normative condemnation and legal obstruction of personal money lending. This means that the government created a risky market while knowing about its dangers; and in this it was supported by the financial system and banks, by trade unions and a social movement invoked by the Communist Party. Without exaggeration it can be said that a consensus did exist in political and economic organizations about the advantageousness of a consumer credit market at the time of its creation. Creditors were banned from refusing loan applications on any grounds other than for economic reasons, whilst having a political right encouraged consumers to apply for a loan.

The reconstruction of the consumer credit market was conceptualized as a part of the 'Microeconomic Reform Strategy' of the presidency of Thabo Mbeki. It moved the responsibility for economic success from the level of collective political planning towards the individual's risk-taking propensity. However, the exact role of a consumer credit market in this political strategy remained unclear. Programmatic papers failed to outline intended effects on the supply side of the economy, nor did they provide a more detailed strategy for the borrowers on the demand side.

All that can be concluded from the later debates on the effects of the NCA is that the government hoped for a flourishing financial business, and some additional employment deriving from credit bureaux, debt counselling and other service providers of the consumer credit industry. Concerning the expectations with regard to the credit customers and their facilitated access to consumer goods, the policy framework of 2004 contained far reaching but vague statements about the possibilities of accumulating assets and exploiting economic opportunities. At the same time, the risks of over-indebtedness involved in a consumer credit market were not ignored (DTI 2004c: 6). The complex arrangement of the institutions of the NCA was meant to cut this Gordian knot by forbidding reckless lending on the part of credit providers and by demanding instrumentally rational household budget calculation on the part of borrowers. Besides this, the legislators seemed to be convinced of the generally beneficial effects of an expanded consumer credit market.

However, the crisis that was revealed by the public statements of the National Credit Regulator from March 2012 onwards left no doubt that the basic problem of the free market could not be prevented by the NCA. Despite the detailed regulations and the prohibition of certain practices, too many loans were granted at high prices to people who could not afford them. At times more than 10 million South Africans, representing more than 18 per cent of the total population, showed 'impaired credit records', documenting that they had problems with serving their instalments. An increasing number of them were classified as long-term over-indebted, which means that they were excluded from, instead of involved in, the market economy. These problems motivated the Department of Trade and Industry to publish a review of its policy framework in May 2013, based on research by the National Credit Regulator. It resulted in the amendments of the Regulations of the NCA from March 2015, published in the Government Gazette No. 38557. They contained not a single measure of debt relief in the entire 235 pages. Neither could already financially stressed debtors expect alleviation of their burdens, and nor were already over-indebted borrowers released from their trap. All that remained was a new procedure of affordability measurement that was imposed on credit providers, which encouraged them to calculate at a newly defined margin. Compliance with the procedures and forms of the NCA and its Regulations resulted in legal protection of their claims.

In 2017, a debate on a 'debt intervention' measure began, which finally could offer a clearance of debts to a small number of over-indebted citizens following the completion of a lengthy procedure. However, millions of long-term indebted borrowers will not benefit from this, and the basic construction of the consumer credit market will remain untouched.

This path of development presents a final analytical question that demands an answer: why did the legislators adhere to market principles that promised general welfare effects but generated very high levels of over-indebtedness?

This question arises in light of the development that started from the expectation of general social benefits resulting from a market which rests on the economic rationality of all actors, and that ended in a political stalemate in which legislators denied options of debt relief to most of the financially over-burdened borrowers because they still wanted to enforce the efficiency of a market that brought about this desperate over-indebtedness in the first place.

On the basis of this study, the answer to this question lies in a social differentiation between an economy that was institutionalized as a realm of private free-will social interaction on the one hand, and the legal foundations of this sphere in the relentless South African property right that offered no escape from private debts on the other. It is important to acknowledge that this differentiation was not limited to an analytical distinction but that it was a socially enacted one. Voluntary interaction and the autonomous negotiations of the economy were strictly separated from the commanding area of enforced debt reclaim.

Explaining this division of two allegedly distinct social realms, which were, however, closely connected under the surface, was the main purpose behind reconstructing the social theories of Georg Simmel and Max Weber in the previous chapter.

First of all, Simmel explained the social foundation of the appealing idea of a self-regulating market economy, which allowed this political project to survive even after the fierce critique of capitalism by Karl Marx and the labour movement had become popular. He was able to do so because he focussed on the capacity of money to function as a tool of comparison and measurement in the first place. In contrast to this, many theorists zeroed in on the exchange function or value storage function of money, but Simmel showed how money changes the common perception of the world by quantitatively interrelating very different goods and services. This makes it possible to include these items in the social practice of negotiating exchange values and swapping commodities. Yet, this monetary quality not only extends the market economy, it also enlarges the economic society because more people are able to offer something for exchange, and to participate in society.

This explains the attractiveness of consumer credit markets because the easy access to loans augments market society in two ways, by increasing the potential turnover and by increasing the number of participants.

Simmel justified the idea that money does not require a back-up of utility value, an understanding that underlies the product of unsecured loans, which caused the crisis of the South African consumer credit market. Unsecured loans are the most characteristic product of financialized consumer credit markets because they provide borrowed money to customers without any collateral. According to Simmel the enlargement of monetary supply by granting unsecured loans would only require a simultaneous enlargement of the exchange values in order to keep the economy in a general equilibrium. The precondition for generating such an economic expansion of commodities, which would balance the increased amount of money, Simmel saw in the performance of a specific rationality by social actors.

The appropriate point of reference for analysing rationalities of social action is Max Weber. With regard to markets, his general framework of four different 'ideal types' of social action was limited to the one of instrumental rationality that prefers ends over means. The reason for this reduction was seen in a latent, compulsory, but non-violent conflict between economic actors, whereas the demarcation from violent enforcement that would destroy economic freedoms was seen in the free-will capability of borrowers to serve their debts.

The crucial characteristic of economic interaction was seen in the attachment of a specific meaning to social action: economic actors intend to make provision for future needs, so they apply considerations about utility to their actions. This understanding is in full accordance with Simmel. Both Weber and Simmel conceptualized the economy as a social realm of calculation. They identified a close kinship between the economy and mathematics because market economies would be concerned with planning, understood as the calculation of expected utilities in the first place.

This close connection between markets and calculation creates two tendencies. The first effect of mathematical modelling of the economy consists in conceptualizing this social field as a kind of closed system, which stands apart from the rest of society. This is a direct effect of the intention to calculate future results of present actions because this procedure can be improved by focussing on known facts and excluding unknown variables. The removal of possibly disruptive factors effectuates a tendentially plain and clean economic world model. The second tendency of this mathematization lies in the strategy of solving problems by extending the scope of the calculation. If the promised results of economic models do not materialize, the option exists to blame limitations of economic freedoms and resources for it. Just as expanding a fraction in mathematics can be a way of solving an arithmetical problem, so the call for the inclusion of more capacities, more freedom of action or more resources tends to be a role model suggestion in the case of economic problems. This tendency could be empirically observed in the treatment of the South African consumer credit crisis from 2012 to 2014.

Limited or mis-configured individual rationality was identified by governmental actors as the main reason for the financial problems and hardships of South African debtors. Or, formulated in the terms of Max Weber, the question was: why did the reduction of rationalities of social action not materialize? The answer requires one to identify the core reason for the limitation of rationalities, and Max Weber's answer is quite convincing – but with a surprising effect. Weber sees the latent conflict in the economy as caused by scarcity. Instrumental rationality becomes the only meaningful solution to the problem of scarcity, a social situation in which competing actors strive for exclusive access to a resource. It is evident that in such a situation the one who prioritizes means over ends more rigidly and efficiently will succeed. So, every kind of influence of solidarity, emotions or traditions would interfere with the goal of this kind of social action. However – and this is the important part of Weber's argument – the social phenomenon of scarcity is caused by according property rights. In his own conceptualization property rights are part of state enforcement and law, and we have seen that this distinction of economy and law is socially enacted. They belong to a fundamentally different sphere because the very nature of a property right is its legal fixation, which opposes the demand for freedom of action in the economy. The negotiation of prices is a private affair of individuals and companies, whereas all questions concerning property rights are handed over to the legal system, which in current market economies is usually enforced by state power. This means that the fulfilment of loan contracts is performed against the background of fixed property rights.

This border between the economy and the law is crossed when a borrower becomes over-indebted, which means that his income is lower than his repayment obligations in the long run. At this point the status of over-indebtedness requires calculation: every borrower has debts by definition, which is basically an unproblematic fact. Only the expectation of being unable to repay a loan turns indebtedness into a social and economic problem, and over-indebtedness represents its extreme form. In traditional personal lending, this was a conflict between lender and borrower. In a financialized consumer credit market, however, this represents a problem for the whole of society. Now, defaulting unsecured loans are threatening the basic principles of the market society because either the debtor remains excluded from economic activity and – due to a loss of autonomy – from democracy, or the contract cannot be fulfilled, which would present a fundamental violation of market principles, as these require the compliance with promises made in regard to future-oriented calculations.

So, over-indebted borrowers as a consequence of consumer credit markets present a problem of social welfare and stability, and of democratic justice. Hence, most countries that have established such a market have had to cope with the problem. Many of them introduced options of consumer bankruptcy and insolvency in order to put an end to fruitless reclaims and to prevent the permanent exclusion of debtors from social life. Bankruptcy and insolvency represent a modification of property rights and contract law on a case-to-case basis: to preserve the basic principles of the overall system, ad hoc exceptions are introduced. A review of those cases that informed the South African legislators revealed that the NCA represents one of the most rigorous variants of property and contract law among the countries with financialized consumer credit markets.

This means that the South African National Credit Act represents a very strict attempt to discipline consumers into an instrumental rationality by confronting them with the inescapable consequences of a repayment default. The ideology that was applied here was that of 'moral harzard' (Baker 1996), according to which every protection against economic hardship would only induce levity and financial largesse. South African borrowers should be forced into parsimony under all circumstances.

For a South African debtor there exists a sole option: paying back a loan with money. The decisive political mistake at this point consists in treating money and loans as ordinary commodities. Yet, money is not a commodity like others that could be procured or renounced like any other. Instead, a lack of this fictitious commodity keeps customers from the satisfaction of all of their necessities, and not just from the product they are barred from, and the only way of obtaining money consists in selling one's own working power, i.e. by offering one's own person as a commodity in the labour market (Polanyi 2001: 71–80). In a consumer credit market, this means that the rationality of customers may be steered by very urgent demands, which encourages them to disregard long-term consequences. For instance, the repayment of debts with new loans was quite common in South Africa (Shevel 2013). It has to be emphasized once again that the prospect of difficulties of repayment was synonymous with the outlook on increased earnings on the side of creditors, due to a property right that was intended to enforce economic rational action.

The contradiction of this effect can only be fully grasped by recalling the historical development. Starting from the insight that 'imbalances in negotiation power' (s 3(e) NCA) had caused the free consumer credit market of the 1990s to destroy the legitimacy as well as the functioning of the lending business, the government created the legal framework in which lenders would offer surplus capital to borrowers in the expectation of profits. The reason given for the imbalances was that they emanated from an insufficient distribution of knowledge among the contracting parties.

On account of this, loan contracts were intended to endow borrowers with clear price signals. Prices were conceptualized as providing sufficient knowledge to prevent over-borrowing by motivating credit customers to perform rational calculations. However, the feasibility of a lending business serving a relatively poor clientele and the financial stability of the economy depended on limiting the demand to those customers who would perform strictly rational calculations. Guided by the intention not to intervene in private economic interactions, the only way of urging consumers into economic rationality lay in a deterrence of over-borrowing by enforcing the final settlement of all pecuniary obligations of loan contracts. This was achieved by providing creditors with access to institutions that could enforce their claims in case of conflict. In the end, this institutional setting deprived over-indebted borrowers of any option to negotiate after their repayment capabilities had failed. Hence, it increased the imbalance of power to a maximum degree. So, starting from the notion of unequal power resources, which had to be levelled, the establishment of a consumer credit market ended in the aggravation of the 'imbalances in negotiation power' due to the attempt to enforce voluntary rational calculations on the side of the borrowers. In other words, the attempt to secure the freedom of interaction in the economy ended in the total deprivation of liberty on the demand side of the market. The core of this predicament was to be found in the confusion of unequal access to social power with a shortage of information and knowledge.

The social theory of Georg Simmel made it clear that a development of knowledge about the relative exchange value of commodities in monetary societies requires flexibility in order to allow adjustments and learning processes on the basis of individual experiences. Yet, in South Africa the political intention to foster the socially shared imagination of a self-regulating consumer credit market was finally effected in the enforcement of a purely cognitive knowledge of simple price signals on the side of borrowers, and in an encouragement to sell high-risk loans at high prices on the side of lenders. The inescapable commitment to repay on the demand side, combined with the almost unlimited protection of property on the supply side, created an institutional imbalance, which could not be levelled by the distribution of information and knowledge.

The legitimization of the NCA rested on a free-market ideology, which insisted on the principle of non-interference in private economic interactions despite the experiences of the devastating social effects of an unregulated market in the 1990s. On the one hand, this legitimization represented the continuity of the understanding of monetary principles, which had been sustained during decades of different political regimes. This study has reconstructed the history of the political motive of 'sound money' from the times of bullion money to the end of the apartheid regime. On the other hand, this legitimization kept the promise of providing financial means to the majority of the population, which had been barred from economic progress since the beginning of a South African state in 1652. The Microeconomic Reform Strategy built the framework for the hope, expressed in section 3(a) of the NCA, to develop 'a credit market that is accessible to all South Africans, and in particular to those who have historically been unable to access credit under sustainable market conditions'. This combination of an affirmation of renowned economic principles with the outlook of a profitable market that supplied its customers with the option to participate in the amenities of capitalism saved the South African government from attacking the traditional political and social structure of society. The mismatch between promises of help to the over-indebted citizens and the undeterred defence of property rights during the reform discussions after 2012 suggests an unwillingness of the government to interfere in the existing distribution of wealth.

The logic of the South African consumer credit market lay in a simple, formed market that signalled profitability for the supply side of the market, and freedom of choice for the demand side. The legislators claimed as a justification that the final decision to buy a loan lay in the responsibility of customers, who had been forced into rational action by prices and the deterrent scenario of over-indebtedness. This means that the reduction in the sale of inappropriate loans by lenders was expected from the withdrawal of demand by rationally acting borrowers. Hence, the South African government systematically negated the economic constraints which governed the demand for consumer credit and the social consequences generated by the practically unlimited protection of the creditors' claims during the reform process since 2012.

The incapability of governmental actors to identify the correct cause of the absent welfare effects of their rational market is to be found in the 'social imaginary', understood as the popular and socially effective legitimization of the consumer credit market (Castoriadis 1997). It expected an economic equilibrium to derive from non-interference in the mechanisms. According to that notion, the value-oriented, affectual or traditional motivations of actors, possibly caused by political attempts to correct unwanted outcomes, would prevent the general expectation of an optimization of the economy by all actors coming true. The appeal of the idea of non-interference also derived from the possibility of promising a maximum of free action to all citizens of a democracy. This prioritization of freedom over democracy overlooked the insight that the main economic problem of South Africa was to be found in the massive lack of income opportunities which would enable citizens to participate as autonomous and, hence, rational actors in a constraint-free market economy in the first place. This was ignored by the South African government.

Once the ideology of a self-regulating market economy is accepted, an escape becomes unlikely because any failures of this market construction are put down to imperfect market conditions. Instead of a change to the mechanisms, their purification and intensification are demanded.

This effect was seen very clearly by Karl Marx ([1867] 1996: 162). In the chapter entitled 'The Transformation of Money into Capital' of the first volume of *Capital* he describes how the transformation of qualitative relations into purely quantitative terms turns the optimization of economic interaction into an autonomous and possibly never-ending circulation:

> The repetition or renewal of the act of selling in order to buy, is kept within bounds by the very object it aims at, namely, consumption or the satisfaction of definite wants, an aim that lies altogether outside the sphere of circulation. But when we buy in order to sell, we, on the contrary, begin and end with the same thing, money, exchange value; and thereby the movement becomes interminable.

The technique used for the process, i.e. calculation, turns from a means into an end. In a consumer credit market, however, these processes of calculation are regularly interrupted and retranslated into material effects. The NCA enabled creditors to leave the market process when the repayments of borrowers were interrupted. Thereafter, credit customers were turned into guilty debtors, that is to say, they were legally bound – and not economically motivated – to impose limits on their living standards and mobilize all resources to settle the claims, 'based on the principle of satisfaction by the customer of all responsible financial obligations' (s 3(g) NCA).

The brilliant effects of the enhanced capacities resulting from mathematical economics blinded even Max Weber, who defined economic calculation as being the ultimate meaning of the economy despite the fact that he had to root its rationality in scarcity, which is brought about by rigid property rights. This understanding was realized in the legal framework of the South African consumer credit market, which defended the idea of an enforcement of instrumental rationality of actors against the evident result of a great number of indefinitely indebted citizens. However, Weber also understood that respect for the voluntariness of all economic actors would end on the supply side of the market as soon as forceful alternatives appeared. The South African NCA enabled creditors to expect this transformation of economic trade into legal proceedings upfront, and to include it in the terms of their contracts. The detailed 'terms and conditions' of loan contracts showed that South African banks anticipated their legal options to secure their earnings, once the repayment obligations proved to be overwhelming for the borrower. Collateralized by this back-up, they could sell high-risk loans to customers with a high probability of repayment default (Riles 2011).

The South African government basically denied the effect of its consumer credit market, which consisted of a huge number of over-indebted citizens deprived of all options to negotiate a modification of their loan contracts, akin to a traumatized person who suppresses the reasons for the detrimental consequences of a practice it receives enjoyment from. The joy of 'corporatised liberation' (McKinley 2017) of the South African government consisted in delegating the task of the socio-economic inclusion of the victims of colonialism and apartheid to the private and individual economic interaction in an allegedly self-regulating market.

The South African government acted in a self-deluded way on both levels of symbolic interaction. On the functional level, it proposed the idea of an enforcement of voluntary rational calculations, and on the level of public communication it was obsessed by the idea of non-interference in a self-regulating market. However, both perceptions were deceiving.

The economic interaction of the consumer credit market did not consist of two private and autonomous contracting parties who calculated the profitability or the feasibility of a loan offer. And market actors did not represent natural entities free from political interference. Instead, this study has revealed how the economic setting produces a complex network revolving around 'distributed agency' (Muniesa, Millo and Callon 2007). This means that market participants were transformed into calculative actors by a complex setting of controls, as shown in Illustration 6.1 as a summary of the analytical chapters of this study.

The illustration shows in detail the following: the payment system monitored all financial transactions and cancelled them only after completion. If it was not monitored by this system, a loan contract was illegal. The legal system enforced this compliance and the submission to all other legal requirements of the NCA.

Inside this channel of interaction a complex network of mutual controls was enacted. The National Consumer Tribunal and the National Credit Regulator checked the market participants, and the central bank kept a special eye on the organizations on the supply side. Credit bureaux scrutinized the financial actions of borrowers. Lenders and borrowers were controlled from multiple angles, and a competitive market meant that they had to control each other, too.

Seen from this perspective, the idea of freely interacting market participants dissolves. The same is true of the social imaginary of a self-regulating market. The most decisive event analysed in this study in this regard was the management of the crisis after the collapse of African Bank in August 2014. Although the market eventually showed resilience in the face of this crisis, its main cause was the punishment of African Bank by the financial markets after it had reduced its sale of expensive high-risk loans to customers. The turmoil was contained thanks to

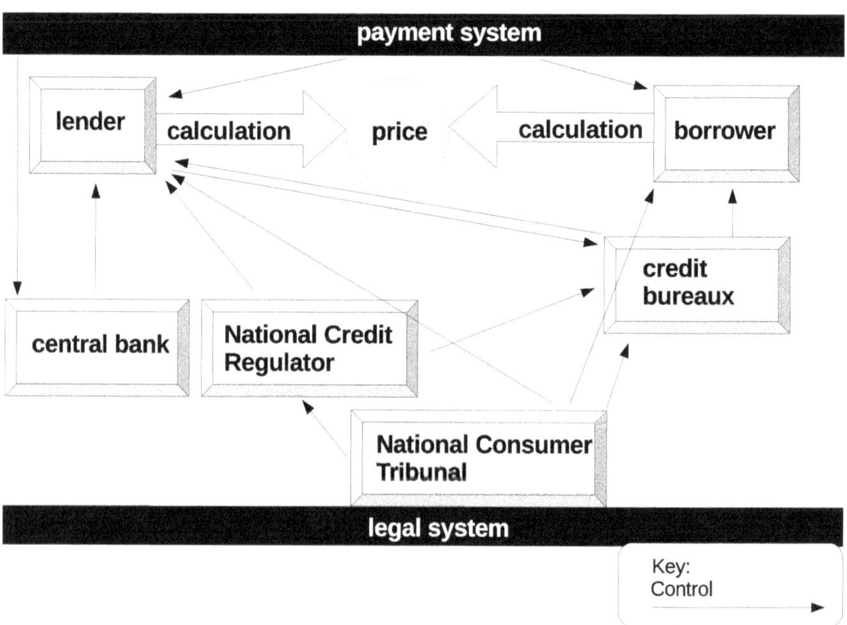

Figure 6.1. Model of distributed agency. Created by the author.

the concerted interaction of government and banking companies. This means that political and business intervention saved the market from a collapse, whereas self-regulation had driven the lending business into crisis in the first place, as the downgrading by international rating agencies had confirmed.

Both the public legitimization of the South African consumer credit market and the idea of naturally and freely interacting economic actors are revealed as deceptions. In fact, the market is politically established whilst calculating actors are institutionally generated. The economic outcome of the market is profitable for the banking business but disastrous for a fifth of the population. With regard to domestic demand, the effect of the market for most credit customers leads to a double payment of commodities: first, they pay for the commodity, and then they repay their loan. It is a way of increasing the prices of consumer goods and allowing another business to participate in the profits. To expect general economic progress from this is fatuous.

However, the theoretical conclusion to this study in understanding the South African consumer credit market as a politically created institutional setting of 'distributed agency' also allows us to extrapolate modifications and a change in its legitimization. We will not offer an alternative model here; that would require practical testing anyway. But we want to show that alternatives are possible.

These will now be explained with reference to Keith Hart (2000) and Robert Shiller (2003). Hart argued that the generalization of market economies, especially after the industrialization of the eighteenth and nineteenth century, had depended on the depersonalization of monetary exchanges, but that the digital communication network, which has become known as the Internet, would enable us to re-personalize the economy. Under the term 'memory bank' he refers to the visibility of traces that emanate from digital economic interactions and considers options for diversifying the possible reactions to the results of monetary calculations.

Indeed, our comparison of international consumer credit legislations in the fourth chapter showed that many countries justify debt relief by referring to a kind of substituting service in return by debtors. In common law countries, this lies in the willingness to re-enter the accident-prone process of a market economy, and in many civil law countries the reward can be seen in the form of financially more prudent consumers. The argument of Hart, in connection with the established alternatives of other consumer societies, proposes the political idea of providing non-monetary ways as an option for settling the claims of creditors or justification of legal debt relief measures.

Appropriate options have already been developed by Shiller. His models essentially consist of extensions of the probability-based calculations of the financial markets which allow the benefits to be generalized. Basically, he asks why it should not be possible to develop social institutions in which the options of risk sharing, something that is successfully and profitably practised in financial markets, are applied for the benefit of a democratic society.

The answer given in this study is that this would require a modification of property rights, as well as the development of institutions which would support economic actors on the demand side of the market in the same way that they do on the supply side. This is more than a political utopia. The comparison of different consumer bankruptcy and insolvency legislations has presented modifications of property rights that already exist, by way of conditionally extending or limiting the powers of disposal of economic actors. Debt relief means that the right to claims of creditors ends when the costs of indebtedness for society exceed its general benefits. In reference to single credit contracts, this simply means distributing the risks of credit default more justly, and it is not impossible to demand of creditors that they accept their share of loan defaults, considering their potential earnings.

Shiller has emphasized the fact that there is no need to take these risks individually. Instead, they could be institutionally shared among all participants on the supply side of a market. In fact, the South African banks practised exactly this when they took their share of losses of the collapsed African Bank in August 2014. Turning this emergency measure into a general business principle, for instance, by transferring a tax on every loan to a fund that finances debt relief measures, could help to solve the problem of over-indebtedness.

Two further options refer to Hart's concept of a human economy (Hart, Laville and Cattani 2011), and his economic reflections about the possibilities of a globally digitalized monetary and communication system (Hart 2000). To begin with, the debt counselling rulings of the NCA could be complemented by a credit counselling apparatus, i.e. institutions which give advice to credit customers about the utilization of their loans. This suggestion rests on the crucial insight that the necessary information about the reasonableness of a loan develops only after a contract is made (Esposito 2011: 18–36). The political organization of the options offered by the Internet would allow credit customers to be provided with more signals than just the price of a loan. Instead of demanding instrumentally rational calculations with regard to precarious future income, it would be more promising to organize collective endeavours in the application of money by those who lack sufficient income to finance their wants and necessities. There is no reason why a complex society, endowed with the option of cheap distribution of knowledge and information, should rest all its hopes for an appropriate application of credit money on the single signal of a price, in combination with the deterrent effect of over-indebtedness. Secondly, the very same distribution of information could be used to offer alternatives to pecuniary repayments of defaulting loan contracts. The French model of insolvency legislation established local committees that counselled the cases of debtors. It is easy to imagine such committees that would consider options other than monetary repayments as the service in return for the granting of debt relief. In an advancement of the mechanisms that Mauss (2002) analysed in traditional communities, it could be determined which non-monetary performances a democratic community would accept as an alternative.

The development of market societies in general, and the institutionalization of consumer credit markets in particular, have shown the transformation of the original meaning of property as a demonstration of political power into a secondary support of symbolically performed monetary transactions. Such economic progress suffers from its embedding in a landscape of backward political institutions. The democratic capacities of consumer credit could be unleashed by transferring the functional capacities from the level of individual initiative to a democratic collective deliberation. We all know the language of money, but the possibilities of its grammar remain the capacity of a privileged elite.

References

'Abil Shares Plummet 17% on Trading'. 2013. *Business Day Live*, 3 May 2013.

Alexander, P. 2010. 'Rebellion of the Poor: South Africa's Service Delivery Protests – a Preliminary Analysis', *Review of African Political Economy* 37(123): 25–40.

Altman, E.I., and A. Saunders. 1998. 'Credit Risk Measurement: Developments over the Last 20 Years', *Journal of Banking & Finance* 21: 1721–42.

Appadurai, A. 2012. 'The Spirit of Calculation', *The Cambridge Journal of Anthropology* 30(1): 3–17.

Baker, T. 1996. 'On the Genealogy of Moral Hazard', *Texas Law Review* 75(2): 237–92.

Bamu, P., and D. Collier. 2005. *Reforming the Microcredit Industry in South Africa: Will the Proposed National Credit Bill Address Existing Problems and Developmental Concerns?* (Development and Labour Monographs Series Occasional Paper 1/2005.). Cape Town: Institute of Development and Labour Law, University of Cape Town.

Banking Association of South Africa. 2013. *2012 South African Banking Sector Overview*. 2013.

Bateman, M. 2014. 'South Africa's Post-Apartheid Microcredit-Driven Calamity', *Law, Democracy & Development* 18: 92–135.

Bauman, Z. 2005. *Work, Consumerism, and the New Poor*. Maidenhead: Open University Press.

———. 2007. *Consuming Life*. Cambridge and Malden, MA: Polity Press.

Benjamin, C. 2013. 'African Bank Faces Possible R300m Fine for Reckless Lending', *Mail and Guardian*, 4 July 2013.

Berger, P.L., and T. Luckmann. 1991. *The Social Construction of Reality: A Treatise in the Sociology of Knowledge*. London and New York: Penguin Books.

BIS (Bank for International Settlement). 2006. *Payment Systems Worldwide: A Snapshot. Outcomes of the Global Payment Systems Survey. State 12 December 2005*. Basel.

———. 2012. *Committee on Payment and Settlement Systems: Payment, Clearing and Settlement Systems in South Africa*. Basel.

———. 2013. *Committee on Payment and Settlement Systems: Statistics on Payment, Clearing and Settlement Systems in the CPSS Countries. Figures for 2012. September 2013. Preliminary Release*. Basel.

Bonochis, R., and A.J. van Vuuren. 2014. 'African Bank Splits to Isolate Loans in Reserve Bank Rescue', *Mail and Guardian*, 11 August 2014.

Boraine, A., and M. Roestoff. 2002. 'Fresh Start Procedures for Consumer Debtors in South African Bankruptcy Law', *International Insolvency Review* 11: 1–11.

Brand, R., and N. Khanyile. 2014. 'African Bank's Failure Puts SA's Sovereign Rating at Risk', *Business Day Live*, 22 August 2014.

Braudel, F. 1992. *The Wheels of Commerce: Civilisation and Capitalism 15th–18th Century.* Berkeley and Los Angeles, CA: University of California Press.

Breckenridge, K. 1995. '"Money with Dignity": Migrants, Minelords, and the Cultural Politics of South African Gold Standard Crisis 1920–1933', *The Journal of African History* 36(2): 271–304.

———. 2014. *Biometric State. The Global Politics of Identification and Surveillance in South Africa, 1850 to the Present.* Cambridge: Cambridge University Press.

Bryan, D., and M. Rafferty. 2017. 'Reframing Austerity: Financial Morality, Savings and Securitization', *Journal of Cultural Economy* 10(4): 339–55.

Burton, D. 2008. *Credit and Consumer Society.* London and New York: Routledge.

Calder, L. 1999. *Financing the American Dream: A Cultural History of Consumer Credit.* Princeton, NJ: Princeton University Press.

Callon, M. (ed.). 1998a. *The Laws of the Markets.* Oxford and Malden, MA: Blackwell Publishers.

———. 1998b. 'Introduction: The Embeddednes of Economic Markets in Economics', in *The Laws of the Markets.* Oxford and Malden, MA: Blackwell Publishers, pp. 1–57.

———. 2007. 'An Essay on the Growing Contribution of Economic Markets to the Proliferation of the Social', *Theory, Culture & Society* 24(7–8): 139–63.

Campbell, J. 2007. 'The Excessive Cost of Credit on Small Money Loans under the National Credit Act 34 of 2005', *South African Mercantile Law Journal* 19(3): 251–71.

Carruthers, B.G. 2005. 'The Sociology of Money and Credit', in *Handbook of Economic Sociology.* Princeton, NJ and Oxford: Princeton University Press, pp. 355–78.

Castoriadis, C. 1997. *The Imaginary Institution of Society.* Cambridge and Malden, MA: Polity Press.

Collins, D. 2008. 'Debt and Household Finance: Evidence from the Financial Diaries', *Development Southern Africa* 25(4): 469–79.

Collins, D., J. Morduch, S. Rutherford, and O. Ruthven. 2009. *Portfolios of the Poor. How the World's Poor Live on $2 a Day.* Cape Town: University of Cape Town Press.

Cooren, F. 2004. 'Textual Agency: How Texts Do Things in Organizational Settings', *Organization* 11: 373–93.

COSATU. 2005. *Submission the National Credit Bill B18-2005.* Johannesburg.

Crush, J. 1999. 'Fortress South Africa and the Deconstruction of Apartheid's Migrations Regime', *Geoforum* 30: 1–11.

Cumming, C. 1987. *The Economics of Securitization* (No. Autumn 1987), Quarterly Review. New York: Federal Reserve Bank of New York.

Donnelly, L. 2014. 'African Bank Rescue Evades Key Questions', *Mail and Guardian,* 15 August 2014.

DTI (Department of Trade and Industry). 2003. *Credit Law Review August 2003. Summary of the Findings of the Technical Committee.* Pretoria.

———. 2004a. *Credit Law Review: Setting the Scene.* Media release. Pretoria.

———. 2004b. *Draft Green Paper on the Consumer Policy Framework 09/04: Driving Competitiveness, Consumer Confidence and Business Excellence* (Government Gazette No. 26774). Pretoria.

———. 2004c. *Making Credit Markets Work: A Policy Framework for Consumer Credit.* Pretoria.
———. 2013a. *Consumer Will Still Be Responsible for Their Debts Despite Credit Amnesty.* Media release, 27 November 2013. Pretoria.
———. 2013b. *Government Moves to Protect Consumers and Assist Over-Indebted Households.* Media release, 12 December 2013. Pretoria.
———. 2014a. *Removal of Adverse Consumer Credit Information and Information Relating to Paid Up Judgements.* Media release, 27 February 2014. Pretoria.
———. 2014b. *The New Credit Law Will Enable Government to Crack on Illegal Lenders.* Media release, 20 May 2014. Pretoria.
Eichengreen, B. 2008. *Globalizing Capital: A History of the International Monetary System*, 2nd edn. Princeton, NJ and Oxford: Princeton University Press.
Esposito, E. 2011. *The Future of Futures: The Time of Money in Financing and Society.* Cheltenham and Northampton, MA: Edward Elgar.
Feinstein, C.H. 2005. *The Economic History of South Africa: Conquest, Discrimination and Development.* Cambridge: Cambridge University Press.
Fontaine, L. 2001. 'Antonio and Shylock: Credit and Trust in France, c 1680 – c 1780', *Economic History Review* LIV(1): 39–57.
Gelpi, R.-M., and F. Julien-Labruyère. 2000. *The History of Consumer Credit: Doctrines and Practices.* London and New York: Palgrave Macmillan.
Glenn, H.P. 2010. *Legal Traditions of the World*, 4th edn. Oxford and New York: Oxford University Press.
Goodwin-Groen, R. 2006. *The National Credit Act and Its Regulations in the Context of Access to Finance in South Africa.* Johannesburg: FinMark Trust.
Gorton, G.B., and G.G. Penacchi. 2015. 'Banks and Loans Sales Marketing Nonmarketable Assets', in G.B. Norton (ed.), *The Maze of Banking: History, Theory, Crisis.* Oxford: Oxford University Press, pp. 504–27.
Graeber, D. 2011. *Debt: The First 5000 Years.* New York: Melville Publishing House.
Granovetter, M. 1973. 'The Strength of Weak Ties', *American Journal of Sociology* 78(6): 1360–80.
———. 1985. 'Economic Action and Social Structure: The Problem of Embeddedness', *American Journal of Sociology* 91(3): 481–510.
GTZ (Gesellschaft für Technische Zusammenarbeit; German Association for International Cooperation). 2008. *The Incidence of and the Undesirable Practices Relating to Garnishee Orders in South Africa.* Pretoria.
Gumede, W.M. 2007. *Thabo Mbeki and the Battle for the Soul of the ANC.* Cape Town: Zebra Press.
Hahlo, H.R., and E. Kahn. 1960. *The Union of South Africa: The Development of Its Laws and Constitution.* London: Steven and Sons Ltd.
Hart, G. 2014. *Rethinking the South African Crisis: Nationalism, Populism, Hegemony, Geographies of Justice and Social Transformation.* Athens, GA: University of Georgia Press.
Hart, K. 1986. 'Heads or Tails? Two Sides of the Coin', *Man* 21(4): 637–56.
———. 1990. 'Kinship, Contract and Trust: The Economic Organization of Migrants in an African Slum', in D. Gambetta (ed.), *Trust: Making and Breaking Cooperative Relations.* Oxford: Basil Blackwell, pp. 176–93.
———. 2000. *The Memory Bank: Moneys in an Unequal World.* London: Profile Books.

———. 2012. 'A Note on Arjun Appadurai's "The Spirit of Calculation"', *The Cambridge Journal of Anthropology* 30(1): 18–24.

——— (ed.). 2015. *Economy For and Against Democracy*. Oxford and New York: Berghahn Books.

Hart, K., J.-L. Laville and A.D. Cattani (eds). 2011. *The Human Economy: A Citizen's Guide*. Cambridge and Malden, MA: Polity Press.

Hart, K., and J. Sharp (eds). 2014. *People, Money, and Power in the Economic Crisis*. Oxford and New York: Berghahn Books.

Harvey, D. 2005. *A Brief History of Neoliberalism*. New York: Oxford University Press.

Hawkins, P. 2003. *The Cost, Volume and Allocation of Consumer Credit in South Africa*. Pretoria: Department of Trade and Industry.

Heerden, C.M. van, and J.M. Otto. 2007. 'Debt Enforcement in Terms of the National Credit Act 34 of 2005', *Journal of South African Law* 2007(4): 655–84.

Hiilamo, H. 2018. *Household Debt and Economic Crisis: Causes, Consequences and Remedies*. Cheltenham: Edward Elgar.

Hirschman, A.O. 2013. *The Passions and the Interests: Political Arguments for Capitalism before Its Triumph*. Princeton, NJ and Oxford: Princeton University Press.

d'Holbach, P.T. Baron de. 1889. *System of Nature: Or Laws of the Moral and Physical World*. Boston, MA: J.P. Mendum.

von Holdt, K., and E. Webster. 2005. 'Work Restructuring and the Crisis of Social Reproduction: A Southern Perspective', in E. Webster and K. von Holdt (eds), *Beyond the Apartheid Workplace: Studies in Transition*. Scottsville: UKZN Press, pp. 3–40.

Holmes, T. 2014. 'Banks Flee Risky Loan Business', *Mail and Guardian*, 30 May 2014.

Hooper-Box, C. 2002. 'Low-Cost Homes Leave Banks R1bn in the Red', *IOL News*, 17 August 2002.

Houghton, D.H. 1973. *The South African Economy*, 3rd edn. Cape Town, London and New York: Oxford University Press.

Hulme, D. 2008. *The Story of the Grameen Bank: From Subsidised Microcredit to Market-Based Microfinance*, Working Paper 60. Manchester: Brooks World Poverty Institute, University of Manchester.

Hunt, R.M. 2006. 'Development and Regulation of Consumer Credit Reporting in the United States', *The Economics of Consumer Credit*. London and Cambridge, MA: The MIT Press, pp. 301–45.

James, D. 2012. 'Money-Go-Round Personal Economies of Wealth, Aspiration and Indebtedness', *Africa* 82(1): 20–40.

———. 2013. 'Regulating Credit: Tackling the Redistributiveness of Neoliberalism', *Anthropology of This Century* (6).

———. 2015. *Money from Nothing: Indebtedness and Aspiration in South Africa*. Stanford, CA: Stanford University Press.

Johannesburg Stock Exchange. 2008. *African Bank: Acquisition of Ellerine Holdings Limited ('Ellerines')* Johannesburg: Stock Exchange News Service.

———. 2010. *African Bank: Integration of Ellerines Financial Services into African Bank*. Johannesburg: Stock Exchange News Service.

Jungmann, N., and N. Huls. 2009. 'Debt Counselling in The Shadow of the Court: The Dutch Experience', in J. Niemi, I. Ramsay and W.C. Whitford (eds),

Consumer Credit, Debt and Bankruptcy: Comparative and International Perspectives. London and Portland, OR: Hart Publishing, pp. 419–39.

Kelly-Louw, M. 2007. 'Better Consumer Protection under the Statutory in Duplum Rule', *South African Mercantile Law Journal* 19(3): 337–45.

———. 2008. 'The Prevention and Alleviation of Consumer Over-Indebtedness', *South African Mercantile Law Journal* 20(2): 200–26.

———. 2009. 'Prevention of Over-Indebtedness and Mechanisms for Resolving Overindebtedness of South African Consumers', in J. Niemi, I. Ramsay and W.C. Whitford (eds), *Consumer Credit, Debt, and Bankruptcy: Comparative and International Perspectives*. London and Portland, OR: Hart Publishing, pp. 175–97.

Kilborn, J.J. 2004. 'The Innovative German Approach to Consumer Debt Relief: Revolutionary Changes in German Law, and Surprising Lessons for the US', *Northwestern Journal of International Law and Business* (24): 257–303.

———. 2007. *Comparative Consumer Bankruptcy*. Durham: Carolina Academia Press.

Klug, H. 2010. *The Constitution of South Africa: A Contextual Analysis*. Oxford and Portland, OR: Hart Publishing.

Knight, F.H. 1921. *Risk, Uncertainty and Profit*. Boston, MA and New York: Houghton Mifflin Company.

Krige, D. 2011. *Power, Identity and Agency at Work in the Popular Economies of Soweto and Black Johannesburg* (PhD thesis University of the Witwatersrand).

———. 2014. '"Letting Money Work for Us": Self-Organisation and Financialization from Below in an All-Male Savings Club in Soweto', in K. Hart and J. Sharp (eds), *People, Money, and Power in the Economic Crisis*. Oxford and New York: Berghahn Books, pp. 61–81.

Krippner, G.R. 2011. *Capitalizing on Crisis: The Political Origins of the Rise of Finance*. Cambridge, MA and London: Harvard University Press.

Langenohl, A. 2008. '"In the Long Run We Are All Dead": Imaginary Time in Financial Market Narratives', *Cultural Critique* 70(1): 3–31.

Langley, P. 2010. *The Everyday Life of Global Finance*. Oxford and New York: Oxford University Press.

———. 2014. 'Consuming Credit', *Consumption Markets & Culture* 17(5): 417–28.

Latour, B. 2010. *The Making of Law: An Ethnography of the Conseil D'état*. Cambridge and Malden, MA: Polity Press.

Lefebvre, H. 1991. *The Production of Space*. Oxford and Cambridge, MA: Blackwell.

Lefifi, T.A. 2013. 'Bloodletting as Unsecured Loan Bubble Pops', *Business Day Live*, 5 May 2013.

Leslie, R. 1933. 'South Africa and the Gold Standard', *The Economic Journal* 43(169): 88–92.

Leyshon, A., and N. Thrift. 2007. 'The Capitalization of Almost Everything the Future of Finance and Capitalism', *Theory, Culture & Society* 24(7–8): 97–115.

Luhmann, N. 1989. *Ecological Communication*, trans. J. Bednarz. Cambridge: Polity Press.

———. 1992. 'Operational Closure and Structural Coupling: The Differentiation of the Legal System', *Cardoso Law Review* (13): 1419–41.

MacKenzie, D. 2006. *An Engine, Not a Camera*. Cambridge, MA and London: The MIT Press.
Makgetla, N. 2018. 'Inequality in South Africa', *The Crisis of Inequality, New South African Review* (Vol. 6). Johannesburg: Wits University Press, pp. 14–42.
Manzo, K.A. 1996. 'Mimosas of the Veld: White and Rainbow Nations in South Africa', in *Creating Boundaries: The Politics of Race and Nation*. Boulder, CO and London: Lynne Rennier Publishers, pp. 71–112.
Marais, H. 2011. *South Africa Pushed to the Limits: The Political Economy of Change*. London and New York: Zed Books.
March, J.G., and H.A. Simon. 2004. 'Organizations Cognitive Limits on Rationality', in F. Dobbin (ed.), *The New Economic Sociology: A Reader*. Princeton, NJ and Oxford: Princeton University Press, pp. 518–32.
Maris IT. 2006. *Impact of the New National Credit Act on the Debt Recovery and Credit Bureau Industries*. Pretoria: Maris IT Credit Risk Management Solutions.
Martin, R. 2002. *The Financialization of Everyday Life*. Philadelphia, PA: Temple University Press.
Marx, C. 2008. *Oxwagon Sentinel: Radical Afrikaner Nationalism and the History of the Ossewabrandwag*. Pretoria: UNISA Press.
Marx, K. 1996. 'Capital A Critique of Politic Economy Volume I', *Collected Works*, Volume 35. New York: International Publishers.
Mason, R., and J. Duns. 2003. 'Developments of Consumer Bankruptcy in Australia', in J. Niemi-Kiesiläinen. I. Ramsay and W.C. Whitford (eds), *Consumer Bankruptcy in Global Perspective*. Oxford and Portland, OR: Hart Publishing, pp. 227–46.
Mauss, M. 2002. *The Gift: The Form and Reason for Exchange in Archaic Societies. With a Foreword by Mary Douglas*. London and New York: Routledge Classics.
McKinley, D.T. 2017. *South Africa's Corporatised Liberation*. Johannesburg: Jacana.
Meyerhenrich, J. 2008. *The Legacies of Law: Long-Run Consequences of Legal Development in South Africa, 1652–2000*. Cambridge and New York: Cambridge University Press.
Muniesa, F., Y. Millo and M. Callon. 2007. 'An Introduction to Market Devices', in M. Callon, Y. Millo and F. Muniesa (eds), *Market Devices*. Malden, MA, Oxford and Victoria: Blackwell Publishing, pp. 1–12.
NCR (National Credit Regulator). 2007. *Credit Bureau Monitor: Third Quarter September 2007*. Pretoria.
———. 2008a. *Consumer Credit Market Report: Second Quarter June 2008*. Pretoria.
———. 2008b. *Credit Bureau Monitor: Second Quarter June 2008*. Pretoria.
———. 2009a. *Consumer Credit Market Report: Second Quarter June 2009*. Pretoria.
———. 2009b. *Credit Bureau Monitor: Second Quarter June 2009*. Pretoria.
———. 2010a. *Consumer Credit Market Report: Second Quarter June 2010*. Pretoria.
———. 2010b. *Consumer Credit Market Report: Third Quarter September 2010*. Pretoria.
———. 2011a. *Consumer Credit Market Report: Fourth Quarter December 2011*. Pretoria.
———. 2011b. *Consumer Credit Market Report: Second Quarter June 2011*. Pretoria.
———. 2011c. *Consumer Credit Market Report: Third Quarter September 2011*. Pretoria.
———. 2011d. *Credit Bureau Monitor: Fourth Quarter December 2011*. Pretoria.

———. 2011e. *Credit Bureau Monitor: Second Quarter June 2011*. Pretoria.
———. 2012a. *Consumer Credit Market Report: First Quarter March 2012*. Pretoria.
———. 2012b. *Consumer Credit Market Report: Fourth Quarter December 2012*. Pretoria.
———. 2012c. *Consumer Credit Market Report: Third Quarter September 2012*. Pretoria.
———. 2012d. *Credit Market Activity Suggests* the Need for Caution. Media release. Pretoria.
———. 2012e. *Credit Performance of Consumer Accounts Deteriorates in the First Quarter of 2012*. Media release. Pretoria.
———. 2012f. *Financial Health of Consumers Plummets*. Media release. Pretoria.
———. 2012g. *Research on the Increase of Unsecured Personal Loans in South Africa's Credit Market*. Pretoria.
———. 2012h. *Strong Growth in Unsecured Personal Loans*. Media release. Pretoria.
———. 2013a. *Consumer Credit Market Report: Fourth Quarter December 2013*. Pretoria.
———. 2013b. *Consumer Credit Market Report: Second Quarter June 2013*. Pretoria.
———. 2013c. *Consumer Credit Market Report: Third Quarter September 2013*. Pretoria.
———. 2013d. *Credit Bureau Monitor: Fourth Quarter December 2013*. Pretoria.
———. 2013e. *Credit Bureau Monitor: Second Quarter June 2013*. Pretoria.
———. 2013f. *Credit Bureau Monitor: Third Quarter September 2013*. Pretoria.
———. 2014a. *Consumer Credit Market Report: Fourth Quarter December 2014*. Pretoria.
———. 2014b. *Consumer Credit Market Report: Second Quarter June 2014*. Pretoria.
———. 2014c. *Consumer Credit Market Report: Third Quarter September 2014*. Pretoria.
———. 2014d. *Credit Bureau Monitor: Fourth Quarter December 2014*. Pretoria.
———. 2014e. *Credit Bureau Monitor: Second Quarter June 2014*. Pretoria.
———. 2018a. *Consumer Credit Market Report: First Quarter March 2018*. Pretoria.
———. 2018b. *Consumer Credit Market Report: Fourth Quarter December 2018*. Pretoria.
———. 2018c. *Consumer Credit Market Report: Second Quarter June 2018*. Pretoria.
———. 2018d. *Consumer Credit Market Report: Third Quarter September 2018*. Pretoria.
———. 2018e. *Credit Bureau Monitor: Fourth Quarter December 2018*. Pretoria.
Nattrass, J. 1981. *The South African Economy: Its Growth and Change*. Cape Town: Oxford University Press.
Ndzamela, P. 2014a. 'Embattled African Bank Gets Bailed Out', *Business Day Live*, 11 August 2014.
———. 2014b. 'African Bank Gets Ready for Licence Bid', *Business Day Live*, 12 August 2014.
Ndzamela, P., and M. Mittner. 2014. 'Capitec Moves to Reassure Funders', *Business Day Live*, 19 August 2014.
Neethling, L. 2006. 'Blacklisting of a Debtor as Credit Risk – Infringement of a Debtor's Rights to Creditworthiness and Earning Capacity as Personal Immaterial Property Rights', *South African Mercantile Law Journal* 18(3): 376–82.

Netshitenzhe, M. 2017. *Presentation to Portfolio Committee on the Proposed Draft National Credit Policy Review for Debt Relief and the National Credit Amendment Bill, 2017 Developed by the Portfolio Committee on Trade and Industry.* 17 May.

Niemi, J., I. Ramsay and W.C. Whitford. 2009. *Consumer Credit, Debt and Bankruptcy. Comparative and International Perspectives.* London and Portland, OR: Hart Publishing.

Niemi-Kiesiläinen, J., I. Ramsay and W.C. Whitford. 2003. 'Introduction', in J. Niemi-Kiesiläinen, I. Ramsay and W.C. Whitford (eds), *Consumer Bankruptcy in Global Perspective.* Oxford and Portland, OR: Hart Publishing, pp. 1–14.

Numbeo. 2019. Cost of Living in South Africa. Retrieved 13 June 2019 from https://www.numbeo.com/cost-of-living/country_result.jsp?country=South+Africa.

Nyaruwata, G. 2009. *Addressing Over-Indebtedness in South Africa: What Role Should Supply-Side and Demand-Side Interventions Play?* Conference Paper presented at the Postgraduate Student Conference, 15 April 2009.

O'Meara, D. 1983. *Volkskapitalisme: Class, Capital and Ideology in the Development of Afrikaner Nationalism, 1934–1948.* Johannesburg: Ravan Press.

Otto, J.M. 2009. 'Over-Indebtedness: An Application for Debt Review in Terms of the National Credit Act: Consumers Beware! Firstrand Bank Ltd v Olivier', *South African Mercantile Law Journal* 21: 272–78.

———. 2010. *The National Credit Act Explained*, 2nd edn. Durban: Lexis Nexis.

Parliament of the Republic of South Africa. 2018a. *Protection and Promotion of Indigenous Knowledge Bill and National Credit Amendment Bill Approved by the National Council of Provinces and the National Assembly Respectively.* Media release. Cape Town.

———. 2018b. *Trade and Industry Committee Adopts National Credit Amendment Bill.* Media release. Cape Town.

Peebles, G. 2010. 'The Anthropology of Credit and Debt', *Annual Review of Anthropology* (39): 225–40.

Polanyi, K. 1977. 'Money Objects and Money Uses', in H.W. Pearson (ed.), *The Livelihood on Man.* New York, San Francisco, CA, London: Academic Press, pp. 97–121.

———. 2001. *The Great Transformation: The Political and Economic Origins of Our Time.* Boston, MA: Beacon Press.

Porteous, D. 2004. *Banking on Change: Democratising Finance in South Africa 1994–2004 and Beyond.* Cape Town: Double Story Books.

Prashad, V. 2014. *The Poorer Nations: A Possible History of the Global South.* London and New York: Verso Books.

Ramsay, I. 2003. 'Bankruptcy in Transition: The Case of England and Wales – The Neo-Liberal Cuckoo in the European Bankruptcy Nest?', in J. Niemi-Kiesiläinen, I. Ramsay and W.C. Whitford (eds), *Consumer Bankruptcy in Global Perspective.* Oxford and Portland, OR: Hart Publishing, pp. 205–25.

Riles, A. 2011. *Collateral Knowledge: Legal Reasoning in the Global Financial Markets*, Chicago Series in Law and Society. Chicago, IL and London: University of Chicago Press.

Ritchie, G. 2018. 'Wary Consumers Start Saving', *Mail and Guardian*, 5 October 2018.

Roestoff, M., and H. Coetzee. 2012. 'Consumer Debt Relief in South Africa Lessons from America and England; and Suggestions for the Way Forward', *South African Mercantile Law Journal* 24(1): 53–76.

Roestoff, M., and S. Renke. 2005. 'Debt Relief for Consumers – the Interaction between Insolvency and Consumer Protection Part 1', *Orbiter* 2005: 561–74.

———. 2006. 'Debt Relief for Consumers – the Interaction between Insolvency and Consumer Protection Part 2', *Orbiter* 2006: 98–110.

Rosanvallon, P. 2006. *Democracy Past and Future*. New York: Columbia University Press.

Rose, R. 2002. 'Reinvestment Bill Being Redrafted', *Business Day*, 21 August 2002.

Rossouw, J.J. 2008. *Inflation in South Africa 1921 to 2006: History, Measurement and Credibility.* (Unpublished PhD thesis University of KwaZulu-Natal).

SACP. 2013. 'SACP Condemns Theft of Its Red October Campaign'. Retrieved 15 October 2013 from http://www.sacp.org.za/main.php.

Schraten, J. 2014. 'The Transformation of the South African Credit Market', *Transformation. Critical Perspectives on Southern Africa* (85): 1–20.

———. 2015. 'Habits of Austerity Financialization and New Ways of Dealing with Money', in K. Hart (ed.), *Economy For and Against Democracy*. Oxford and New York: Berghahn Books, pp. 19–38.

———. 2016. 'Credit as a Source of Debts and Wealth', *Przeglad Socjologiczny* 65(3): 81–110.

Schumpeter, J.A. 1996. *History of Economic Analysis*. London and New York: Routledge.

Schwartz, S. 2003. 'Personal Bankruptcy Law: A Behavioural Perspective', *Consumer Bankruptcy in Global Perpective*. Oxford and Portland, OR: Hart Publishing, pp. 61–82.

Shevel, A. 2013. 'Easy-Credit Bomb Set to Explode', *Business Day Live*, 4 August 2013.

Shiller, R.J. 2003. *The New Financial Order: Risk in the 21st Century*. Princeton, NJ and Oxford: Princeton University Press.

Simmel, G. 1990. *The Philosophy of Money*. London and New York: Routledge.

Skeel Jr., D.A. 2001. *Debt's Dominion: The History of Bankruptcy Law in America*. Princeton, NJ and Oxford: Princeton University Press.

Smith, A. 1981. *An Inquiry into the Nature and Causes of the Wealth of Nations*. 2 Volumes. Indianapolis, IN: Liberty Classics.

———. 1984. *The Theory of Moral Sentiments*. Indianapolis, IN: Liberty Classics.

Smith, D.E. 1999. *Writing the Social: Critique, Theory, and Investigations*. Toronto and Buffalo, NY and London: University of Toronto Press.

———. 2001. 'Texts and the Ontology of Organizations and Institutions', *Studies in Cultures, Organizations and Societies* 7(2): 159–98.

South African Reserve Bank. 2005. *The National Payment System in South Africa 1995 to 2005*. Pretoria.

———. 2012a. *Financial Stability Review March 2012*. Pretoria.

———. 2012b. *Financial Stability Review September 2012*. Pretoria.

Stanley, M. 1968. 'Nature, Culture and Scarcity: Foreword to a Theoretical Synthesis', *American Sociological Review* 33(6): 855–70.

Statistics South Africa. 2007. *Mid-Year Population Estimates. 3 July 2007. Statistical Release P0302*. Pretoria.

———. 2009. *Mid-Year Population Estimates. 27 July 2009. Statistical Release P0302*. Pretoria.

———. 2010. *Monthly Earnings of South Africans, 2010. 30 November 2010. Statistical Release P0211.2*. Pretoria.

———. 2011. *Mid-Year Population Estimates. 27 July 2011. Statistical Release P0302*. Pretoria.

———. 2013. *Mid-Year Population Estimates. 14 May 2013. Statistical Release P0302*. Pretoria.

Stoop, P.N. 2009. 'South African Consumer Credit Policy: Measures Indirectly Aimed at Preventing Consumer Overindebtedness', *South African Mercantile Law Journal* 21(3): 365–86.

———. 2010. *Disclosure as an Indirect Measure Aimed at Preventing Over-Indebtedness*. Draft paper presented at the International Conference on Over-Indebtedness and Credit Regulation at the Law Clinic of University of Pretoria.

Sztompka, P. 2003. *Trust: A Sociological Theory*. Cambridge: Cambridge University Press.

Tabb, C.J. 1991. 'The Historical Evolution of the Bankruptcy Discharge', *American Bankrupcty Law Journal* (65): 325–71.

Taylor, C. 2002. 'Modern Social Imaginaries', *Public Culture* 14(1): 91–124.

Telfer, T.G.W. 2003. 'New Zealand Bankruptcy Law Reform: The New Role of the Official Assignee and the Prospects for a No-Asset Regime', in J. Niemi-Kiesiläinen, I. Ramsay and W.C. Whitford (eds), *Consumer Bankruptcy in Global Perspective*. Oxford and Portland, OR: Hart Publishing, pp. 247–68.

Terreblanche, S. 2002. *A History of Inequality on South Africa 1652–2002*. Scottsville: UKZN Press.

Treasury (Ministry of Finance of South Africa). 2012a. *Joint Statement By The Minister Of Finance And The Chairperson Of The Banking Association Of South Africa: Ensuring Responsible Market Conduct For Bank Lending*. Media release. Pretoria.

———. 2012b. *Media Statement on Finance Minister's Meeting with the Banking Industry*. Pretoria.

———. 2017. *Debt Relief Bill: Portfolio Committee Presentation*. Pretoria.

Tshwane, T. 2018. 'Debt Relief Won't Be a Quick Fix', *Mail and Guardian*, 14 September 2018.

Verhoef, G. 2009. 'Concentration and Competition: The Changing Landscape of the Banking Sector in South Africa 1970–2007', *South African Journal of Economic History* 24(2): 157–97.

Vessio, M.L. 2008. 'What Does the National Credit Regulator Regulate?', *South African Mercantile Law Journal* 20(2): 227–42.

Weber, M. 1978. *Economy and Society*. Berkeley, CA, Los Angeles, CA and London: University of California Press.

Welsh, D. 2009. *The Rise and Fall of Apartheid*. Johannesburg and Cape Town: Jonathan Bell Publishers.

Wennerlind, C. 2011. *Casualties of Credit: The English Financial Revolution, 1620–1720*. London and Cambridge, MA: Harvard University Press.

West, E. 2013a. 'Abil Witnesses 26% Drop in Headline Earnings', *Business Day Live*, 20 May 2013.

———. 2013b. 'Abil Reels as Dividend Cut Disappoints Investors', *Business Day Live*, 21 May 2013.

Westhuizen, C. van der. 2007. *White Power and the Rise and Fall of the National Party*. Cape Town: Zebra Press.

World Bank Group. 2019. *GINI Index (World Bank Estimate)*. Retrieved 22 June 2019 from https://data.worldbank.org/indicator/SI.POV.GINI.

Ziegel, J. 2003. *Comparative Consumer Bankruptcy Regimes – A Canadian Perspective*. Oxford and Portland, OR: Hart Publishing.

Index

www.ingramcontent.com/pod-product-compliance
Ingram Content Group UK Ltd.
Pitfield, Milton Keynes, MK11 3LW, UK
UKHW021838100926
8556IPUK00004B/425

9 781789 20638